Listening for Theatrical Form in
Early Modern England

Edinburgh Critical Studies in Renaissance Culture

Series Editor: Lorna Hutson

Titles available in the series:

Open Subjects: English Renaissance Republicans, Modern Selfhoods and the Virtue of Vulnerability
James Kuzner

The Phantom of Chance: From Fortune to Randomness in Seventeenth-Century French Literature
John D. Lyons

Don Quixote in the Archives: Madness and Literature in Early Modern Spain
Dale Shuger

Untutored Lines: The Making of the English Epyllion
William P. Weaver

The Girlhood of Shakespeare's Sisters: Gender, Transgression, Adolescence
Jennifer Higginbotham

Friendship's Shadows: Women's Friendship and the Politics of Betrayal in England, 1640–1705
Penelope Anderson

Inventions of the Skin: The Painted Body in Early English Drama, 1400–1642
Andrea Ria Stevens

Performing Economic Thought: English Drama and Mercantile Writing, 1600–1642
Bradley D. Ryner

Forgetting Differences: Tragedy, Historiography, and the French Wars of Religion
Andrea Frisch

Listening for Theatrical Form in Early Modern England
Allison K. Deutermann

Forthcoming titles:

Perfecting the Law: Literature and Legal Reform in Shakespeare's England
Virginia Lee Strain

Visit the Edinburgh Critical Studies in Renaissance Culture website at edinburghuniversitypress.com/series/ecsrc

Listening for Theatrical Form in Early Modern England

Allison K. Deutermann

EDINBURGH
University Press

Edinburgh University Press is one of the leading university presses in the UK. We publish academic books and journals in our selected subject areas across the humanities and social sciences, combining cutting-edge scholarship with high editorial and production values to produce academic works of lasting importance. For more information visit our website: www.edinburghuniversitypress.com

© Allison K. Deutermann, 2016

Edinburgh University Press Ltd
The Tun – Holyrood Road
12(2f) Jackson's Entry
Edinburgh EH8 8PJ

Typeset in 10.5/13 Adobe Sabon by
Servis Filmsetting Ltd, Stockport, Cheshire

A CIP record for this book is available from the British Library

ISBN 978 1 4744 1126 4 (hardback)
ISBN 978 1 4744 1127 1 (webready PDF)
ISBN 978 1 4744 1128 8 (epub)

The right of Allison K. Deutermann to be identified as the author of this work has been asserted in accordance with the Copyright, Designs and Patents Act 1988, and the Copyright and Related Rights Regulations 2003 (SI No. 2498).

Contents

Acknowledgements		vi
Series Editor's Preface		viii
1.	Introduction: 'Audiences to this Act'	1
2.	Sound in Mind and Body: Hearing Early Modern Revenge Tragedy	22
3.	'Sprinkled Among your Ears': Ben Jonson, John Marston and the Cultivation of the Listening Connoisseur	63
4.	'Caviare to the General'?: Taste, Hearing and Genre in *Hamlet*	104
5.	Listening for Form at the Cockpit Theatre	140
6.	Epilogue	173
Bibliography		178
Index		192

Acknowledgements

It is a great pleasure to be able to thank all of the people who helped bring this book into being. At the very top of that list is Jean Howard, without whom so many of us in the field would never have built careers, written books, or finished our dissertations. Her brilliance and exacting standards are known to all who have had the very good fortune to work with her. I owe her much as a mentor and friend.

The intellectual community of Columbia University first helped me form the questions that remain at the heart of this book. Julie Crawford, David Kastan and Alan Stewart were instrumental in shaping the project from the start, as were the members of Columbia's early modern dissertation seminar. I am especially grateful to András Kiséry, Musa Gurnis, Tiffany Werth, Matthew Zarnowiecki, Lianne Habinek and Adam Hooks for their many years of insight, advice and friendship.

When the dissertation died so that this book might live, I was teaching at Amherst College, where I benefited enormously from the support of Adam Zucker, Jane Hwang Degenhardt, Peter Berek, Andrew Parker and Arthur Kinney. Amherst taught me how to teach (a skill it seems we are not necessarily born with). I cannot thank the faculty, students and staff there enough. The members of the Massachusetts Center for Interdisciplinary Renaissance Studies were invaluable in helping me to rethink what would become my third chapter.

The bulk of this book was written in New York while working at Baruch College, where I have had the sensational luck to join a department that is both warmly collegial and intellectually rigorous. Above all, I must thank Baruch's Lauren Silberman, John Brenkman, Nancy Yousef, Tim Aubry, Sean O'Toole, Stephanie Hershinow and Laura Kolb for their unceasing willingness to talk things through. My CUNY writing group has, on more than one occasion, saved me from myself. Thank you Gavin Hollis, Andrea Walkden, Vimala Pasupathi and Patricia Akhimie: my secrets are I hope safe with you. At various points in the writing process, I have benefited greatly from the sharp critical eyes of Henry S. Turner, Tanya Pollard, Shankar Raman, Lowell Gallagher, Molly Murray, Dehn Gilmore and Valerie Traub, and I have learned much in ongoing conversations with Miriam Jacobson, Benedict Robinson, Zachary Lesser, Adam Smyth, Rob Carson, Pamela Brown and Gordan McMullan.

This book was completed with the support of the Whiting Foundation and with a fellowship from the Huntington Library, where I was able to comb through the spectacular holdings in early modern science and rhetoric, and where I had the great joy of the company of Heather James, Heidi Brayman Hackel and Marjorie Rubright. I also owe much to Richard Wistreich and Carla Zecher, whose NEH seminar at the Newberry Library on music books, materiality and performance transformed my thinking about the ways in which print helps to shape auditory reception. I was able to complete research necessary for my fifth chapter with the help of the Dean's office and a succession of much-needed grants from PSC-CUNY, which paid for a semester in London at the British Library. Grants-in-aid to the Folger Shakespeare Library supported research at the dissertation stage that has remained a crucial part of the project from beginning to end. Lorna Hutson, the editor for this series, offered invaluable feedback at each stage of publication; she has made this a much better book than it otherwise would have been. I also want to thank my anonymous readers, as well as Jackie Jones, James Dale and Adela Rauchova at Edinburgh University Press, for their clear-eyed advice, support and patience. My fourth chapter evolved out of an essay of the same title, "'Caviare to the general'?: Taste, Hearing, and Genre in *Hamlet*." Copyright © 2011 Folger Shakespeare Library. This article was first published in *Shakespeare Quarterly* 62.2 (2011), 230–55. Reprinted with permission by Johns Hopkins University Press.

One more thing: Ann, Val, Liz, Caroline, Erica, Sarah, Joselin, Sari, Musa, András and Dehn: thank you for your care and support through the toughest of times. This book is dedicated to my mom, whose intelligence, compassion and strength are superhuman, and to my daughter, who was born somewhere in the middle of my fifth chapter. As I type these lines, she is sitting on my lap, slapping the keys on my laptop and shouting, 'I do it! I help mama!' More than you know, duck. I love you.

Series Editor's Preface

Edinburgh Critical Studies in Renaissance Culture may, as a series title, provoke some surprise. On the one hand, the choice of the word 'culture' (rather than, say, 'literature') suggests that writers in this series subscribe to the now widespread assumption that the 'literary' is not isolable, as a mode of signifying, from other signifying practices that make up what we call 'culture'. On the other hand, most of the critical work in English literary studies of the period 1500–1700 which endorses this idea has rejected the older identification of the period as 'the Renaissance', with its implicit homage to the myth of essential and universal Man coming to stand (in all his sovereign individuality) at the centre of a new world picture. In other words, the term 'culture' in the place of 'literature' leads us to expect the words 'early modern' in the place of 'Renaissance'. Why, then, 'Edinburgh Critical Studies in *Renaissance Culture*'?

The answer to that question lies at the heart of what distinguishes this critical series and defines its parameters. As Terence Cave has argued, the term 'early modern', though admirably egalitarian in conception, has had the unfortunate effect of essentialising the modern, that is, of positing 'the advent of a once-and-for-all modernity' which is the deictic 'here and now' from which we look back.[1] The phrase 'early modern', that is to say, forecloses the possibility of other modernities, other futures that might have arisen, narrowing the scope of what we may learn from the past by construing it as a narrative leading inevitably to Western modernity, to 'us'. *Edinburgh Critical Studies in Renaissance Culture* aims rather to shift the emphasis from a story of progress – early modern to modern – to series of critical encounters and conversations with the past, which may reveal to us some surprising alternatives buried within texts familiarly construed as episodes on the way to certain identifying features of our endlessly fascinating modernity. In keeping

[1] Terence Cave, 'Locating the Early Modern', *Paragraph*, 29:1 (2006) 12–26, 14.

with one aspect of the etymology of 'Renaissance' or 'Rinascimento' as 'rebirth', moreover, this series features books that explore and interpret anew elements of the critical encounter between writers of the period 1500–1700 and texts of Greco-Roman literature, rhetoric, politics, law, oeconomics, *eros* and friendship.

The term 'culture', then, indicates a license to study and scrutinise objects other than literary ones, and to be more inclusive about both the forms and the material and political stakes of making meaning both in the past and in the present. 'Culture' permits a realisation of the benefits to be reaped after two decades of interdisciplinary enrichment in the arts. No longer are historians naïve about textual criticism, about rhetoric, literary theory or about readerships; likewise, literary critics trained in close reading now also turn easily to court archives, to legal texts, and to the historians' debates about the languages of political and religious thought. Social historians look at printed pamphlets with an eye for narrative structure; literary critics look at court records with awareness of the problems of authority, mediation and institutional procedure. Within these developments, modes of research that became unfashionable and discredited in the 1980s – for example, studies in classical or vernacular 'source texts', or studies of literary 'influence' across linguistic, confessional and geographical boundaries – have acquired a new critical edge and relevance as the convergence of the disciplines enables the unfolding of new cultural histories (that is to say, what was once studied merely as 'literary influence' may now be studied as a fraught cultural encounter). The term 'Renaissance' thus retains the relevance of the idea of consciousness and critique within these textual engagements of past and present, and, while it foregrounds the Western European experience, is intended to provoke comparativist study of wider global perspectives rather than to promote the 'universality' of a local, if far-reaching, historical phenomenon. Finally, as traditional pedagogic boundaries between 'Medieval' and 'Renaissance' are being called into question by cross disciplinary work emphasising the 'reformation' of social and cultural forms, so this series, while foregrounding the encounter with the classical past, is self-conscious about the ways in which that past is assimilated to the projects of Reformation and Counter-Reformation, spiritual, political and domestic, that finally transformed Christendom into Europe.

Individual books in this series vary in methodology and approach, sometimes blending the sensitivity of close literary analysis with incisive, informed and urgent theoretical argument, at other times offering critiques of grand narratives of the period by their work in manuscript transmission, or in the archives of legal, social and architectural history, or by social histories of gender and childhood. What all these books have in common, however, is the capacity to offer compelling, well-documented and lucidly written critical accounts of how writers and thinkers in the period 1500–1700 reshaped, transformed and critiqued the texts and practices of their world, prompting new perspectives on what we think we have learned from them.

Lorna Hutson

Chapter 1

Introduction: 'Audiences to this Act'

I iudge Cookes and Painters the better bearing, for the one extendeth his art no farther then to the tongue, palate, and nose, the other to the eye, and both are ended in outwarde sense, which is common to us with bruite beastes. But these, by the priuie entries of the eare, slip downe into the heart, & with gunshotte of affection gaule the minde, where reason and vertue shoulde rule the roste.

Stephen Gosson, The School of Abuse (London, 1579)

Language and matter, with a fit of mirth
That sharply savours more of air than earth,
Like midwives, bring a play to timely birth.
But where's now such a one in which these three
Are handsomely contriv'd? or, if they be,
Are understood by all who hear to see?

John Ford, The Lady's Trial (London, 1639)

'Audiences to this Act'

In 1579, just three years after London's first commercial theatre opened, the erstwhile playwright Stephen Gosson attacked his fellow dramatists for penning lines that 'by the priuie entries of the eare, slip downe into the heart, & ... gaule the minde'.[1] Decades later, in a prologue most likely written in collaboration with John Ford, the actor Theophilus Bird complained that few plays were 'understood by all who hear to see'.[2] Writing from opposite ends of the roughly 60-year history of early modern English drama, Gosson and Bird occupy different cultural moments and, of course, hold contrary agendas. The dramatist-turned-antitheatricalist Gosson's attack on the theatre aims to persuade would-be playgoers to stay away, while Bird's complaint, which introduces Ford's *The Lady's Trial*, is more of an advertisement for the play that follows. Yet there is much in their perspectives that is shared. For both men, early modern theatre is primarily aural. Whether its language slips into the 'priuie entries of the eare' to corrupt the listener from within or fires the imaginations of those who 'hear to see', drama is consumed by the ear, and its power or impotence is determined by its aural efficacy. Gosson imagines these effects as inevitable and deep. Sound slips inside the body whether the listener wishes it to or not, transforming the hearer fundamentally and absolutely. Bird and Ford imagine these effects as less guaranteed and as far more varied: dramatic appreciation, or even understanding, requires listeners' thoughtful, informed engagement.

In their attention to the sounds of the stage, Gosson, Bird and Ford are far from unusual. For most early modern dramatists and playgoers, as well as for many of the stage's most vociferous opponents, theatre was above all something to be *heard*. This does not mean that it was not also something to be seen – or, as historians of the book would remind us, to be read.[3] But *Listening for Theatrical Form* argues for a fundamental, historical difference in how early modern men and women conceived of theatrical performance: as an affective, dynamic process that was largely aural in its experience. We find evidence for such thinking in a range of texts, including antitheatrical screeds like Gosson's, rhetorical manuals and in many of the frustratingly few first-hand, anecdotal accounts of playgoing that survive; but above all, we find it in the plays themselves. Sixteenth- and seventeenth-century drama is positively saturated with moments that draw attention to ears and hearing. This preoccupation crosses genres, companies and playhouses, and it shapes the work of every major dramatist, often in seemingly contradictory ways. Undoubtedly, the theatre's fascination with hearing reflects and participates in a broader cultural investment in audition, which the following chapters seek to chart; but ultimately I am arguing for a deeper, and much more fundamental, relationship between the two.[4] Audition was not just a subject of dramatic interest. It was essential to the theatre's very existence. From its beginnings in the open-air amphitheatres of the late sixteenth century, up through the final decade of its operation in the indoor and outdoor playhouses of Caroline London, English commercial theatre was built out of dramatists' persistent, even obsessive, interest in how and what theatregoers should hear. Paying attention to audition is vital if we are to understand how the codes and conventions through which the drama became legible took shape on the early modern stage.

While the impact of the two auditory models discussed above was felt throughout sixteenth- and seventeenth-century theatre, their influence was most profound on revenge tragedy and city comedy – arguably the most popular, longest lasting early modern genres. I argue that the not only parallel, but dialectical, development of these dramatic forms was rooted in competing conceptualisations of sound – particularly the sound of dramatic speech – and its reception. Consider the final scenes of *The Revenger's Tragedy* (first performed 1606).[5] Stabbed to death in the middle of his own coronation banquet, Lussurioso concludes his brief and sententious farewell speech, 'My tongue is out of office'. Hearing this, the courtier Vindice cries out for air, presumably causing those who have surrounded the two men to back away. He then addresses the dying duke:

> VINDICE: Now thou'lt not prate on't, 'twas Vindice murdered thee –
> LUSSURIOSO: O!
> VINDICE: Murdered thy father –
> LUSSURIOSO: O!
> VINDICE: And I am he.
>   Tell nobody.—So, so, the duke's departed. (5.3.77–80)[6]

Vindice reveals his hatred for Lussurioso now, when it is safe to do so, with obvious relish. But there is much more to this exchange than simply a revelling in or even a revelation of revenge. It is as if the revenger's spoken confession helps to enact, or is in fact necessary to the completion of, the very murder being confessed. Each of Vindice's lines forces from Lussurioso a moan ('O') that echoes the 'O, O' that he first cries out while being stabbed in this same scene (5.3.48). Vindice's words, like his sword, produce wounds against which the duke proves fatally defenceless.

It is one of the central claims of this book that in this scene, and in the countless others like it that appear in tragedies of revenge, it is not just the meaning of Vindice's words that matters, but the material out of which they are formed. Their sound, as well as their sense, pierces Lussurioso's body to deadly effect. This is a lesson, I will show, that is taught by early modern rhetorical and anatomical theory, which held that sound – *any* sound – signalled by its very presence that the hearer was undergoing a profound transformation. But it is a lesson that was also frequently taught by the stage itself. That sounds might hurt their hearers was a presupposition of London commercial theatre almost from its inception. One of the first trends, or fashions, to develop in the public playhouses of the 1580s was a fixed association between brash, loud noises and physical violence. The battle plays of the late sixteenth century represent warfare sonically, as an ear-splitting assault of drums, trumpets and alarums. Robert Greene's *Alphonsus, King of Aragon* is filled with what Venus calls the 'great noise' of 'men at arms';[7] while in his *James the Fourth*, trumpets are said to 'sound a dreadful charge'.[8]

George Peele's *Battle of Alcazar* commands its audience to hear the 'dreadful shrieks and clamours that resound' as 'war begins his rage and ruthless reign'.[9] Exuberantly noisy plays like these, which Ben Jonson would later mock for their 'rolled bullet' thunder and 'tempestuous drum[s]', forged practical and thematic associations between aural and physical violence that would permeate the drama for decades.[10] But increasingly, this network of associations became central to, and a more lasting component of, one kind of play in particular. Revenge tragedies locate the source of the stage's sonic assaults not in the drums, trumpets and alarums of battle, but in what George Peele's *David and Bethsabe* calls 'revenging lips' and 'breathie swords' – that is, in the revenger's violently potent vocal matter.[11] This book argues that part of what made revenge tragedy recognisable as such by 1606, when *The Revenger's Tragedy* was first performed, was its representation of sound and audition, and particularly the reception of dramatic speech. The deadly energy of Vindice's words and the duke's defencelessness against them are as conventional as a number of other features common to the genre – its comingling of the tragic and the comic; its incorporation of metatheatrical set pieces, such as a masque or a play-within-a-play, as tools for dramatic discovery and revelation; its foreign settings; its ghosts; and its staging of the revenger's madness.

This is not to say that after 1600 sound's violent potential is unleashed only in tragedies of revenge. Ben Jonson, that persistent mocker of supposedly old-fashioned, noisy theatre, incorporated gruesome aural violence into his own comedies. His *Epicoene, or the Silent Woman*, which was staged a few years after *The Revenger's Tragedy*, in 1609, features a character who 'can endure no noise', and who wears 'a huge turban of nightcaps on his head, buckled over his ears' in a futile attempt to keep out the sounds of the city.[12] Jonson's London pulses with the commercial din of shopkeepers, barbers, gallants – and, above all (as Karen Newman put it), the 'talkative women' who 'gallivant about the city streets spending breath as well as money'.[13] Yet sound functions very differently in this play than it does in *The Revenger's Tragedy*. It is not a weapon – or, rather, it is not *always* a weapon, to everybody – but a good to be consumed thoughtfully, and knowledgeably, by people of taste. *Epicoene* ridicules the turban-wearing Morose's inability to manage the city's sounds, implying that such control is not only possible but in fact necessary to cultivate. Morose's failure to limit the ferocity of sound's impact (whether that sound is a braying trumpet, a thump at the door or the long-winded witty rants of the gallant Truewit) identifies him as insufficiently male and as insufficiently urbane – an effeminate old man out of touch with, and therefore unworthy of participating in, the sometimes boorishly loud, aurally garish city of London that forms not only the soundtrack to so many of Jonson's comedies, but also their inspiration. In its staging of sound as a good to be sampled selectively by tasteful consumers, *Epicoene* is as representative of the city comedy genre as *The Revenger's Tragedy* is of tragedies of revenge. Time and again, these plays, which are deeply interested in exploring the kinds of cultural competencies necessary for achieving social, sexual and financial success in sixteenth- and seventeenth-century London, represent problems of auditory reception as social failures. Much like Morose's inability to manage the city's soundscape, mishearings are social 'tells', as devastatingly revealing of social pretension as a poorly deployed Latin phrase or an over-fondness for French fashion.

How did we get here? How did these two seemingly incompatible ways of thinking about sound – as something that slips down into the heart unbidden, and 'gaules' the mind, or as something that can be sampled, even if only by a select and privileged few – manage to coexist on the early modern stage? And how did they affect theatregoers' experience of this largely aural art form? These are the questions that drive this book, and I argue that they are central to the formal and cultural history of early modern theatre.

Sound, Sense and Form

From Plato onwards, a tradition has existed privileging sight as the highest, most refined of the senses; and yet, such thinking is by no means the only, or even the primary, means through which men and women experienced or conceptualised of their sensory perception. Touch, taste, hearing and smell have all been the subjects of recent studies that seek to restore a sensory balance, or to challenge historical hierarchies of the senses altogether.[14] We know from this work that hearing has held (and, indeed, continues to hold) a fascination for a number of cultures, across multiple periods. This fascination is evidenced and encouraged by the growing, interdisciplinary field of sound studies, which includes scholarship as diverse as the anthropologist Charles Hirschkind's *The Ethical Soundscape* (a study of the circulation and reception of Islamic cassette sermons in Cairo) and neuroscientist Seth S. Horowitz's *The Universal Sense: How Hearing Shapes the Mind*.[15] Historians and literary scholars interested in sounds and soundscapes have examined their role in shaping early American culture, the Victorian novel and mid-twentieth-century American modernism.[16] Yet we know that hearing occupied, if not a uniquely privileged position in early modern English culture, then certainly an especially central one. Its significance in this period has been well documented by Bruce R. Smith and Gina Bloom, among others, who have helped us to imagine the soundscapes of early modern England and to better access the experiences of the men and women who moved within them.[17] None of these studies take up the relationship between auditory reception and theatrical form which is the central subject of this book, but they provide the necessary texture and context for understanding why that relationship matters. Hearing was a subject of urgency in early modern England. This intensified interest in audition was driven by several factors: the growth of anatomy as a discipline and practice,[18] which turned new attention in the sixteenth and seventeenth centuries to the ways in which all aspects of the body performed and functioned, including the senses; the stated Protestant preference for words over images, which, in a culture with relatively low literacy rates, meant that the ear was by necessity the organ of salvation;[19] early modern training in rhetorical theory and practice; and, finally, the drastic changes to English soundscapes brought on by rapid urban growth, which were forever changing how and what people heard.[20] Any discussion of sound in early modern English theatre has to take into account these factors, since the auditory experiences of the men and women who wrote, performed and consumed its plays as entertainment were so vitally conditioned by them.

As such thinking suggests, I understand dramatic genres as emerging largely through performance, and out of a collective, often deliberately collaborative, process. This process of creative production was one in which playwrights, actors and audiences all had a part.[21] While sixteenth- and seventeenth-century dramatists drew from classical and medieval traditions, the forms they produced for the stage were, in many ways, altogether new. Their development was interactive, messy and inexact, the product of experimentation and competition between specific playwrights as well as between the companies and playhouses for which they wrote.[22] Early modern dramatists made stylistic and structural choices based not only on inherited theatrical models and practices but also on grittier, more pragmatic concerns: to meet the demands of the market, or to pass the scrutiny of the Master of the Revels, as well as to make sense of present social and cultural realities. They improvised and repeated patterns that worked, and, in the process, established 'rules' of playing through which dramatic tropes, conventions and structures – including generic categories – came into being. The codes of signification through which early modern plays were produced and made meaningful developed gradually, and through a dynamic, multiply directed process.

Sound, one of the basic building blocks of the theatre, was elemental to this process. Dramatists experimented with sound effects and styles of versification, pronunciation and tone in ways that invited theatregoers to tune in to their own auditory experience. We can find traces of this experimentation in the multilingual puns Patricia Parker has helped us to hear, as well as in the stage music (songs, ballads, incidental music, jigs) whose sound, meaning and dramatic function musicologists and theatre historians have done so much to recover.[23] This book argues that revenge tragedy and city comedy were born directly out of such sonic play. In tragedies of revenge, sound, particularly the sound of vehement speech, is deadly violent. It slices into hearers' bodies on and off the stage, becoming a crucial weapon in the revenger's arsenal that can be wielded bluntly or with astonishing precision. It is this signature formal feature that city comedy's earliest dramatists – Ben Jonson in particular – began to ridicule at the start of the seventeenth century. Skewering both the sound and style of reception associated with revenge's rumbling speeches, these dramatists touted their own comedies' self-professedly less noisy, and more musical, 'stage poetry', insisting that it required a more thoughtful and selective auditory practice. The two genres are thus competitively interconnected with a shared and lasting history.

What made these competing ways of imagining hearing possible – and, at the same time, what made hearing itself so irresistible, and so persistent, a dramatic subject – was the intense scrutiny brought to this sense by the period's religious and natural philosophical discourses, as well as by the rhetorical training that was so central to early modern grammar school and university education. Rhetoricians were deeply concerned with sound, both as an essential component of style and as a means to an end.[24] If persuasion was the orator's goal, then achieving that goal depended largely on hearers' receptive reception of what was being said. As Wayne Rebhorn has shown, in Renaissance Europe this process was often figured as a kind of assault, in which the orator conquers his listening subjects with weaponised words.[25] Henry Peacham's *The Garden of Eloquence* (London, 1593) describes metaphor as being 'forcible to persuade' since, 'In respect of their firme impression in the mind, & remembrance of the hearer, they are as seales upon soft waxe, or as deep stamps in long lasting metall' (pp. 13, 14). Impressing, stamping, and otherwise marking the hearer, well-chosen metaphors have considerable effect, but their success is also partly dependent on the hearer's knowing and willing reception, and it is this seeming contradiction that lies at the heart of my study. Further on in his discussion of metaphors, Peacham cautions that some are doomed to fail: the 'similitude' should not be 'farre fetcht', for example, 'as from strange things unknowne to the hearer' (p. 14). Without the receptivity born of mutual understanding, in other words, the 'soft waxe' of the listener will remain smoothly unaffected. Most English writers on the subject of rhetoric seem to have been similarly attuned to the power of language, and particularly of speech, to affect its hearers, while at the same time acknowledging that this potent weapon might misfire or fail to go off at all.

A similar fascination with sound, as well as a great deal of uncertainty as to how, or even whether, its reception could be managed, can be found in sixteenth- and seventeenth-century anatomy texts. Helkiah Crooke's *Microcosmographia*, for example, which contemporary scholars have mined extensively for insight into the history of the body, concludes its discussion of sound and hearing with an apology to the reader: '[T]here are some passages in my Author[s], wherein I haue bene intangled', Crooke writes, 'partly by the difficultie of the matter, partly by the fault of the Printer' (p. 612).[26] He promises that he has 'followed their words' 'as neere as I could', or 'at least their meaning, if they vnderstood themselues, as of some of them I make much doubt' (p. 612). Like other university-educated anatomists of the period, and indeed like his classical sources, Crooke seems to have struggled most over the question of just what, exactly, a sound *is*. While the objects of the other senses – sight, touch, taste, smell – could be defined more or less precisely as substances, sound's Aristotelian categorisation remained elusive.[27] Ultimately, Crooke concludes that sound is a quality rather than a substance, and a passive (rather than a sensitive) one at that. It is not an active force, but an effect that is produced and transmitted through a medium:

> Others do define it to be A sensatiue quality striking the hearing and the proper obiect of that Sense. But we will thus define it, *A Sound is a passiue and successiue quality produced from the interception and breaking of the Aire or Water which followeth upon the collision or striking of two sounding bodyes, & so fit to moue the Sense of Hearing*. (p. 693, emphasis original)

Sound is a 'passive' and seemingly almost liquid quality that ebbs towards the ear. Its progress is passive and mysterious, and as it moves (or rather, as it *is moved*), it not only transforms the air surrounding the hearer but also reshapes the hearer herself. For all its apparent passivity, then, sound is both a product and a sign of force. It can only be produced through the violence of two bodies colliding with or striking one another, and it can only be heard through the intrusive transformation of the body. Though lacking in ontology (since it is neither 'subject' nor 'object'), it is anything but imperceptible or insignificant. It is almost more verb than noun.

I will have much more to say about anatomists' descriptions of sound in the pages that follow, but first I want to dwell on a surprising point of intersection between early modern thinking about sound and dramatic form: both are elusive, existing only (as Crooke says elsewhere about sound) '*ens fluxum*', or in the moment of being produced (p. 691).[28] And yet both are efficacious, even transformative. In the middle of a lengthy section summarising classical and contemporary authorities' thinking on sound, Crooke writes that Archangelus 'hath it on this manner as neere as I can vnderstande him. *The thing that maketh the sound sealeth or stampeth in the ayre the species or forme of the sound*, and withall driueth it on vnto the Instrument of hearing' (p. 611, emphasis added). The 'forme of the sound' is impressed, or marked, into the air, which is thereby transformed into something heard – something that is in fact 'driven' into the listener's body. This is more than a happy coincidence of vocabulary between seventeenth-century anatomists and twenty-first-century literary scholars, a justification for imagining both sound and form as dynamic forces shaping raw material. Since the theatre was itself a largely aural art form, absorbed either consciously and selectively or involuntarily through the ear, in a very real sense, the 'forme of the sound' and theatrical form were fundamentally, materially linked in performance. Thinking about one may even have helped shape the theorisation of the other. This is not because early modern dramatists were reading natural philosophy, necessarily, but because sound and hearing were practical and thematic preoccupations for the period's playwrights, and because sound and theatrical form could both be said to exist *ens fluxum* – that is, in the moment of their potentially transformative reception.

If sound and dramatic form were linked both practically and materially, then the process of learning to recognise and make sense of formal features was, in many ways, an aural one, even outside the theatre. The question of how to hear God's word was a frequent subject in Protestant, and especially in Puritan, sermons. Often citing Paul's assertion that 'faith cometh by hearing', ministers represented listening as a spiritually necessary but also difficult skill that could only be mastered through deliberate care and practice.[29] They therefore sought to train listeners in the performance of fruitful, productive audition by providing explicit instructions in how to hear, and by encouraging the lasting, memorable reception of their own words through the use of poetic devices.[30] Stephen Egerton's how-to book on hearing, *The Boring of the Eare* (London, 1623), advises parishioners to strive to 'vnderstand, and marke the method and order of the Preacher ... Because it is a great helpe to the memorie, and serueth ... as a threed or line without which hee shall bee entangled as in a Maze' (sig. E^r). This 'method' and 'order' refers not only to the overall structure of the sermon itself, but also to the shape of its sentences. The hearer is urged to 'ponder as well one part of the sentence, as another, & not take things to halues' (sig. D6^v):

> for hence it commeth that things spoken comparatiuely are wrested, as if they were spoken simply. Hence it is that the proposition of a similitude is marked, and the application neglected, with diuers other inconueniences from whence arise Errours, Scoffings, Cauellings, &c. (sig. D6^v)

In order to avoid mistakes, Egerton insists, listeners must pay attention to each sentence in its entirety ('as well one part of the sentence, as another'). They must learn to recognise a 'similitude' when they hear one, and to understand the relationship between its components ('proposition' and 'application'). Spiritually productive listening demands the cultivation of a formally sophisticated ear attentive to structure, order and method as well as to the use of similes and other devices. What emerges in these sermons is a sense of the ear as the organ of salvation but also, uncomfortably, of aesthetic judgement, since, as Egerton admits, some ministers are better at 'keep[ing] a good order' than others (sig. E^v).

All this interest in sound and its reception, whether driven by dramatic, rhetorical, scientific or religious concerns, would necessarily have been coloured by what one heard – a sensory experience which, in early modern London, was changing drastically. Between 1550 and 1600, London's population quadrupled in size, and the volume and variety of its soundscape swelled.[31] While the city's loudest noises (church bells, cannon fire) may have remained more or less the same, the ones that made up its regular hum were becoming lastingly transformed: the sounds of commerce and manufacturing, street traffic and the chatter of those moving through this increasingly cosmopolitan centre of trade.[32] Both the experience and the theorisation of hearing drew attention, in other words, to some of the challenges newly posed by city life, such as how to make sense of the practice and social meaning of consumption, and how to negotiate the relationship between the body and its environment in noisy, crowded spaces. The study of early modern audition therefore has much to add to recent work on the history of consumption, as well as the history of the body. By asking how individuals thought about and experienced audition both inside and outside the playhouse (itself a commercial space), *Listening for Theatrical Form* reveals just how fully theatrical models of selective reception helped to shape an abstract, aesthetic sense of taste in this period. It also demonstrates how the body's inescapable vulnerability to certain kinds of sounds would have undercut any developing sense of a bounded self. Like the four humours (blood, phlegm, yellow bile and black bile), sound is something both inside and outside the body that must be regulated, providing opportunities for self-mastery as well as for potentially embarrassing failures of self-control.[33] Sound's passage into and out of the self helps to mark the boundaries that exist between the individual and his or her environment and, at the same time, points out their porousness.

These are subjects that scholars have repeatedly looked to the content of the period's theatre to help make sense of and understand, but I suggest that the creation of its raw material was driven by, and in some instances was itself a spur to, thinking through such questions. While this is a book about the theatre, then, it is also a book about the culture that produced it, and about the interface or relationship between the two. I see this relationship as productive, active and mutually constitutive – an assumption that a number of early modern playgoers, authors and antitheatricalists would have shared. And, like them, I see it as knit together largely through shared, though also distinctly varied, sonic experience. The sounds of the stage and the sounds of the city not only echoed one another, but also marked or failed to mark their hearers in much the same way. The chapters that follow listen in on this process.

Listening for Theatrical Form

One of my goals in this book is to take seriously the question of what it is that the theatre *does*. That it does do something was, to Stephen Gosson and other antitheatricalists, a given; it was also a given to those who wrote in defence of the stage during the sixteenth and seventeenth centuries; and it continues to be so for many of the scholars and critics currently writing about this period's literature.[34]

Since the late twentieth century, when literary scholars began arguing for 'the historicity of texts and the textuality of histories', the dominant critical assumption has been that literature and culture are enmeshed within one another.[35] Exactly how they are enmeshed, and what this might mean, are questions that have not always been answered clearly. For phenomenological critics, the nature of the interface between literature and culture is best approached from the perspective of the individual. How did (and do) we experience the world around us, including its literature? What physical, material effects might literature, and drama in particular, have on the human body? Bruce R. Smith's work has been crucial to this thinking, opening up new possibilities for a scholarship of 'experience' and 'sensation' by imagining early modern drama as something thrillingly felt in performance. His *The Acoustic World of*

Early Modern England introduced a historical reconstruction of soundscapes long lost to us while arguing for the need for a 'phenomenology of listening' based on 'an amalgam of biological constants and cultural variables'.[36] My work owes much to Smith's, but I understand sensory experience as historically contextualised rather than as biologically predetermined, and as more heterogeneous than uniform. Even the biological body is experienced *through* rather than apart from history and culture, and it is not experienced identically by every body. I have therefore based my work not on twenty-first-century scientific theory, but on the early modern material in which sound and audition are richly theorised, including anatomy texts, sermons, poetic manuals, music books and plays. I have also resisted the tendency found in much phenomenological criticism, as well as in much of the recent work on affect, to speak in universalising terms about *the* theatrical experience, as though all men and women heard and felt things the same way. Defined as the 'intensities' and 'resonances' that 'pass [from] body to body', affect has become (as Katharine Craik and Tanya Pollard put it) an 'ambiguous and powerful concept' for contemporary scholars.[37] But in examining 'public sensations', or the 'qualities of experience', this work has often ignored the historical specificity of such sensations and experience, let alone the possibility of their individuation.[38]

The desire to correct this universalising impulse shapes much of Gina Bloom's *Voice in Motion*, particularly its chapter on Shakespeare's late plays, and I take Bloom's cue in arguing for a variety of auditory experiences and possibilities.[39] This is a problem that is improved upon, but not solved, by breaking down the universal into the particular – for example, into categories of gender (as in Bloom's account) or class. Undoubtedly, identity categories shaped how and what people heard; they also determined by and large how others expected them to do so; but this is not the whole story. Theatrical reception was necessarily varied, individuated and particular, and to speak in broad terms about auditory experience is to disregard this fact. At the same time, to break down the discussion of audition to the level of the individual is not to make claims so much as to offer interesting observations from which we can extrapolate nothing. The balance I have struck in this book is to focus on the ways in which the plays themselves anticipate and seek to train their audiences in particular modes of reception, and to seek out evidence of how that effort either succeeded or failed. Doing so sheds new light on what early modern audiences were like as well as on what the period's dramatists thought about them, and about the theatre culture, they helped to establish.

The next four chapters trace the formal evolution of revenge tragedy and city comedy over six decades of theatre history, focusing on specific moments, and specific plays, that I see as key to the two genres' development. I begin by eavesdropping on the public commercial theatres of the 1580s and early 1590s. Many of the plays performed during this decade seem to delight in their sonic excess, combining cannon fire, thunder and alarums with trumpet calls, drums and, finally, the rumbling thunder of bombastic speech. These raucously noisy productions, which I am proposing we consider as a distinct dramatic form, frequently link unpleasantly loud sounds with violent action and, especially, with the performance of vengeance. Revenge is said to 'thunder' into bodies, or to 'shriek' and 'cry' out; at the same time, noise itself is often deployed as a weapon against one's enemies. This dramatic feature is given force by contemporary scientific thinking and, at the same time, by repurposed classical theories of theatrical influence and effects. If sounds function as weapons in these plays, however, they do not always do so in exactly the same way. Increasingly, revengers' speeches become weapons that can be wielded precisely – that is, that can be directed into the ears of specific, intended victims rather than released indiscriminately into large crowds of hearers. I track this development through three plays, each of which I read against the backdrop of the late-sixteenth-century theatrical marketplace: Thomas Kyd's *The Spanish Tragedy*, Shakespeare's *3 Henry VI* and finally his *Titus Andronicus*.[40] By the close of the sixteenth century, revenge tragedy proves intimately bound up in thinking about what sound can do to listeners both on and off the stage, making it a theatrical form explicitly invested in the question of what it means to hear plays in performance.

My third chapter takes up the subject of city comedy, arguing that the form's turn-of-the-century innovators – Ben Jonson chief among them – positioned it as a sophisticated sonic alternative to the booming (in every sense) revenge plays of the 1580s and 1590s. To hear city comedy, and to appreciate it, was represented as requiring a more selective ear, one that could tune out unwanted noises while making sense of the sounds that mattered. By listening well, theatregoers could demonstrate their membership in an elite social and critical collective of well-informed, tasteful playgoers; failing to do so, by contrast, would mark listeners out as social impostors. Hearing becomes in these plays one of a number of new social skills that must be mastered in order to participate fully in city life – in short, it becomes the stuff, or the subject matter, of city comedy. But it also becomes a mode of consumption that the theatre is especially equipped to teach men and women to perform, and to perform well. Simply put, city comedies train men and women to hear in the very ways that, supposedly, only the privileged few could: to tune, or focus, their ears, filtering sounds according to an array of criteria. What began as a strategic competitive move on the part of some dramatists, as they sought to distinguish their own plays from the noisy blockbusters on offer elsewhere, eventually became something more, a valediction of (and, for many playgoers, an introduction to) new auditory practices that could fundamentally transform their experience of London's soundscapes.

My fourth chapter turns to the play of the period that is perhaps most interested in, and most self-consciously about, hearing: Shakespeare's *Hamlet*. Possibly a revision of an earlier revenge play, also called *Hamlet*, Shakespeare's tragedy is vitally shaped by the formal contests emerging at the turn of the century.[41] In my reading, Hamlet becomes a kind of Jonsonian mouthpiece, articulating a model of selective and tasteful theatrical reception, whose own hearing trouble frequently, and tragically, undermines the possibility of performing such audition. Hamlet's longing for complete and absolute control over his body's intake and release of sounds is juxtaposed against Horatio's more measured, partial reception, and it is only in the play's final moments that the dying Hamlet is released from this doomed and tortured struggle. Shakespeare's tragedy recuperates revenge from charges of embarrassing obsolescence by suggesting that all sounds can be processed thoughtfully, consciously and carefully – that no one dramatic sound or form forces its audiences to hear it so unthinkingly, or so violently, as revenge's critics would imply. The chapter closes by tracing *Hamlet*'s influence on a handful of Jacobean revenge tragedies and city comedies, arguing that *Hamlet*'s formal and auditory experiments would have a profound effect on the sound and structure of early modern drama.

The outcome of the contests in which *Hamlet* intervenes is the subject of my fifth chapter, which focuses on the repertoire of a single West End playhouse, the Cockpit, during the final decade of the early modern theatre's existence. In this somewhat seedy rival to the more fashionable Blackfriars, new revenge tragedies and city comedies continued to be written and performed, but the two forms were becoming increasingly hybridised, their sonic and auditory investments less distinct. I argue that a set of supra-generic conventions, each deeply attentive to sound and space, began to emerge across the plays performed in this playhouse, and that, collectively, these helped to shape a kind of Cockpit 'brand'. Combining a survey of the Cockpit's 1630s repertoire with focused attention to two representatively hybrid plays (James Shirley's revenge-comedy *The Ball* and John Ford's urban tragedy, *'Tis Pity She's a Whore*), I ask how this playhouse's scrutiny of the formal and sonic contests outlined above participated in the development of early modern theatre as a cultural institution. Together, these chapters demonstrate that the formal development of early modern drama was driven not just by playwrights' innovative, creative repurposing of classical and medieval traditions and materials, but also by focused attention to the theatre's sound and aural effects.

Seeing Sound

I want to close by turning away from the theatre, briefly, to two images that help to make vivid the competing models of hearing that will be discussed throughout this book: Theodore van Thulden's *Hercules and Omphale* (mid-1600s) and Rembrandt's *The Mennonite Preacher Cornelis Anslo and His Wife Aeltje Gerritsdr. Schouten* (1641). In the first, Omphale's dominance of Hercules, who has been forced to surrender his lion skin to the nymph and made to hold her distaff, is further figured by the way in which she grasps his ear. Flattened against the canvas and opened up to the viewer's penetration, the great god's ear becomes a portal into his thrashing, uncomfortable body. Its placement at the centre of the painting makes the viewer complicit in Hercules emasculation. This is a supremely vulnerable ear, belonging to no less powerful a figure than Hercules; and unlike the distaff it is a permanent physical feature shared among all men, and all women.[42] In the second painting, Rembrandt's striking double portrait, a man and woman are seated in an apparently domestic space before an open Folio. The man leans toward the woman while gesturing to the book, as though enthusiastically pressing his point. She, her lips slightly open, could be preparing to ask a question or even to disagree with the speaker, though her rapt expression is usually taken as evidence of his mesmerising oratorical skill.[43] Her face is focused, taut, and perhaps a little pained, suggesting how intently she is listening – an effect that is further emphasised by the oddly ear-shaped edge of her cap. Her posture suggests tension, and her right arm, which is bent inward, is suspended mid-gesture. Here, listening is a full-body activity engaging the eyes, mouth and hands as well as the ear. It seems to require effort, or work, and to be anything but automatic or inevitable. If the first painting represents the ear as vulnerable and feminised, then the second imagines it as a consciously attuned sensory organ, helping to unsettle assumptions about the female listener's passivity or the male speaker's dominance. Rembrandt's double portrait also reminds us that listening played a vital role in decidedly non-spiritual concerns. Anslo was a cloth merchant as well as a minister, and the painting celebrates the Dutchman's success in

Figure 1.1 *Hercules and Omphale* (oil on canvas), Theodore van Thulden (1606–79) © Tokyo Fuji Art Museum, Tokyo, Japan / Bridgeman Images

both professions. The room's lush fabrics, like the sitters' fur-lined clothing, point to the changing material conditions of Amsterdam and, with a little imagination, of early modern London, shifting our attention to the social as well as the spiritual functions of audition in urban, commercial centres. Hearing is just one of the acts of consumption on display in this scene – crowded as it is with books and cloth as well as with the sound of Cornelis Anslo's voice.

Together, these paintings remind us that audition was not just of theatrical, or dramatic, interest in this period, and they hint at the extent

Introduction: 'Audiences to this Act'   17

Figure 1.2   Der Mennonitenprediger Cornelis Claesz Anslo (1592–1646) und seine Frau Aeltje Gerritsdr Schouten (1589–1657) (oil on canvas), Harmensz van Rijn Rembrandt (1641) © Gemäldegalerie, Staachliche Museen zu Berlin Preußischer Kulturbesitz.

to which hearing was a subject of concern on the Continent as well as in England. Van Thulden's *Hercules and Omphale* and Rembrandt's double portrait give texture to my study of early modern audition by helping to locate it in time and space, both real and imagined. They place attention on this sense in mythical and in everyday domestic settings, highlighting it as a source of anxious scrutiny and as something to be celebrated, in addition to representing it as a practical necessity. They also show the extent to which sounds were 'good for thinking' (to borrow anthropologists Mary Douglas and Baron Isherwood's famous phrase).[44] How and what one heard could signal relationships between individuals and communities – such as, for example, between the gendered pair of Hercules and Omphale, or of Cornelis Anslo and Aeltje Gerritsdr. Schouten; or between the godly Protestant couple pictured in Rembrandt's portrait and the painting's spectators, who are necessarily positioned on the outside, looking (and listening) in. Finally, and perhaps most importantly, the paintings show the extent to which listening could be observed by others as well as experienced individually – that even when performed in private it was potentially a publicly meaningful act, which carried its own codes of social as well as aesthetic or artistic signification.

As I turn to the formal and cultural implications of specific modes of theatrical audition in the pages that follow, I want to keep these points, and the images that help to make them vivid, in play. Doing so will allow us to look for traces of early modern hearing not just in personal, historical accounts of individual reception, but also in the period's plays, since early modern English dramatists repeatedly used representations of audition to think about the questions and debates outlined above – that is, about the relationship between the body and its environment, or about how to create and signal affiliations between individuals in increasingly crowded, anonymous urban spaces. These are questions that, to a large extent, are still with us. But their exploration in early modern English drama represents a formally, aesthetically productive intervention of unique cultural urgency. The persistent, focused examination of audition in this period contributed to no less than the formation of the theatre itself – both at the formal, generic level, where it was rubbed into the grain of revenge tragedy and city comedy, and at the more global level of the drama as a whole; and, finally, at the level of the theatre as an institution. Its codes of signification, its rules of playing and its at times strikingly self-conscious cultural contributions, were often rooted in the theatre's investigation of its own aural impact. These are the stories that the following chapters aim to tell by investigating how playgoers learned (as Bird and Ford put it) 'to hear to see'.

Notes

1. Gosson, *The Schoole of Abuse*, sig. B6^v–B7^r.
2. Ford, *The Lady's Trial*, Prologue, ll. 1–5.
3. As Andrew Gurr reminds us, the Latin terms from which the English words 'audience' and 'spectator' derive (*audire*, to listen; *spectare*, to watch) gave the Romans their theatregoing *auditors* and *spectators* – terms they seem to have used interchangeably, and which the English used as well. See Gurr, *Playgoing in Shakespeare's London*, pp. 102–24. In thinking of these plays as performed, I am working from the related assumption that the period's dramatists wrote primarily for the stage. Lukas Erne makes a compelling argument for the opposite approach in *Shakespeare as Literary Dramatist*.
4. As my emphasis on the sound of dramatic speech suggests, I am using 'audition' in a very different sense from Harry Berger, whose *Imaginary Audition* argues for a mode of theatrical reading that considers how characters hear their own and each other's speeches within the world of the play. My inter-

est, instead, is in how dramatic speeches – spoken aloud in early modern playhouses before sixteenth- and seventeenth-century audiences – were expected to be heard, and were actually heard, in performance.
5. On the dating and authorship of this play, see MacDonald P. Jackson's introduction to *The Revenger's Tragedy* in *Thomas Middleton: The Collected Works*, pp. 543–7.
6. All citations to *The Revenger's Tragedy* are taken from *Thomas Middleton: The Collected Works*.
7. Robert Greene, *Alphonsus, King of Aragon*, in *The Dramatic Works of Robert Greene*, vol. 2, Act 5, p. 54 (the edition is not lineated).
8. Greene, *James the Fourth*, in *The Dramatic Works of Robert Greene*, vol. 2, Act 5, p. 152.
9. Peele, *The Battle of Alcazar*, in *The Stukeley Plays*, Prologue, 2.1.10; Prologue, 2.1.1.
10. Jonson, *Every Man in His Humour*. The quote is taken from the Prologue to the 1616 Folio edition, ll. 18–19.
11. Peele, *David and Bethsabe*, in *The Dramatic Works of George Peele*, at l. 1286 and l. 1830.
12. Jonson, *Epicoene or The Silent Woman*, 1.1.141–2, 139–40.
13. Newman, 'City Talk: Women and Commodification in Jonson's *Epicoene*', p. 507.
14. See Harvey, *Sensible Flesh*; Dugan, *The Ephemeral History of Perfume*; and Bruce R. Smith, *The Acoustic World of Early Modern England*. See also Gallagher and Raman, *Knowing Shakespeare*; and Craik and Pollard, *Shakespearean Sensations*.
15. Hirschkind, *The Ethical Soundscape*; Horowitz, *The Universal Sense*.
16. Rath, *How Early America Sounded*; Picker, *Victorian Soundscapes*; Emily Thompson, *The Soundscape of Modernity, 1900–1930*. See also Johnson, *Listening in Paris*.
17. See Bruce Smith, *The Acoustic World of Early Modern England* and Gina Bloom, *Voice in Motion*. I return to both below. See also Tanya Pollard's 'Vulnerable Ears: *Hamlet* and Poisonous Theater', in *Drugs and Theater in Early Modern England*, pp. 123–43; Wesley Folkerth's *The Sound of Shakespeare*; Reina Green's '"Ears Prejudicate" in *Mariam* and *Duchess of Malfi*'; and Leslie C. Dunn and Nancy A. Jones's edited collection, *Embodied Voices*. Work by historians on sound and its reception in early modern England includes Adam Fox's *Oral and Literate Culture in Early Modern England, 1500–1700* and Arnold Hunt's *The Art of Hearing*.
18. See Katharine Park, 'The Criminal and the Saintly Body'; David Hillman, *Shakespeare's Entrails*; Valerie Traub, 'Mapping the Global Body' and 'The Nature of Norms in Early Modern England'; see also Christian Billing, 'Modelling the Anatomy Theatre and the Indoor Hall Theatre'; Hillary M. Nunn, *Staging Anatomies*; Jonathan Sawday, *The Body Emblazoned*; Michael Neill, *Issues of Death*; Carla Mazzio and David Hillman, *The Body in Parts*; and Richard Sugg, *Murder After Death*.
19. See Hunt, *The Art of Hearing*; Crockett, *The Play of Paradox*; Folkerth, *The Sound of Shakespeare*; and Tiffany, '*Hamlet* and Protestant Aural Theater'. On the continuing importance of the visual to mainstream Protestant culture, see Crawford, *Marvelous Protestantism*.

20. On English soundscapes, see Smith, *The Acoustic World of Early Modern England*. Studies of selections of that soundscape can be found in Eric Wilson, 'Plagues, Fairs, and Street Cries'; and Korda, *Labors Lost*, pp. 144–73.
21. On the audience's role in the production of theatrical meaning, see Jeremy Lopez, *Theatrical Convention and Audience Response in Early Modern Drama*; Jennifer A. Low and Nova Myhill, *Imagining the Audience in Early Modern Drama*; Steven Mullaney, 'Affective Technologies'; and Thomas Cartelli, *Marlowe, Shakespeare, and the Economy of Theatrical Experience*.
22. See Roslyn L. Knutson, *The Repertory of Shakespeare's Company*; Scott McMillin and Sally-Beth MacLean, *The Queen's Men and their Plays*; Mary Bly, *Queer Virgins and Virgin Queans on the Early Modern Stage*; Gurr, *The Shakespeare Company, 1594–1642*; Lucy Munro, *Children of the Queen's Revels*.
23. See especially Patricia Parker's 'Shakespeare's Sound Government: Sound Defects, Polyglot Sounds, and Sounding Out', 'The Novelty of Different Tongues' and *Shakespeare from the Margins*. On stage music, see especially Austern, *Music in Children's Drama of the Later Renaissance* and Lindley, *Shakespeare and Music*.
24. See Murphy, 'One Thousand Neglected Authors' and Gerald P. Mohrmann's 'Oratorical Delivery and Other Problems in Current Scholarship on English Renaissance Rhetoric'.
25. Rebhorn, *The Emperor of Men's Minds*, p. 43.
26. Crooke, *Microcosmographia* (1615). In his confusion, I will show, Crooke is representative rather than unusual among early modern anatomists.
27. This difficulty is shared by Crooke's classical authorities (Aristotle, Plato, Galen, etc.) and those he calls the 'later writers' (Andreas Vesalius, Renaldo Colombo and Casper Bauhine, among others) (Crooke, p. 611). See Michael Frede's 'Categories in Aristotle'.
28. As Crooke puts it, 'that is, such a *being* as is then onely existent while it is a doing and in the time of his generation' (p. 691). The original reads '*eus fluxum*' [sic].
29. Romans 10:17.
30. Folkerth and Bloom have highlighted the conventional use of the sower's parable in these sermons, which explicates what the Preacher William Harrison called 'the difference of hearers'. Lori Anne Ferrell argues for a 'Protestant kinetics' that involves ear, eye and hand (for note-taking). I share Bloom's interest in engaged, thoughtful listening in the sermons, as well as Ferrell's understanding of fruitful spiritual audition as a full-bodied practice. Ferrell, 'How-To Books, Protestant Kinetics, and the Art of Theology'.
31. See Sacks and Lynch, 'Ports 1540–1700'.
32. On England's changing commercial culture, see Brenner, *Merchants and Revolution* and Braudel, *The Wheels of Commerce*. Bruce Smith describes the 'cross-currents of multiple speech communities' that could be heard in sixteenth- and seventeenth-century London as a consequence of this growth (pp. 53, 55).
33. On the humoral body see especially Paster, *The Body Embarrassed* and Schoenfeldt, *Bodies and Selves in Early Modern England*.

34. See especially Jean-Christophe Agnew's *Worlds Apart*, which argues for a mutually productive, rather than a merely reflective, relationship between early modern theatre and market culture.
35. Montrose, 'New Historicisms' and 'Renaissance Literary Studies and the Subject of History'.
36. Smith, *Acoustic World*, p. 284. See also his *Phenomenal Shakespeare*, which turns to audiences' 'sensations, feelings, emotions, aesthetic pleasure' (p. 7).
37. The terms of definition are Gregory J. Seigworth and Melissa Gregg's, in 'An Inventory of Shimmers', p. 1. See Craik and Pollard, 'Introduction', in *Shakespearean Sensations*, pp. 1–28, at p. 2.
38. The first phrase is Erin Hurley and Sara Warner's in 'Affect/Performance/Politics'; the second, Brian Massumi's, in *Parables for the Virtual*, p. 6. Even Smith, though he is deeply attentive to the difficulties in laying 'claim to [a] share[d] . . . "intersubjectivity"' with historical subjects, nonetheless emphasises that 'every speaking human starts with the same equipment for seeing and speaking: a body' (*Phenomenal Shakespeare*, pp. 23, 25).
39. See also Allison Hobgood's *Passionate Playgoing in Early Modern England*, which brings a distinctly 'early modern cultural history of affect' to the study of audiences' emotional experience (p. 9).
40. In calling *3 Henry VI* and *Titus Andronicus* Shakespeare's, I do not mean to discount the claims of collaborative authorship advanced for either play. See my discussion in Chapter 2.
41. The assumption that Shakespeare's *Hamlet* is a revision of an earlier play of the same title has been challenged by Bourus, *Young Shakespeare's Young Hamlet*.
42. Rubens's *Hercules Mocked by Omphale* (c. 1606) depicts Hercules's subjugation to Omphale similarly, with the nymph tweaking the god's ear (which is flattened, and shown as vulnerably open, at the centre of the canvas). A student of Rubens's, van Thulden may have been involved in copying a similar image from the mid-sixteenth-century frescoes by Francesco Primaticcio and Niccolo dell' Abbate at Fontainebleau. Later painters would represent this scene from Ovid similarly. Cf. Francois Lemoyne, *Hercules and Omphale* (1724), in which Hercules's open ear is turned toward the viewer at the centre of the painting.
43. See Susan Rather's brief mention in 'Stuart and Reynolds', p. 72.
44. Douglas and Isherwood, *The World of Goods*, p. 91.

Chapter 2

Sound in Mind and Body: Hearing Early Modern Revenge Tragedy

Introduction

This chapter traces the emergence of revenge tragedy as a distinct dramatic form on the early modern stage.[1] While the term 'revenge tragedy' is a twentieth-century invention, the body of plays to which it refers share a number of important features that early modern theatregoers likely would have recognised as recurring: the use of foreign settings; the frustrated revenger's descent into madness, whether real or feigned; the presence of ghosts. I argue that part of what made revenge tragedies recognisable as such was their vividly violent representation of sound, which slices and seeps into the bodies of those who hear it both on and off the stage. While stabbing or wounding words appear in a wide variety of plays, and are by no means the exclusive property of any one dramatic genre, they occur in tragedies of revenge with such ferocious frequency as to serve as a generic tag or mark. This recurring dramatic feature would have shaped thinking about the genre's reception in performance in important ways, and, since the revenge tragedy form would prove to have such longevity on the early modern stage, its violent speeches helped to keep current a sense of the theatre's awesomely transformative potential well into the seventeenth century.

I locate the development of this trend in a fashion for sonic excess that dominated the commercial theatre of the late sixteenth century. Filled with blaring trumpets, explosions, thunder and other sound effects, these early plays (a mix of comedies, tragedies and heroic romances) positively revel in their own noisiness. Revenge figures heavily in many of these productions, but it functions less as a central motive of the plot than as an exhaustively deployed motif, its performance as seemingly purposeless, and its effects as diffuse, as the cacophonous sounds that suffuse the action. It is not until the very end of the sixteenth century that a single, delayed act of vengeance becomes the driving force of the plot, a structural shift that I tie to the increasingly fixed association in performance of vengeance with violent speech.

Although I am arguing for a shift, or development, in dramatic form, I am not making an evolutionary claim of the sort criticised by Alan Dessen, in which various formal features emerge out of an almost inevitable process of increasing literary sophistication.[2] What I am suggesting instead is that one dramatic trend was eventually replaced by another, and that in seeing these two trends as connected, we can uncover much about how the revenge tragedy genre was thought to work in performance. In later sixteenth-century revenge plays, and in the numerous seventeenth-century productions that would take their cue from them, revengers wield words as weapons, sometimes with apocalyptic indiscrimination and at other times with fearsome precision. If we know a revenge tragedy when we see one, then I hope to show that early modern theatregoers would have known a revenge tragedy when they heard one, and to suggest that how they heard it mattered to the formal development and reception of early modern drama.

Revenge and Noise in Late-Sixteenth-Century Theatre

> Now will we passe the river all this night,
> And in the morning sound the voice of warre,
> The voice of bloudie and unkindly warre.
> George Peele, *David and Bethsabe* (London, 1599)[3]

In the 1580s, a handful of printed tracts began appearing on the subject of blank verse, debating its aesthetic value and bemoaning its dominance of the theatrical marketplace. What seems to be at issue, above all, is how this blank verse sounds and who has the right to pen it. In the letter to the 'Gentlemen Students of both Universities' that opens Greene's *Menaphon* (London, 1589), Thomas Nashe complains that 'vainglorious tragedians', or players, are being puffed up by 'deepe read Grammarians' who 'think to outbraue better pens with the swelling bumbast [*sic*] of a bragging blanke verse' (sigs **1^r–**1^v). By 'deepe read Grammarians', Nashe presumably means those playwrights who lack a university education, and who are accused of trying to outdo, or 'outbrave', their poetic betters – the university-educated dramatists Marlowe, Greene and Nashe himself.[4] The previous year, Robert Greene had complained that he had become an object of 'derision' because he 'could not make my verses jet vpon the stage in tragicall buskins, euerie worde filling the mouth like the faburden of Bo-Bell, daring God out of heauen with that Atheist *Tamburlan* . . .'[5] Since Greene himself would write, and by 1588 had in fact already written, in this same mouth-filling style, it seems likely that it was both the sound and the content (and, of course, the success) of Marlowe's play that were, for him, the problem. Similarly, Nashe's letter does not attack the bombastic sound per se, but the appropriation of it by those playwrights who are said to be socially and pedagogically unqualified to pen it. There is a protectiveness, in other words, of this sound, and a kind of jealousness of its success, which together suggest how widespread and how popular it had become.[6]

Comprised of words that 'fill[] the mouth' and that are low in pitch (like a 'faburden' or undersong), these plays' speeches are imagined by Nashe and Greene as ringing out into the audience's ears like the proverbially loud bell of St Mary-le-Bow. The effect is not altogether pleasant, which seems in fact to be the point. *Tamburlaine*'s Prologue frames the play that follows as an iconoclastic aural assault:

> From jigging veins of rhyming mother wits
> And such conceits as clownage keeps in pay,
> We'll lead you to the stately tent of war,
> Where you shall hear the Scythian Tamburlaine
> Threat'ning the world with high astounding terms
> And scourging kingdoms with his conquering sword.
> View but his picture in this tragic glass,
> And then applaud his fortunes as you please. (Prologue, 1–8)[7]

What is promised here, famously, is a play in a cutting-edge poetic style, one far different from and more sophisticated than the 'jigging' and 'rhyming' of earlier plays, which were written primarily in fourteeners. It is a style that will be heard, and that will sound a certain way: threatening, astounding. This poetic style mirrors the syntax, tone and perhaps even the volume with which Tamburlaine will address his foes, conquering kingdoms with 'high astounding terms' as well as with swords.[8] To say Tamburlaine's power is bound up in his oratorical skill is to repeat a critical truism, but the point I am making is somewhat different. Tamburlaine's oratory *sounds* a certain way, and it is for this reason that its effects are imagined as being so potent. Marlowe's audience is invited to be thunderstruck: to 'view' and 'hear' these scenes at their own risk.[9]

Greene's and Nashe's complaints essentially take *Tamburlaine*'s Prologue at its word, imagining the play as 'scourging' hearers with mouth-filling bombast, while their own plays often emulate its poetic style and sound.[10] It is not just Marlowe's 'mighty line', as Ben Jonson would later characterise it, that Greene and others echo, but his play's overall noisiness – what we might call its dramatic soundscape. Like other battle plays of the period, a category that includes not only heroic romances like *Tamburlaine*, but also a number of histories, Marlowe's play is loud: drums, trumpets and alarms are used to signal the eruption and conclusion of battles, and perhaps even to replicate aurally the battles themselves. In a very real sense, noise both signals and is a threat in these plays. After Tewkesbury, the battle with which *Henry the Sixth, Part Three* concludes, the victorious Edward declares an end to England's 'tumultuous broils', figuring the restoration of peace as a cessation of noise and clamour as well as of fighting.[11] And at the start of *Richard III*, which begins in the midst of this same peace, Richard declares, 'Our stern alarums [are] changed to merry meetings, / Our dreadful marches to delightful measures', drawing an opposition between the noise of battle and the comparatively softer (if, for Richard, nauseously cloying) sounds of peace.[12] In the epigraph from George Peele's *David and Bethsabe* that begins this section, 'warre' is said to have a 'voice' that 'sounds' in the midst of battle, a voice as 'bloudie' and 'unkindly' as the violence it bespeaks. In performance, war would have been made vivid for early modern audiences not just through the actors' spectacular stunt work, but also, or even especially, through brash sound effects. Battles commence with 'alarums', drums and trumpets, and the many 'excursions' that are called for in the stage directions would have rung with the sounds of actual 'conquering sword[s]' striking armour-clad actors. At times this noisiness is even commented on, or gestured to, metatheatrically. In *Alphonsus, King of Aragon*, the start of a skirmish is signalled by the army's approaching drums, which an enemy soldier recognises and onomatopoeically imitates, 'Hark, how their drums with dub a dub do come!'[13] While in Thomas Lodge's *The Wounds of Civil War*, Anthony calls out from inside the gates of Rome, 'Hark! by this thund'ring noise of threatening drums, / Marius, with all his faction, hither comes.'[14]

Although a wide variety of plays written and performed in the 1580s and early 1590s incorporate such noises, it is in the tragedies, English histories and foreign histories that they figure most regularly. Collectively, these plays represent a dramatic category that seems to have been tremendously popular on the late-sixteenth-century stage. A partial list would include Marlowe's *I Tamburlaine* (1587–8) and *II Tamburlaine* (1587–8), as well as his *Edward II* (1591–3); Greene's *Alphonsus, King of Aragon* (1587–8), *The Scottish History of James IV* (1590–1), *I Selimus* (1586–93) and (with Thomas Lodge) *A Looking-Glass for London and England* (1587–91); Peele's *David and Bethsabe* (1580s–90s), *The Battle of Alcazar* (1588–9) and *Edward I*

(1590–3); Thomas Lodge's *The Wounds of Civil War* (1587–92); Shakespeare's *First Part of the Contention betwixt the two Famous Houses of York and Lancaster* (1590–2), his *True Tragedy of Richard Duke of York* (1590–2), and his *Henry VI, Part 1* (1592), as well as his *King John* (1591–8); and the anonymous *King Leir* (1588–94) and *Locrine* (1591–5). This is, again, only a partial list, and there is much variety among the plays within it. But the heavily martial sound effects called for in their speeches and stage directions help to link these plays together while distinguishing them from other contemporary productions.[15]

Roughly contemporaneous with this fashion for loud, sonically assaultive drama, and often overlapping with it, is a persistent and almost obsessive interest in revenge. Rather than being the guiding motive of a single, focused character or set of characters, revenge is often invoked in these plays by nearly everyone who appears onstage, and it is used to describe a bewildering range of acts. Often the vengeance these characters pursue is the result not of long and careful plotting, but is instead immediate, accidental or providential. At the start of Robert Greene's *Alphonsus, King of Aragon* (1587–8), for example, Alphonsus longs to 'revenge [the] traitorous act' of his uncle, who usurped his father's throne; this goal has already been accomplished, however, by the end of Act Two, when he kills Flaminius in battle.[16] It is not Alphonsus's desire to avenge his father that drives the action of the play, but the series of military conquests that ensues, each of which contains its own vengeful episodes. In fact, the term 'revenge' appears at least another twelve times over the course of the next three acts, and is used by no fewer than five characters. 'Revenge' is similarly ubiquitous in Thomas Lodge's *The Wounds of Civil War* (1587–92), which contains at least nineteen occurrences of variants on 'revenge', 'avenge' and 'vengeance', and which pits the exiled Roman war hero Marius and his son against the tyrannical Scilla in a series of *coups d'états* (each of which is styled as 'revenge'). 'Revenge' is used thirteen times in Anthony Munday's *Rare Triumph of Love and Fortune* (1582) and is thematically central to his *Fedele and Fortunio* (1579–84), a comedy. The word seems to have been used as a kind of intensifier, a way of indicating the speaker's passion as much as, if not more than, a way of categorising a certain set of acts. It even seems, at times, to refer to a passion or emotion that can be felt and communicated to others through facial expressions and gestures.[17] In *King Leir* (c. 1588–94), the messenger who watches Ragan peruse Gonoril's letter interprets her gestures for the audience, 'See how she knits her brows and bites her lips / And stamps and makes / a dumb-show of disdain / Mix'd with revenge and violent extremes' (4.3.16–18). While in *A Looking-Glass for London and England* (1587–91), Radagon, the farmer's son who has risen to become the King's flattering counsellor, threatens his parents (of whom he has now grown ashamed), 'Dare you enforce the furrowes of reuenge / Within the browes of royall Radagon?' (2.2.1075–6). Both scenes draw on oratorical practice, in which stylised gestures are used to communicate specific emotions, but the overall effect is to suggest that 'revenge' is not just an act but a mood or feeling, like 'disdain', which can be read by others in a furrowed brow.

While many, if not most, of the plays performed in the 1580s and 90s invoke revenge in some form or another, vengeance is called for with particular frequency in those plays that participate in the fashion for noisiness discussed above. By my admittedly rough count, some of the late-sixteenth-century plays with the highest tally of words with the root 'venge' (i.e. revenge, avenge, venge, vengeance, revengeance, revengement) would include, in roughly chronological order by date of first performance, *Fedele and Fortunio* (1579–84, eighteen venge words); *The Spanish Tragedy* (1582–92, thirty-five venge words); *Alphonsus, King of Aragon* (1587–8, sixteen); *The Wounds of Civil War* (1587–92, nineteen); *The Battle of Alcazar* (1588–9, twenty-six); *Locrine* (1591–5, twenty-three); *The True Tragedie of Richard Duke of York* (1590–2, sixteen; the much longer Folio text of *Henry VI, Part 3* includes twenty-four); *Massacre at Paris* (1593, fifteen); and *Titus Andronicus* (1594, forty-three).[18] These plays vary significantly in their form and content, not to mention in the number of venge-root words they use. But their collective participation in two late-sixteenth-century dramatic trends warrants attention: the use of booming sound effects and 'bombastic' blank verse that celebrates its own apocalyptic power with a deep investment, both rhetorically and thematically, in revenge.

Given the frequency with which revenge and noise were linked in early modern commercial drama, it seems likely, even inevitable, that the two would have been linked both practically and conceptually in performance. Consider, for example, the theatre's use of thunder, which Linda Woodbridge calls 'theatrical shorthand for heaven's angry voice demanding retribution' (p. 33). Thunder often sounds at the precise moment when characters vow or are commanded to avenge a wrong, as when Talbot promises to 'avenge [Salisbury] upon the French' and his words are echoed by *'an alarum, and it thunders and lightens'* in *Henry VI, Part 1* (1.4.93, 96 SD, italics original).[19] It is not just that thunder signals divine retribution, or even that the classical sources from which early modern playwrights took their revenge plots feature thunder too, but that stage thunder seems to enact on a physical level something like the violence of revenge itself. In Greene's *The Scottish History of King James IV*, the English King threatens his son-in-law, whom he rightly suspects of trying to kill his daughter, 'I come for to revenge my daughter's death . . . / That this thy thirsty soil, chok'd up with blood, / May thunder forth revenge upon thy head.'[20] Here, to 'thunder' revenge is to call for it, or portentously demand it, but it is also to make it happen – to thunder revenge upon the heads of one's enemies. Thunder even seems at times to help perform retribution. In Greene and Lodge's *Looking-Glass for London and England*, King Rasni's sister, Remilia, is struck by lightning in her sleep after having agreed to be his wife: '*Lightning and thunder wherewith* Remilia *is strooken*' (2.1.499 SD). Rasni's response, 'What wondrous threatning noyse is this I heare', emphasises the threat that thunder embodies both as a signal and as a force within the play (l. 500). Again and again, revenge is dramatically figured, or even triggered, through sound.

There are practical reasons for such associations between noise and violence. Sixteenth- and seventeenth-century anatomists repeatedly describe sound as a force against which the body is all but defenceless, and to which it is constantly, vulnerably open.[21] Apparently without exception, anatomists and barber surgeons from the period refer to the ear as the 'hole of hearing', a gaping orifice through which noises and other foreign matter, such as bugs, can enter the body.[22] Once sound reaches the ear, it alters the form of the ear's outward air – that is, of the air that is found either outside the body or in the outermost part of the ear, beyond the tympanic membrane. This alteration is in turn communicated to the inward air, or the air inside the auditory canal, which (according to Helkiah Crooke) is as much a part of the listener's body as his or her heart or lungs. It is left over from the fetal stage of development, 'made of the ayry part of the seede and that very pure, to which the purest ayry part of the mothers blood applyeth it selfe'.[23] As John Banister puts it, the ears are 'continually open, and prest to receiue the sound of euery speach, or other noyse'.[24] Banister's 'prest' suggests both the material transformation of the body's inward air, the air that is found behind the tympanic membrane, and the involuntary and potentially uncomfortable quality of that transformation. It recalls 'pressing', the process whereby individuals were made to confess by having increasingly heavy stones placed on their bodies.[25] To listen in these texts is to open up the body to somatic transformation, as hearing entails the reshaping of the very matter out of which the body is formed. Providing a list of the sounds most likely to cause pain or damage to the ear, Crooke includes 'vehement and violent noyse such as the shooting of ordenance, thunder & such like' (p. 588). Such 'vehement

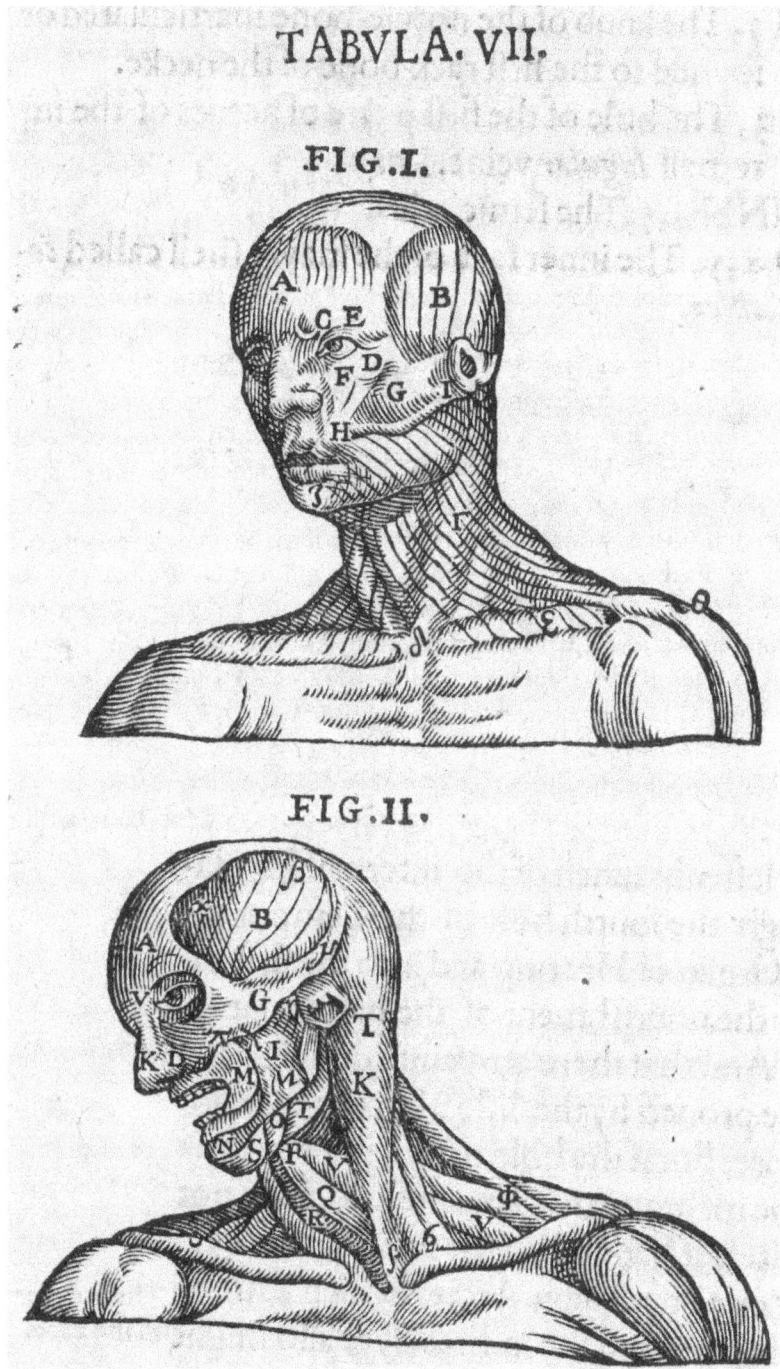

Figure 2.1 Helkiah Crooke, *Microcosmographia* (London, 1616), sig. Dddd2v. STC 6062.2. RB 53894, The Huntington Library, San Marino, California.

and violent noise[s]' are found throughout these plays, in the thunder, trumpets, alarums and dub-a-dubbing drums that *Alphonsus*'s soldier imitates. But if we, like Greene and Nashe, take Marlowe's Prologue at its word, then they might also be found in the 'high astounding terms' of 'swelling bombast'. In the passage quoted above, Crooke uses 'vehement' to mean 'loud' or 'intense', yet the term could also refer to 'passionately uttered or expressed' language, or to speech that 'result[s] from, and [is] indicative of, strong feeling or excitement'.[26] This second definition helps to highlight an important aspect of much late-sixteenth-century commercial theatre: the fact that speech, particularly when it is both loudly and passionately uttered, seems capable of paining or wounding its hearers. In *Fedele and Fortunio*, when Fedele accuses Victoria of having been unfaithful to him, he promises to 'be revenged' by 'blow[ing]' 'bruit of thy reproach throughout the city' so that 'every wounding tongue shall make thine honor now to bleed'.[27] This reproach, the rumour of sexual scandal, may be spread by whispering tongues (although the term 'bruit', from the French *bruire*, 'to make a noise, roar') could signify 'noise, din, clamour').[28] But Fedele's impassioned threat itself, which builds in intensity and possibly in volume, is said by Victoria to 'thunder in mine ear' (2.4.71). In both its sound and its sense, as well as in the feeling of its source, such speech could be said to harm its hearers.

The Prologue that opens Act Two of Peele's *The Battle of Alcazar* nicely frames the network of associations these plays develop between noise, bombast and vengeance. Deeply indebted to Marlowe's *Tamburlaine* for both its plot and the sound of its verse, *The Battle of Alcazar* is thoroughly preoccupied with the 'sound[ing]' of revenge:

> Hark, lords, as in a hollow place afar,
> The dreadful shrieks and clamours that resound
> And sound revenge upon this traitor's soul,
> Traitor to kin and kind, to gods and men.
> Now Nemesis upon her doubling drum,
> Moved with this ghastly moan, this sad complaint,
> 'Larums aloud into Alecto's ears,
> And with her thundering wakes whereas they lie,
> In caves as dark as hell and beds of steel,
> The furies, just imps of dire revenge.
> 'Revenge', cries Abdelmunen's grievèd ghost,
> And rouseth with the terror of this noise,
> Those nymphs of Erebus. 'Wreak and revenge',
> Ring out the souls of his unhappy brethren,
> And now start up these torments of the world,
> Worked with the thunder of Rhamnusia's drum,
> And fearful echoes of those grieved ghosts.[29]

In these lines, revenge is thundered forth, rung out, and fearfully echoed, but it is also 'shriek[ed]' and 'crie[d]', an effect that the Prologue replicates as well as describes. Its blank verse seems to be of a piece with the cries, drums and thunder that it references, boldly 'sound[ing] revenge' 'aloud' in its audience's hearing. All of these sounds are represented by the Prologue as piercing listeners, and as therefore participating in the enactment of vengeance itself. The violence of revenge is signalled, and even made experientially vivid, for the audience through sound – the loud, thunderous sound effects referenced by the Prologue, but also the resonantly voiced blank verse of the Prologue itself.

Peele's Prologue suggests that noise and revenge were fundamentally linked on the early modern stage, and even that playwrights may have thought about the one through the other. The battle plays most preoccupied with revenge are also richly acoustic, positively thick with sound. They suffuse audiences in all the sonic material the theatre could muster, celebrating sound's awesome potential to thunder, to wound, to astound and to destroy. By the start of the seventeenth century, revenge plays would look and sound altogether different – less like *The Battle of Alcazar*, and more like *Hamlet*. In his seminal study of early modern revenge tragedy, Fredson Bowers draws a sharp distinction between 'tragedies of blood' and 'revenge tragedy', in which vengeance features as 'the leading motive and the force behind the action' (p. 63). '*Locrine*', he writes, 'is no revenge tragedy' (p. 103). This is a distinction that may have been less apparent, and certainly less important, to early modern audiences, who would have experienced the gradual and uneven transformation of the genre from one kind of revenge play into another: as Muly Mahamet's son puts it in *The Battle of Alcazar*, 'The news, my lord, is war, war and revenge' (1.2.12). It is to three plays that I see as pivotal in this process of transformation – from plays of 'war and revenge' into what Bowers and others would more readily classify as revenge tragedies – that I turn in the following sections.

Outrageous Theatre: *The Spanish Tragedy*

Thomas Kyd's *The Spanish Tragedy* is usually considered the first extant early modern revenge tragedy, and certainly it shares features with other, later tragedies of revenge that many of the plays discussed above do not.[30] Like much 1580s theatre, *The Spanish Tragedy* makes liberal use of the word 'revenge' and incorporates multiple revenge plots. Unlike those plays, its use of vengeance is focused rather than diffuse. Multiple revengers seek justice, but they pursue a shared set of enemies, and the revenge that is called for by Don Andrea's ghost at the start of the play is not achieved until its final moments. *The Spanish Tragedy* is also relatively quiet. Guns are fired onstage and sennets and trumpets are heard far less frequently than in a play like *Alphonsus, King of Aragon*, in which battles are staged rather than described. At the same time, Kyd's play shares with his contemporaries' a fixed association between revenge and aural violence. It is not thunder or other brash sound effects that are the acoustic markers of vengeance in this play, but speech – and more specifically, theatrical speech.

This association becomes clearest in the play's final scene. Enabling the performance of actual violence by distracting its onstage witnesses, providing a screen for the true 'acting of [Hieronimo's] revenge', this bloody performance has most often been understood as revealing cultural anxieties about the failures of language or the incomprehensibility of violence (4.3.29).[31] Such readings tend to underplay the significance of the 'oration' with which Hieronimo's play in sundry languages concludes, a lengthy, rhetorically ornate speech that serves as epilogue to that performance (4.1.176). In what follows, I suggest that what makes Hieronimo's oration work is, first, its sound; second, the manner and setting of its delivery, which accords with early modern English vernacular manuals on effective, enflaming oratory; and third, its physical potency, which builds throughout the play. In *The Spanish Tragedy*, grief produces physical discomfort from which it initially seems only revenge will provide relief. 'To know the author were some ease of grief', Hieronimo tells his wife, Isabella, after finding the mutilated body of their murdered son: 'For in revenge my heart would find relief' (2.5.40–1). But it soon appears that physical discomfort can also be lessened through lament. For Isabella, tears, sighs and passionate speech together produce a kind of meteorological release: 'Oh, gush out, tears, fountains and floods of tears! / Blow, sighs, and raise an everlasting storm! / For outrage fits our cursèd wretchedness' (ll. 43–5). 'Outrage', as it is used in this speech, is best defined not just as anger or indignation, but also as a 'Violent clamour; an outcry, a loud cry', or 'violence of language, insolence'.[32] This release, or 'outing' of rage through verbal expression, tears and sighs is what 'fits' the cursed wretchedness of Hieronimo and Isabella, and until their revenge plots can be put into action it is the only form of relief available to them.

Yet if Horatio's death must be lamented aloud, or out-raged, in order for Hieronimo and Isabella to experience relief, it must also be kept secret, close and silent to be avenged. This paradox – necessitated by the structure of Kyd's play, in which the performance of revenge is delayed until the play's conclusion – is one on which Hieronimo repeatedly dwells, and which seems to produce physiological as well as emotional discomfort. In the midst of their swelling lament, Hieronimo suddenly urges Isabella to 'cease thy plaints, / Or at the least dissemble them awhile' (ll. 60–1). This self-stifling will enable them to 'sooner find the practice out, / And learn by whom all this was brought about' (ll. 62–3). Only by keeping 'quiet', in other words, will Hieronimo and Isabella discover who is in fact responsible for their son's death. Hieronimo later vows to seek vengeance 'Not . . . / With open but inevitable ills, / As by a secret yet a certain mean, / Which under kinship will be cloaked best' (3.13.21–4). Keeping his revenge plot secret seems to be synonymous with keeping quiet, or with putting an unnatural stop to the circulation of sounds: 'Thus therefore will I rest me in unrest', Hieronimo explains, 'Dissembling quiet in unquietness' (3.11.29–30). The line is later echoed by Revenge: 'Nor dies Revenge, although he sleep awhile', he warns the increasingly frustrated Don Andrea, 'For in unquiet, quietness is feigned' (3.15.23–4).

Keeping 'outrage' in is uncomfortable and possibly even unhealthy, as it threatens to pollute the circulation system linking ears, mouth and brain. What connects these organs is the body's inward air, the corporeal material out of which sound is formed. Although this air is created at conception, it becomes contaminated over time and must be vented: Crooke explains that the 'chollericke excrement of the brain' mingles with the inward air, which 'through the veins attaineth to the membrane of the Tympane and thorough it sweateth into the hole of Hearing' (p. 586). This purged air must, in turn, be replenished, and so new air is breathed in through the nose and mouth. (Proof of this circulation system's existence can be seen, according to Crooke, by the fact that 'when a man yawneth wide hee cannot heare what is spoken' and that 'those that are deafe by outward accident might receyue the sound or voice by their mouths' (p. 587).) As it circulates throughout the body, this air becomes the raw material of the voice and of sounds' reception. Stopping up this circulation system throws the body out of whack, creating a surplus of contaminated air that, like a humoral imbalance, puts the subject's health at risk.[33] Of course, to say that Hieronimo ceases his plaints and remains quiet after Act Two is simply false, since he continues to lament his son's death aloud in his speeches and soliloquies. Even as he does so, however, Hieronimo repeatedly bemoans his *in*ability to express his pain satisfactorily, or the failure of speech to perform its much-needed out-raging function. 'My grief no heart, my thoughts no tongue can tell', he murmurs in Act Three; 'Where shall I run to breathe abroad my woes . . .?' (3.2.67, 3.7.1). His 'lament[s]' have shaken the very earth, but 'still tormented is my tortured soul / With broken sighs and restless passions' (3.7.6, 10–11). The problem is that Hieronimo cannot make his laments heard – not by the heavens, the king or even by Horatio's murderer, since at this point in the play he does not know who that is. The broken sighs and restless passions he exclaims or vents in speech are therefore rebounded back into his own body, forcing him to reabsorb his own 'outraged' matter.

From an emphasis on the frustrated need to vent laments, Kyd's play shifts into an experiment in what happens when laments are too closely kept. By the play's final scenes, these have become both an internal contaminant and the potent, barely controllable weapons of the revenger, a kind of unstable nuclear weapon in the revenger's arsenal. Denied access to the king, who will not hear his suit, and still suffering from the effects of his own reabsorbed complaints, Hieronimo finally unleashes his long-concealed secrets in an apocalyptic performance that destroys 'the whole succeeding hope / [of] Spain' (4.4.199–200). Like the other tokens of his vengeance, the bloody napkin and Horatio's corpse, these secrets are at last 'discovered' to a thunderstruck onstage audience – not, importantly, as part of the play in sundry languages, but in the 'oration', as Hieronimo terms it, that completes this tragedy (4.1.176). Before the show begins, Hieronimo explains that it is 'the conclusion' that

> Shall prove the invention and all was good.
> And I myself in an oration,
> And with a strange and wondrous show besides
> That I will have there behind a curtain,
> Assure yourself, shall make the matter known. (4.1.175–9)

The 'matter' to be made known is, first, the content of his oration (that he has designed this tragedy to avenge Horatio's death), and second, the object that he has tucked behind the curtain: 'Behold the reason urging me to this. / See here my show. Look on this spectacle!' (4.4.88–9). Both the oral confession and the spectacular revelation of Horatio's body are discoveries of 'matter', meaning not only the *res* of what is being said but also the material out of which speech is formed (breath, air, sound) and, finally, the material fact of Horatio's corpse. Like the bloody napkin Hieronimo keeps as a token, or like the dead, decaying body of his son, Hieronimo's lament seems to have gained potency under pressure. It is the conclusion that proves the invention, or that completes his revenge.

Hieronimo's characterisation of his speech as a 'conclusion' points to a specific oratorical form discussed by Cicero and Quintilian and expanded upon by early modern authors, including Thomas Wilson in his *The Art of Rhetoric* (London, 1560). Well-composed conclusions stir their hearers through the use of repetition and enlargement, Wilson writes, producing an involuntary, physiological response:

> Therefore, when the Oratour shall touche any place, which maie giue iust cause, to make an exclamacion, and stirre the hearers to be sory, to be glad, or to be offended: it is necessary to use arte, to the outermoste. Or when he shall come to the repeatyng of an hainous acte, and the maner thereof: he maie set the Judges on fire, and heate them earnestly against the wicked offendour. (sig. hii^v)

And again:

> The other part of a conclusion resteth, either in augmentyng, and vehemently enlargyng that, whiche before was in few woordes spoken, to sette the Judge, or hearers in a heate: or els to mitigate and assuage displeasure conceiued, with moche lamentyng of the matter, and mouyng theim thereby, the rather to shewe mercie. (sig. hii^v)

To set the hearers 'in a heat' is to move them; this is figurative language. And yet as Gail Paster, Katherine Rowe and Mary Floyd-Wilson have shown, in early modern writing about the emotions or passions, such figurative language can and often should be taken literally.[34] The 'heat' being produced by the 'vehemently' speaking orator is part of a somatic response, one that is set in motion by the speaker's words. Such responses are in fact an essential part of emotional experience, as they are required to produce it.

Stretching for seventy-nine lines, Hieronimo's 'conclusion' offers fine examples of repetition and augmentation, and it is clearly intended to 'stir the hearers to be sorry' – not as a goad to justice, but as an end in and of itself. As Wilson rather anxiously acknowledges, conclusions are potentially lethal weapons that must be deployed carefully, and only for the good: 'so I doubt not, but the wittiest wil take moste paines', Wilson insists, for 'the defence of moste honest matters. *Weapons maie bee abused for murder, and yet weapons are onely ordeined for saufgarde*' (sig. hiii^v, emphasis added). Wilson's metaphorical link between words and weapons is rooted in classical representations of the orator as a warrior.[35] But in early modern thinking, sound's physiological force almost always threatens to literalise such metaphors. Setting its hearers aflame, moving and stirring them with its vehemently expressed content, Hieronimo's oration is not intended to persuade, but to punish, to thunder into the bodies of his enemies. It is simultaneously a passionate, well-crafted piece of oratory (a 'conclusion') and an assault, a turbulent venting of out-rage that has been withheld for too long.

To argue that Hieronimo's conclusion assaults its hearers may seem counterintuitive, since it is surprisingly ineffectual. The courtly audience responds as though they have not heard Hieronimo's speech, demanding what would essentially be an exact repetition. ('Why hast thou done this undeserving deed?'; 'Why hast thou murdered my Balthazar?'; 'Why hast thou butchered both my children thus?' (4.4.163–5).) Despite such questions, the King, Castile and the Viceroy can hardly be insensible to what has happened, or to who has stage-managed the grisly tableau. In fact, at the conclusion of Hieronimo's speech, the King immediately recognises that his 'nephew and thy son are slain' and orders attendants to prevent Hieronimo from hanging himself; it is only later that he demands Hieronimo explain his actions (l. 153). The onstage audience's seeming incomprehension represents instead an attempt to restore the social and political order which this knight marshal's revenge has upended, just as the call for 'tortures' to 'make thee tell' would transform Hieronimo's oration into an involuntarily pressed confession (ll. 179, 180). By refusing to hear (or to have heard) Hieronimo's speech, the court wrests from the revenger the awesome power of sounding out his own secret. In this context, Hieronimo's puzzling assertion ('never shalt thou force me to reveal / The thing which I have vowed inviolate') when he seems already to have revealed all, makes sense (ll. 183–4). It is not that Hieronimo has any secrets left to tell, but that he refuses to be forced to speak what he has already voluntarily discovered – to be sounded out.[36] This insistence on retaining control of his own speech, and by extension his own body, asserts a legal distinction that is understood, experienced and performed through sound's production and retention. When Hieronimo bites out his own tongue 'Rather than to reveal what we required', he reveals most viscerally that this exchange is not just about the symbolic, political power of speaking versus being made to speak – although it also very much about this – but about the materially transformative potential of sound itself, and of who will have the ability to control it.

The physiological effectiveness of Hieronimo's speech, which the court seeks to resist and somehow appropriate for itself, is determined by a number of factors, including its formal, poetic qualities, volume and tone. 'See here my show. Look on this spectacle!' Hieronimo demands, pulling back the curtain to reveal Horatio's body:

> Here lay my hope, and here my hope hath end;
> Here lay my heart, and here my heart was slain;
> Here lay my treasure, here my treasure lost;
> Here lay my bliss, and here my bliss bereft;
> But hope, heart, treasure, joy, and bliss;
> All fled, failed, died, yea, all decayed with this. (ll. 89–94)

This is the crisis point of Hieronimo's speech, when all is at last discovered to his onstage audience. But the content of these lines is all but blotted out by the sudden spectacle of Horatio's corpse, and their sense becomes somewhat lost in the sonorousness of the lines themselves. Hieronimo's speech is heavy with what George Puttenham calls 'auricular figures', conceits that 'make the meter or verse more tunable and melodious' but ultimately 'reach no further than the ear': for example, asyndeton (the deliberate omission of a conjunction) and paroemion (in which each word in a line of verse begins with the same letter).[37] According to Puttenham, these conceits 'affect not the mind but very little', and are therefore 'merely auricular' (pp. 257, 247). Hieronimo's lines would seem almost to be at risk of becoming pure sound, or sound whose sense is somehow secondary – even as they are meant to draw urgent attention to the 'matter' before them, the deictic 'this', 'here' of Horatio's corpse. Built out of conceits that rely on sonic repetition, and most likely delivered powerfully, loudly, in performance, Hieronimo's speech is full of 'woordes that' (to quote again from Thomas Wilson) 'fill the mouth, and haue a sound with them' (sig. hii^v).

In short, sound seems almost as important as sense here, and the desired sound is described in terms strikingly similar to those used by Greene and Nashe in their attacks on bombastic blank verse (in which 'euerie worde fill[s] the mouth like the faburden of Bo-Bell'). The poetic styles and conceits deployed by Kyd and Marlowe may be strikingly different, but the sound of those styles, and more importantly their anticipated effects on hearers, are similar. This is speech as sonic force. In the theatre as well as in the courtroom, such mouth-filling words are thunderous and affective, possessed of the capacity to move (as all successful rhetoric must), but also of the potential to wound or to assault. Part accusation, part wail, part dirge and part plot summary, Hieronimo's speech works here as a weapon, containing all the force of the pent-up sounds his body has held for so long.

I have argued that the effects of Hieronimo's theatrical oration are emphasised by the thunderstruck passivity of its courtly audience, and then by the violence of their reaction. But of course, these are not the only listeners towards whom Hieronimo's nuclear outrage is directed, a fact on which the play's elaborately metatheatrical framing all but compels us to dwell. Hieronimo's play 'in sundry languages' is only the latest in a series of inset performances, and almost the whole of *The Spanish Tragedy* is framed by Revenge and Don Andrea's not always attentive onstage reception (4.4.73). What distinguishes Hieronimo's final production from those preceding it (Hieronimo's dumbshow for the puzzled King of Spain, Revenge's dumbshow for Don Andrea at the end of Act Three), apart from its violence, is how it sounds – or rather the fact that it 'sounds' at all. Unlike the earlier dumbshows, it is a scripted performance, and a decidedly noisy one: a 'mere confusion' and babel of languages rather than a play with a clearly articulated 'argument' (4.1.172, 4.4.9). What this means is that as *The Spanish Tragedy*'s inset productions become more violently effective, they also begin to resemble more closely the kind of play Kyd's audience is seeing and hearing performed. Any complacency theatregoers might have felt in their own insusceptibility to Hieronimo's 'outrage' would potentially be unsettled, moreover, by the mistakes they have just seen Kyd's onstage audience make – mistakes that can be boiled down to their having failed to take what they are hearing and seeing seriously. Hieronimo's 'play in sundry languages' and its 'conclusion' suggest that theatre of the sort Kyd's audiences have been hearing and seeing is more than mimetic; that it has the potential to be materially efficacious; and that it does so, in large part, because it is produced through sound.[38]

The Spanish Tragedy is every bit as striking for the ways in which it differs from the plays with which it was roughly contemporary, then, as it is for the ways in which it has long been assumed to have shaped London's theatre. The battle plays of the late sixteenth century are, essentially, all 'conclusion', exposing their hearers throughout to bombastic speeches and cacophonous sound effects. *The Spanish Tragedy* focuses the aural violence of these other plays into a fearsomely precise theatrical weapon withheld until its final scene. In this sense, it has something of the force and concision of what George Puttenham calls *dirae*, and others call *ara* or *imprecatio*: short, epigrammatic bursts of poetic vitriol inspired by the desire for, and participant in the acting of, revenge. *Dirae*, or curse poetry, relieves the victim's almost physiological discomfort by allowing him 'to rid the gall' possessed 'of all such vindictive men', giving vent to it through language (p. 145). Such 'cursing' and 'wishing', even 'though it never the sooner happened', is itself a source of relief: 'yet was it great easement to the boiling stomach'. Not just a blanket term for virulent, hateful speech, *dirae* are a specific poetic form: 'a forme of speech' and a 'figure'. Puttenham identifies *dirae* as 'the fit instrument ... to express the bitterness of the detestation within us': 'and forasmuch as it sendeth forth the flame of revenge kindled in our affections', he warns, 'it may well be compared to the casting of wildfire, or poisoning of shot, to destroy the enemy'.[39] For this reason, the form is as forbidden to English poets as is the pursuit of revenge itself: 'We Christians', Puttenham writes, 'are forbidden to use such uncharitable fashions and willed to refer all our revenges to God alone' (p. 145). Hieronimo's lengthy oration can hardly be called epigrammatic, and as such it does not qualify as an example of *dirae*, but it works according to similar principles both in the source of its potency and in its intended effects. Assuming that *The Spanish Tragedy* was first performed towards the start of the 1580s, then Kyd's play, with its focused, metatheatrically framed oratorical assault, its *dirae*-like power to set its hearers aflame, seems to have been more of a formal outlier than a model for nearly a decade.[40] In what follows, I turn to a pair of plays by Shakespeare, most likely written in collaboration with other dramatists, which helped to introduce lasting innovations to revenge tragedy as a dramatic form, fundamentally reshaping it for the early modern stage.

Shake-scene-speech: *Henry VI, Part 3* and the Formation of Revenge

Yes trust [the players] not: for there is an upstart Crow, beautified with our feathers, that with his Tygers hart wrapt in a Players hyde, supposes he is as well able to bombast out a blanke verse as the best of you: and beeing an absolute Johannes fac totum, is in his owne conceit the onely Shake-scene in a countrey. O that I might intreat your rare wits to be imployed in more profitable courses: and let those Apes imitate your past excellence, and never more acquaint them with your admired inventions ... seeke you better Maisters; for it is pittie men of such rare wits, should be subject to the pleasure of such rude groomes.

Greene's Groatsworth of Wit (London, 1592)[41]

This famous passage, which includes the earliest known reference to Shakespeare, has much in common with Nashe and Greene's complaints, quoted above. Like Kyd, Shakespeare is accused of either appropriating or at least imitating an existing style of bombastic, scene-shaking speech. The phrase 'Tygers hart wrapt in a Players hyde' parodies York's words to Queen Margaret in Act One, Scene Four of his *Henry VI, Part Three* ('Tiger's heart wrapped in a woman's hide').[42] Greene's accusation has been taken as evidence that Shakespeare is the sole author of the *Henry VI* plays and, at the same time, as proof that these plays are revisions of earlier work by Greene, Marlowe or Peele.[43] Given what we know about early modern theatre practice, it seems more likely than not that *3 Henry VI* is a collaboration, albeit one with which Shakespeare's name was definitely associated. But there is something else at work in this attack, which only becomes clear if we stop thinking of it as an attack on Shakespeare and start thinking of the play itself as the problem. The blank verse that shakes the scenes of *Henry VI, Part 3* is at once both old and new, part of a play that is both familiar and experimental. Like *Tamburlaine* and other 1580s and 1590s battle plays, *3 Henry VI* is loud, suffused with the sounds of battle; it is also bombastic and 'braving'; and, finally, it is liberally decked with references to revenge.[44] At the same time, like Kyd's play, *Henry VI, Part 3* contains focused, sustained and personal revenge plots intermingled with those more diffuse invocations of vengeance. In what follows, I suggest that the play serves as a kind of pivot in the production of the revenge tragedy form, a generic hybrid that blends together elements from the two different kinds of revenge plays discussed in this chapter. And I propose that it is this, *3 Henry VI*'s formal and sonic inventiveness, that is at least partly behind *Greene's Groatsworth*'s attack.

Henry VI, Part 3 looks and sounds a lot like other battle plays of the 1580s and 1590s. This is perhaps even truer of the 1595 octavo edition, *The True Tragedy of Richard Duke of York*, than of the 1623 Folio text. An astonishingly noisy play, *3 Henry VI* is also liberally decked with references to revenge. From the play's opening scene until its final act, the Yorkist and Lancastrian factions are at war with one another. After promising to acknowledge Henry as king during his lifetime (in exchange for being named his heir), York revokes his vow and seeks again to usurp the throne. Queen Margaret, who from the start has rejected Henry's bargain, gathers an army in the north to protect her son's right to the throne. Henry eventually joins her. As in Lodge's *The Wounds of Civil War*, to give just one example, each battle is figured as an act of vengeance. Part of the chaos of King Henry's England lies in how personally motivated each of its nobles are. Revenge is performed not just by proxy – through the deployment of warring armies – but individually. Clifford, Warwick, Richard and others use civil war as a screen for their own ambition and as an expedient for settling scores, which far outweigh their loyalty to any one particular side. Henry makes use of these personal vendettas early on, but cannot control them for long. He reminds Northumberland in the opening scene that York 'slew thy father, / And thine, Lord Clifford, and both have vowed revenge / On him, his sons, his favourites and his friends' (1.1.53–5). But when Henry agrees to make

York and his sons his heirs, Clifford, Northumberland and Westmorland leave the stage in disgust. As Exeter explains to Henry, 'They seek revenge and therefore will not yield' (l. 190). In other words, the desire to avenge their fathers' deaths supersedes any loyalty they feel to Henry. It is not just Henry whose nobles use the war to enact their personal vendettas and fulfil their ambitions, but the Yorkist Edward. Once he has helped Edward to become King, Warwick is so incensed by his decision to jilt the French King's sister that he declares Edward 'No more my King, for he dishonours me' (3.3.184) and vows to 'revenge his wrong to Lady Bona / And replant Henry in his former state' (ll. 197–8). Warwick then conveniently recalls a series of hitherto forgotten wrongs: 'Did I forget that by the house of York / My father came untimely to his death? / Did I let pass th'abuse done to my niece?' (ll. 186–8). As in other plays of the 1580s, then, *3 Henry VI* is suffused with cries for revenge and representations of it, as well as with the noise of battle and the thunderous bombast of blank verse. Characters seek revenge and invoke revenge as an excuse for otherwise questionable acts. They also use the word as a kind of intensifier, as when King Edward assures Lady Grey that those who refuse to accept her as queen 'shall feel the vengeance of my wrath' (4.1.82).

3 Henry VI also shares with the battle plays discussed above, as well as with Kyd's *The Spanish Tragedy*, an emphasis on speech's power to wound and destroy. The drums, trumpets and alarms that signal the start of battle are often paired with volleys of braving speech (taunts, threats, insults) that are themselves likened to bombs, powder and gunfire.[45] And enemies are feared for their ability to threaten and astound as well as to attack. When, after the battle of Towton, Edward comes upon the dying Clifford, he commands:

> Bring forth that fatal screech-owl to our house
> That nothing sung but death to us and ours:
> Now death shall stop his dismal threat'ning sound,
> And his ill-boding tongue no more shall speak. (2.6.56–9)

As most recent editors of the play point out, the phrase 'fatal screech-owl' is proverbial.[46] But to emphasise the line's proverbial meaning is partly to miss the point. It is not just the owl's association with evil omens that Edward is invoking, but its eerie, discordant cry. In fact, the entire progress of Clifford's vendetta against the House of York is here being figured in sonic terms – as a screeching, a singing and a 'threat'ning sound'. For Edward and his supporters, a dead Clifford is above all a silenced Clifford.

This understanding of Clifford as embodied noise will in turn define the brothers' revenge against him. Suspicious that Clifford is 'counterfeit[ing]' death to 'avoid such bitter taunts / Which in the time of death he gave our father', Richard, his brothers and Warwick all decide to 'vex him with eager words' (2.6.66–7, 68). It is Clifford's imperviousness to these 'vexing words' that finally convinces his enemies he is in fact dead, but it is also this imperviousness that, for Richard at least, renders Clifford's death so unsatisfying:

> If this right hand would buy two hours' life,
> That I in all despite might rail at him,
> This hand should chop it off, and with the issuing blood
> Stifle the villain whose unstaunched thirst
> York and young Rutland could not satisfy. (ll. 80–4)

For two hours' railing time, Richard would chop off his own hand. Without such speech – or rather without such speech being *heard* by its intended target – his revenge feels incomplete.

Both Edward's characterisation of Clifford as 'that fatal screech-owl' and Richard's longing to 'rail' draw on the network of associations between aural and physical violence that I have been arguing are at the heart of late-sixteenth-century commercial theatre – associations that are thematic, practical, figurative, literal and even theatre-historical. But the two scenes are also, in a way, perplexing. While Clifford is certainly capable of trading braving speeches with his enemies, in comparison to many of the other Lancastrians he says relatively little. Even as a revenger, Clifford is not much of a talker. His murder of the child Rutland is blunt, brutal and abrupt:

> RUTLAND: I never did thee harm; why wilt thou slay me?
> CLIFFORD: Thy father hath.
> RUTLAND: But 'twas ere I was born.
> Thou hast one son, for his sake pity me,
> Lest in revenge thereof, sith God is just,
> He be as miserably slain as I.
> Ah, let me live in prison all my days,
> And when I give occasion of offence
> Then let me die, for now thou hast no cause. (1.3.38–45)

Later, Clifford becomes even more curtly dismissive: 'Thy father slew my father; therefore die' (l. 47). The awful simplicity of the line highlights the automatic quality of Clifford's revenge, making it seem less heroic than absurd – and possibly more cruel. Clearly permissible, even honourable, within the world of the play, Rutland's murder is nonetheless coded as morally questionable for *3 Henry VI*'s audiences: Shakespeare makes Rutland younger than he is in his sources, and the Tutor's plea ('Ah, Clifford, murder not this innocent child / Lest thou be hated both of God and man' (ll. 8–9)) functions as a kind of choric warning. While Clifford's murder of Rutland is vicious, it is not especially verbose; the crimes of which Edward accuses him (screeching, singing, sounding threats against the House of York) do not quite fit with what we see and hear.

The explanation for this confusion, I think, can be found in the scene that so captured the attention of the author of *Greene's Groatsworth*: Margaret's excruciating torture of the Duke of York. The staging of this scene does something catastrophic to language within the world of the play, swelling its capacity to harm. The scene is unusual among late-sixteenth-century battle plays in that it draws out for the uncomfortable benefit of its on- and offstage audiences the infliction of long-pursued, rather than sudden, vengeance. If we assume that *Henry VI, Part 3* was performed after *Henry VI, Part 2*, which seems likely, then Margaret's desire for revenge against York already took shape in that earlier play.[47] And unlike Rutland, whom we meet only in the moments before he is killed, York is (by that same logic) a familiar character whose animosity with Margaret we have witnessed develop. But the most striking departure from other plays of the late sixteenth century, with the important exception of *The Spanish Tragedy*, is the specific way in which Margaret's vengeance is enacted. With its use of props, staging and costume, her brutally imaginative revenge against York is explicitly metatheatrical, a vicious playlet performed for a large onstage audience of Clifford, Northumberland, the Prince and an unspecified number of soldiers. After being made to 'stand upon this molehill here' at Margaret's command, York is then forced to hear an unrelenting forty-two-line harangue, in which he is told of his son's murder; given a 'napkin' 'stained' with Rutland's blood to 'dry thy cheeks withal'; and made to wear a paper crown (ll. 67, 79, 83). 'Thou shouldst be mad', Margaret explains, 'And I to make thee mad do mock thee thus' (ll. 89–90). After taunting him with the names of his absent sons, she asks,

> Or with the rest, where is your darling, Rutland?
> Look, York, I stained this napkin with the blood
> That valiant Clifford with his rapier's point
> Made issue from the bosom of the boy;
> And if thine eyes can water for his death,
> I give thee this to dry thy cheeks withal. (ll. 78–83)

Like Hieronimo's bloody handkerchief, Margaret's napkin, dipped in York's son's blood, acts as a vivid *memento mori* and a goad to revenge. Her use of deictic pointing words ('*this* napkin'; 'I give thee *this*') turns York's and the audience's attention to the actual, material object of the bloody napkin while coupling it with speech: Margaret shows him the napkin dipped in Rutland's blood, but she also must *tell* him whose blood it is.

The gratuitous application of the napkin is also theatrically gratuitous – Shakespeare's audience, like York, essentially has its noses rubbed in the allusion. The prop pointedly highlights *3 Henry VI*'s revival of a dramatic feature that seems to have fallen out of fashion since Kyd's play was first performed. While in seventeenth-century revenge tragedies, the metatheatrical framing of revengers' wounding words is all but ubiquitous (think of the bloody masques that conclude *The Revenger's Tragedy* and *Women Beware Women*, or the elaborate banquets at the end of *'Tis Pity She's a Whore* and *The Broken Heart*), in the late sixteenth century it seems to have been far less common. George Peele's *David and Bethsabe* (1580s–90s) includes a murderous royal banquet, but this is not nearly so self-reflexively theatrical as Hieronimo's apocalyptically bloody 'play in sundry languages', or even as the cannibalistic feast that Titus hosts 'costumed like a cook' in *Titus Andronicus* (a play I discuss at length below). The scene must have stood out, both to be memorable enough for the author of *Greene's Groatsworth* to quote, and for him to be able to expect his readers would recognise it and know the play from which it had come. Its unusually metatheatrical framing of thunderous, vengeful speech may help to explain why.

From this moment on in the play, Margaret's enemies will persistently associate her with speech that sounds a certain way – we might call it 'scene-shaking'. She is said to 'rail' (Edward calls her 'this railer') and to 'scold'; and her power is intrinsically linked to her ability to 'fill the world with words' (5.5.38, 29, 44). As the term 'scold' suggests, this is partly about the gendering of braving, insulting speech, which in the world of this play belongs to martial men. But it is also about what this scene does to speech itself. It weaponises it and swells its somatic impact. For all the braving, railing speeches exchanged between the men in this play, it is Margaret's lines that first elicit an involuntary physiological response from an onstage hearer: 'Bidd'st thou me rage? Why, now thou hast thy wish. / Wouldst have me weep? Why, now thou hast thy will' (1.4.143–4). York's anguished reply, which is nearly as long as Margaret's 'insult', demonstrates how vehement speech could produce somatic responses in its hearers by moving their passions – a basic tenet of classical and early modern rhetorical training, but one that here plays a crucial part in York's torture (and, just as importantly, in his responsive eloquence) (l. 124). It is an almost meteorological reaction – 'For raging wind blows up incessant showers' – once it has been set in motion, that affects the whole climate of Shakespeare's play (l. 145).

York's lines compel from Northumberland, in turn, an emotional–physiological response of his own ('Beshrew me, but his passions moves me so / That hardly can I check my eyes from tears' (ll. 150–1)). While from Margaret they draw yet more railing, as well as the promise of a jubilant response: 'Stamp, rave, and fret, that I might sing and dance', she commands, imagining their interaction as a kind of mutually productive, endlessly amplifying echo (l. 91).

The audience, too, is part of this dramatic echo chamber. And in the pause in the action, as well as in the *noise*, that Margaret's mini-revenge play carves out of Shakespeare's brash and noisy plot, the audience is similarly invited to 'breathe while we take time to do [York] dead' (1.4.108). This call for a collective taking of breath focuses attention on how words can wound and move, restore and pinch, their affective power complicated and amplified within the space of the theatre when drums and alarums are stilled. Ultimately, *3 Henry VI* offers a very different staging of onstage reception than that found in *The Spanish Tragedy*, which initially stuns its hearers into silence. Instead, the scene combines a set of responses that together model and perhaps even entrain audiences in how they might hear a play that delights in its own potentially painful sonic excess. One of the possibilities that emerges, through York himself, is to hear even the most virulent and violent speeches with a kind of ethically restorative productivity. His hearing represents an affective, transformative mode of reception that is not wholly conscious or deliberate, but that nonetheless can be controlled or channelled in some way. At stake in such moments, I hope to show below, is nothing less than an expolration of how the theatre works, as well as of whether or not its effects can be managed, and to what end.

''Tis True, 'tis True, Witness my Knife's Sharp Point': Weaponised Words and the Making of Theatrical Form in *Titus Andronicus*

Titus Andronicus has been linked with *The Spanish Tragedy* since shortly after it was first performed. 'He that will swear *Jeronimo* or *Andronicus* are the best plays', announces the Induction to Ben Jonson's 1614 *Bartholomew Fair*, 'shall pass unexcepted at here as a man whose judgement shows it is constant, and hath stood still these five and twenty or thirty years'.[48] First performed in 1592–4, *Titus Andronicus* is, like *The Spanish Tragedy*, coded in these lines as old-fashioned and outdated, as well as lastingly memorable. The two plays share formal and structural features that I have been arguing were unusual in late-sixteenth-century drama: revenge figures centrally to both plots, but in both cases its enactment is delayed until the plays' final moments. Jonson's derisive remark suggests that the two plays were linked as examples, or even progenitors, of a certain kind of play. (What is *not* included in Jonson's short list is, in a way, as striking as what is: *Tamburlaine*, which he skewers elsewhere as outmoded, or any of the many plays it helped to shape, including *3 Henry VI*.) By the time *Bartholomew Fair* was first performed, plays like *Titus* and *The Spanish Tragedy* seem to have been recognisable as a discrete dramatic category – one which, at the time *Titus* was being written, may not yet have been considered a genre at all.

As in *3 Henry VI* and *The Spanish Tragedy*, in *Titus* vehement speech is often used as a weapon of precision that can be wielded more directly than a barrage of other noises, such as drums, trumpets and alarms. And as in both of those earlier plays, the self-reflexively theatrical staging of this weapon's deployment draws attention to the theatre's potential impact on its offstage audiences. Throughout *Titus Andronicus*, noise is linked with violence and disorder – or, more precisely, with barely contained chaos. The play opens in a Rome at precarious peace, its 'quietness' punctured with the sounds of war as its soil is trod by multiple armies. Saturninus and Bassianus, rivals for the crown, each speak in braving blank verse of their 'right', addressing imagined crowds of Romans (1.1.1, 9).[49] Their claims are mediated by the equally stentorian Marcus and, eventually, by the war hero Titus, who enters with a third army of 'as many as can be' sounding 'drums and trumpets' (l. 72 SD). Titus rejects the proffered empery, restoring it to the emperor's eldest son, Saturninus, and the crisis is deferred but not averted. After delivering a braving, bombastic speech in honour of his 'five-and-twenty valiant sons', nearly all of whom have died in defence of Rome, he orders the 'eldest son' of the Goth Queen, Tamora, to be hacked apart on a funeral pyre in tribute to the gods (ll. 82, 106). This is the act that precipitates Tamora's plan to 'massacre them all, / And raze their faction and their family', a revenge plot which Saturninus, who has been rejected by Titus's daughter Lavinia, willingly supports (ll. 455–6). The scene ends once again with the sound of trumpets, as the rival factions exit, the seeming peace only thinly covering simmering conflicts.

The opening scene's martial sounds, so familiar from late-1580s theatre (and, quite likely, written at least in part by George Peele, who authored several of the battle plays discussed above), are soon replaced by the noises associated with the more 'civilised' violence of courtly pursuits. Act Two, Scene Two opens with the direction, 'Enter Titus Andronicus and his three sons ... making a noise with hounds and horns' (2.2.1 SD). Titus urges, 'let us make a bay / And wake the emperor and his lovely bride'; he then calls on his companions to 'ring a hunter's peal, / That all the court may echo with the noise' (2.1.3–6). This command is followed by another 'cry of hounds, and wind horns in a peal' (l. 10 SD). Sound serves an ordering function in this scene, albeit one associated with the violence of the hunt – itself a supremely musical pursuit, both in its many onstage representations and in early modern experience.[50] Later, the sounds of the hunt become more menacing, as its object changes from a panther and a hart to Titus's daughter, Lavinia. Aaron has already put this idea into the heads of Chiron and Demetrius when Tamora invites him to 'sit',

> And whilst the babbling echo mocks the hounds,
> Replying shrilly to the well-tuned horns
> As if a double hunt were heard at once,
> Let us sit down and mark their yellowing noise;
> And after conflict such as was supposed
> The wandering prince and Dido once enjoyed,
> When with a happy storm they were surprised . . .
> We may, each wreathed in the other's arms,
> Our pastimes done, possess a golden slumber,
> Whiles hounds and horns and sweet melodious birds
> Be unto us as is a nurse's song
> Of lullaby to bring her babe asleep. (ll. 16–29)

Tamora's reference to a 'double hunt' is aural: the horns, echoing resoundingly off the landscape, have confused the hounds. At the same time, her phrase inevitably calls to mind the shadow hunt for Lavinia, who will be raped, mutilated and silenced by Chiron and Demetrius in this same scene. The noises that Tamora hears – barking hounds, the melodious horns' shrilly returned echoes and birdsong – combine for her into a kind of lullaby, but the implicit violence of this 'yellowing noise' is ever-present. The sound, however beautifully tuned, could not only symbolise but also perform aggression, as the theatrical audience is exposed to the potentially painful din of the repeatedly blaring horns.

It is on Tamora's glancing reference to Dido and her 'wandering prince', however, that I wish to focus. Shakespeare's introduction of this story at this moment, when sound and violence are being symbolically and perhaps literally linked, seems to point to the violent potential of speech as well as of noise – it is Aeneas's stories, famously, that produce the attraction that ultimately destroys Dido and Carthage. The invocation of this dangerously sympathetic listener, as Heather James has argued, often functions in Shakespeare's tragedies of state (including *Titus*) as a mark of the vulnerability of the body politic.[51] It is not Dido's reception of Aeneas's tale that is being referenced here, though, but a later moment in the poem, when Dido and Aeneas huddle together in a cave to avoid a storm. In other words, this allusion to Dido is deployed *not* to conjure up her reception of stories, but of other noises, such as thunder, lightning and the sounds of the hunt, as well as her sexualised 'conflicts' with Aeneas. It therefore fits the context of this scene perfectly. And yet, allusions to Dido are so inevitably freighted with thinking about her seduction through stories that the two cannot be divorced from one another – indeed, the listening Dido will be evoked again at the end of the play. The thunder and lightning heard in Dido and Aeneas's cave, the sounds of the hunt, and the rhetorical flourishes of Tamora's speech all become allusively linked. Like the cave (and later the pit, into which Bassianus's body is thrown), the mouth and the womb – all of which are collapsed together into figures of often horrific consumption – speech, thunder and other noises become overlapping markers of violence in this play.[52]

Of all these sounds, I suggest, it is speech that functions as the most reliably direct instrument of violence in *Titus*. And as the plot advances, it will become a weapon that can be wielded with increasingly brutal accuracy. Speech's assaultive potential is suggested in Demetrius's earlier threats to Chiron, which begin to erode the distinction between spoken language and rapiers. Told by Aaron to put away the sword he has drawn against his brother, Demetrius growls that he will not do so 'till I have sheathed / My rapier in his bosom, and withal / Thrust those reproachful speeches down his throat' (2.1.54–6). 'Reproachful speeches' and rapier alike will be 'thrust' into Chiron. His metaphoric language prefigures the actual thrusting of speech, as well as of tongue, phallus and rapier, into Lavinia's body, underscoring their shared violent potential. By aiming his assault at Chiron's 'throat', Demetrius also anticipates the silencing of their victim. It is by 'cut[ting] out' Lavinia's tongue that Chiron and Demetrius attempt to prevent her rape from being discovered – to prevent her 'sting' (2.3.132). Even when the distinction between words and weapons is reasserted, however (as it is several times in this scene), the language used to do so breaks down. Chiron accuses Demetrius of being a 'Foul-spoken coward, that thunderest with thy tongue, / And with thy weapon nothing dar'st perform' (2.1.58–9). The point is to distinguish between a weapon and a thundering tongue, while insulting Demetrius's masculinity; in doing so, however, Chiron also elides these differences. That Lavinia is later assaulted with tongues, swords and genitals will further and most brutally remove them. In the scene that follows the rape, which is all of the assault that *Titus*'s audience is made to witness, the physical violence we do *not* see is in essence re-performed through the oral violence that we *do* see and hear. Chiron and Demetrius's staggeringly vicious taunts pour in turns into Lavinia's wounded body: 'So, now go tell, and if thy tongue can speak, / Who 'twas that cut thy tongue and ravished thee'; 'Write down thy mind, bewray thy meaning so, / And if thy stumps will let thee, play the scribe'; 'And 'twere my cause, I should go hang myself'; 'If thou hadst hands to help thee knit the cord' (2.4.1–10). Repetitive, unmerciful and unavoidable, these taunts are forced into Lavinia's ears in ways that stand in for but also disconcertingly replicate her rape.

Titus's Rome is not just a world in which, as Gillian Murray Kendall puts it, 'language engenders violence and violence is done to language'.[53] An almost hyperbolically intertextual play, *Titus* is deeply interested in language and the literary, but it is the ability of words once pronounced to wreak havoc on actual bodies that seems to matter most in this play.[54] Time and again, the written word fails Titus in ways that suggest only speech will do – both as an outlet for vented out-rage and as a weapon to be wielded against one's enemies. The pitiable, poignantly ineffective shooting of arrows into Saturninus's court in Act Four, Scene Three, each with a handwritten message addressed to the gods, is a case in point: Saturninus is incensed at the 'Sweet scrolls' that Titus has made 'to fly about the streets of Rome', but 'these outrages', as he calls them, do not do any real physical or political damage (4.4.16, 22). Nor do they unburden Titus, whom we next see still scribbling away: 'Is it your trick to make me ope the door', he asks a disguised Tamora upon exiting his study, 'That so my sad decrees may fly away / And all my study be to no effect?' (5.2.10–12). Like the verse-wrapped arrows, the 'bloody lines' Titus has 'set down' are ineffectual, not a goad to action but a pitiable substitute for it (ll. 14–15). All of this writing is coded within the play as insufficient for unburdening Titus of his grief.

In fact, it is as if this bizarre exchange with his costumed enemies (itself seemingly borrowed from *The Spanish Tragedy*) gives Titus the idea for a new revenge plot, built out of the stuff of early modern English theatre as much as out of Seneca and Ovid. The encounter seems to clarify Titus's muddied thinking, to snap him out of his madness into a kind of steely lucidity. It is at this moment that he suddenly rejects the written 'bloody lines' and 'sweet scrolls' he had turned to earlier, choosing instead to vent his outrage aloud. As soon as he has convinced Tamora to leave her sons behind, Titus delivers a lengthy, repetitive 'oration' (to borrow Hieronimo's term) to Chiron and Demetrius:

> Hark, wretches, how I mean to martyr you:
> This one hand yet is left to cut your throats,
> Whiles that Lavinia 'tween her stumps doth hold
> The basin that receives your guilty blood.
> You know your mother means to feast with me,
> And calls herself Revenge and thinks me mad.
> Hark, villains, I will grind your bones to dust,
> And with your blood and it I'll make a paste,
> And of the paste a coffin I will rear,
> And make two pasties of your shameful heads,
> And bid that strumpet, your unhallowed dam,
> Like to the earth swallow her own increase. (ll. 180–91)

The plot itself is straight out of Ovid, but newly key to its performance is the telling. (Procne's son, Itys, who played no part in Philomel's rape, is not told why or how he will be killed before the women feed him to his father.) Once again amplification and repetition, particularly of the anaphoric 'And' (ll. 87–91), identify this piece as a rhetorically sophisticated performance but also, I think, as a weapon. The repetition of 'hark' (at lines 180 and 186) emphasises how keen Titus is that Chiron and Demetrius should hear his plans; it is not just a matter of understanding the horrific fate that awaits them, but of experiencing the words themselves. A few lines below, Titus repeats the detailed plans he has just explained, now addressing them as instructions to Lavinia: 'come, / Receive the blood, and when that they are dead / Let me go grind their bones to powder small, / And with this hateful liquor temper it, / And in that paste let their vile heads be baked' (ll. 196–200). Stated clearly and directly, but also repetitively, the 'argument' of Titus's revenge plot becomes its own vengeful instrument – a way of making Lavinia's rapists experience something like the unwanted verbal and physical assault she herself has felt. This effect is reinforced by the repeated demands made in this scene to keep the rapists quiet – that is, to prevent them, as they prevented Lavinia, from crying out: 'bind them sure', Titus commands before beginning his speech, 'And stop their mouths if they begin to cry' (ll. 160–1). Different versions of these commands are uttered several more times: 'Stop close their mouths; let them not speak a word' (ll. 164); 'Come, come, Lavinia: look, thy foes are bound. / Sirs, stop their mouths; let them not speak to me, / But let them hear what fearful words I utter' (ll. 166–8). It is as if the spoken allusion to the tale of Philomel now helps to re-enact, and exceed, that story's conclusion: 'Far worse than Philomel you used my daughter, / And worse than Progne I will be revenged' (ll.194–5).

What has happened here, and what will happen again in the final scene of the play, is a brutal literalisation of the metaphorical, one that is enabled, first, by contemporary ways of thinking about hearing and the body; and second, by new possibilities brought into focus by the theatrical marketplace of the late sixteenth century. *Titus*'s weaponised speech brings together the association between noise and violence found in earlier battle plays with *The Spanish Tragedy*'s representation of a spell-binding, oratorical out-rage. It is the theatre, in short, and specifically the early modern English theatre, that makes the imagining of Titus's revenge plot possible. It is therefore fitting that he gets his idea from the theatrical device of a costumed Tamora. When Tamora-as-Revenge first asks Titus to break off his writing, descend from his study and speak to her ('Titus, I am come to talk with thee') he resists: 'No, not a word. How can I grace my talk, / Wanting a hand to give it action?' (5.2.16–18). Like the other laboured puns on 'hands' in Act Three, Scene Two ('O handle not the theme, to talk of hands' (3.2.29)), this talk of wanting hands wryly gestures to Titus's one-handedness while pointing to his (and Lavinia's) cruelly butchered eloquence, an inhumane unmaking of the meaning bodies make. He insists he is unable to execute the gestures which not only grace but also help to give meaning to speech in classical oratory – that is, which 'give it action'.[55] But the word 'action' also carries a broader, more generalised sense of doing, or performing (i.e. Titus cannot transform his words into acts without his hands); and finally, and most suggestively, 'action' connotes dramatic action, or playing.[56] The term 'acting' originally referred not to the entirety of an actor's performance, but specifically to his gestures, with the more familiar sense of the word only coming into usage in the seventeenth century.[57] Titus's final 'action' will be performed through just this sort of acting – that is, not through gesture alone, but through the spectacular and theatrically totalising use of costume, staging, props and script.

Like Hieronimo's in *The Spanish Tragedy*, and like Margaret's in *3 Henry VI*, Titus's revenge is a carefully stage-managed event that enables the 'acting of revenge'. Complete with costumes, props and script, Titus's banquet is very much like a play: according to the stage directions, 'a table [is] brought in' and Titus enters 'like a cook, placing the dishes, and LAVINIA with a veil over her face' (5.3.25 SD). To the puzzled Saturninus's question, 'Why art thou thus attired, Andronicus?' Titus replies, 'Because I would be sure to have all well / To entertain your highness and your empress' (ll. 30–2). The word 'entertain', which means both to host and to delight or amuse, casts Titus in the role of a kind of actor-host. After engaging Saturninus in a seeming grammar school exercise about the meaning of yet another classical text (Livy's description of 'rash Virginius', who killed his daughter 'Because she was enforced, stained and deflowered'), Titus reveals Lavinia's 'shame' and both kills and perhaps unveils her, discovering her identity to the onstage audience: 'Die, die, Lavinia, and thy shame with thee, / And with thy shame thy father's sorrow die' (ll. 36, 38; 45–6). As in *The Spanish Tragedy*, *Titus*'s onstage audience is left struggling to understand the meaning of this performance ('What hast thou done, unnatural and unkind?' (l. 47)). Titus provides only partial answers, which in fact reiterate information he has already offered about the 'pattern' and 'precedent' of Virginius (l. 43). Refusing to be sounded, keeping close until the right moment the information he has withheld since the middle of the play, Titus remains in control of his most potent weapon against Tamora, his own confessional assault:

> *Tam.* Why hast thou slain thine only daughter thus?
> *Tit.* Not I, 'twas Chiron and Demetrius:
> They ravished her and cut away her tongue,
> And they, 'twas they, that did her all this wrong.
> *Sat.* Go, fetch them hither to us presently.
> *Tit.* Why, there they are, both baked in this pie;
> Whereof their mother daintily hath fed,
> Eating the flesh that she herself hath bred.
> 'Tis true, 'tis true, witness my knife's sharp point.
> *He stabs the Empress.* (ll. 54–62 SD)

The discovery of Chiron and Demetrius's guilt, coupled with the 'discovery' of their bodies in the pastry coffins, is a necessary accompaniment to the thrusts of Titus's knife's sharp point. The revelation of Titus's revenge participates in its own enactment. The centrality of this revelation is not new – it appears in Ovid, too – but the manner of its delivery is. Titus's short confession is nothing like Hieronimo's lengthy, rhetorically laden 'oration', or 'conclusion', but it shares in the focalisation of its effects. It is, in fact, almost epigrammatic, and in this sense it has more in common with Puttenham's and Peacham's definitions of *dirae*, discussed above, than does Hieronimo's lengthy speech. Like Hieronimo's 'conclusion', Titus's similarly couples the informational matter, the *res*, of his confession with both the matter out of which speech is formed (breath, air, sound) and the material fact of Tamora's sons' dead bodies, all of which she is being made to consume.

Titus's bloody banquet models theatrically framed reception as both a somatically effective and potentially transformative experience, thrilling in its very danger. But ultimately *Titus*'s reception functions somewhat differently from that of *The Spanish Tragedy*'s dumbstruck onstage audience. Once again, it is Dido who guides our thinking, as she is referenced by the stunned Roman lord, who asks Lucius to explain what has happened:[58]

> Speak, Rome's dear friend, as erst our ancestor,
> When with his solemn tongue he did discourse
> To lovesick Dido's sad-attending ear
> The story of that baleful burning night
> When subtle Greeks surprised King Priam's Troy.
> Tell us what Sinon hath bewitched our ears,
> Or who hath brought the fatal engine in
> That gives our Troy, our Rome, the civil wound.
> My heart is not compact of flint nor steel,
> Nor can I utter all our bitter grief,
> But floods of tears will drown my oratory
> And break my utterance even in the time
> When it should move ye to attend me most,
> And force you to commiseration.
> Here's Rome's young captain, let him tell the tale,
> While I stand by and weep to hear him speak. (ll. 79–95)

The multiple references to listening in this passage are dazzling. They include Dido's 'sad-attending ear', too intently focused on Aeneas's story; the Trojan 'ears' 'bewitched' by Sinon; the onstage listeners, who will be prevented from hearing the lord's broken 'utterance' and drowned oratory; the 'force[d] . . . commiseration' that his tale, were it to be told unbroken, would necessarily inspire; and finally, his (and our own) anticipated reception of Lucius's story. That Lucius responds by first addressing his 'gracious auditory', a phrase that could encompass Shakespeare's audience as well as the listening senators, extends this scene's focus outward, incorporating the offstage listeners into the catalogue of hearers listed above. This catalogue suggests that a range of potential experiences and responses are possible. But it also ends with the dissolution of the Roman lord into a kind of watery collective of speakers and listeners, both onstage and off. Opening his ears to Lucius's story entails emotional and physiological risk, since the 'heart is not compact of flint nor steel', but of much softer stuff. For those watching and listening to *Titus*'s 'entertainment', as well as the kind of play of which it forms a part, a similar set of risks and rewards might very well have seemed possible.

Assault as Entertainment: Hearing Revenge Performed

I want to close this chapter by turning to the Induction that opens the anonymous *A Warning for Fair Women* (first per. 1588–90), which helps to illuminate how revenge as a form was changing at the close of the sixteenth century and shows the extent to which sound served as a generic signal.[59] The Induction opens with Tragedy, carrying a whip and a knife, confronting History, who enters 'with Drum and Ensigne'.[60] '[P]eace with that drume', Tragedy demands, 'Downe with that Ensigne which disturbs our stage. / Out with this luggage, with this fopperie, / This brawling she epeskin [sic] is intollerable' (Ind. ll. 5–8). History is here associated with the signs and symbols of war (drums, a flag) as well as with the noises they produce: the rattling drum, from whose 'brawling sheepskin' Tragedy longs for 'peace'.[61] If History is associated with brawling drums and battle-cries, then Comedy and Tragedy, too, are identified largely by ear. Tragedy complains of Comedy's 'Cats guts' and 'fiddle strings', the 'filthie sound' of which 'Stifles mine ears' (ll. 14–15). And Comedy, in her retort, accuses Tragedy of being yet noisier still:

> . . . a Chorus too comes howling in,
> And tels us of the worrying of a cat,
> Then of a filthie whining ghost,
> Lapt in some fowle sheete, or a leather pelch,
> Comes skreaming like a pigge halfe stickt,
> And cries *Vindicta*, revenge, revenge:
> With that a little Rosen flasheth forth,
> Like smoke out of a Tabacco pipe, or a boyes squib. (ll. 50–60)

According to Comedy, tragedies can be identified not just by their subject matter ('some damnd tyrant' who 'Stabs, hangs, impoysons, smothers, cutteth throats' in order 'to obtaine a crowne'), but also by a particular style of vocal delivery – howling, whining, 'skreaming' like a butchered pig. With their 'brawling' drums, squibs and crying ghosts, Tragedy and History sound much more like one another than they do like Comedy, but Comedy's critique is also striking for what it associates with Tragedy alone. For if both history plays and tragedies alike are loud, only one is linked with cries for revenge. That revenge should be the purview of tragedy rather than of history may make sense retrospectively, but in the 1580s and early 1590s, when cries for vengeance were every bit as central to plays in which the drums and ensigns of history disturbed the stage as they were to tragic drama, any such distinction must have seemed muddier. Comedy then concludes her attack by ridiculing Tragedy's poetic style: '*Pure purple Buskin, blood and murther right*' (ll. 65–9). Like Nashe's 'swelling bombast of a bragging blank verse', these lines are meant to seem bloated, puffed up as well as 'purple'. Comedy's critique would seem to suggest they were becoming more associated with tragic drama than with history, much like the subject of revenge itself.

The observations made in this chapter about the relationship between sound and revenge, and about the transformations to the genre that occur over the final decades of the sixteenth century, ultimately lead to two points. First, that our working definition of revenge tragedy might be wrong, or at the very least incomplete. Plays that are preoccupied with the delayed revenge of a single character and, above all, the ethical implications of that revenge have obscured another, and I think for sixteenth-century audiences just as recognisable, kind of 'revenge' play – one in which a large cast of characters interact in a vast dramatic ecosystem of vengeance, noise and bombast. These two revenge-play forms coexisted with and mutually informed one another (Kyd's *The Spanish Tragedy* and Shakespeare's *3 Henry VI* and *Titus Andronicus* certainly have elements of both). But for the most part, revenge tragedy as we know it – or as we *think* we know it – did not really exist until the close of the sixteenth century. Second, the development of the one revenge tragedy form seems to have depended largely on the existence and popularity of the other. The exuberantly noisy plays of the 1580s and 1590s, which Ben Jonson would later mock for their 'rolled bullet' thunder and 'tempestuous drum[s]', forged practical and thematic associations between aural and physical violence that remain at the heart of later revenge plays.

This second claim may be supported not just by the evidence of the plays themselves, but also by theatre history. We know from the work of repertoire-oriented scholars that specific companies were associated with specific playhouses and styles of playing. It is possible that certain outdoor theatres were even more associated with the 'mouth-filling' sound discussed throughout this chapter than were others, or than were specific players. Not including Shakespeare's *Henry VI* plays, of the nine revenge-filled battle plays I listed above (one of which, *Fedele and Fortunio*, may only have been played at court), at least three were performed at the Rose by a handful of different companies: *The Wounds of Civil War*, *The Battle of Alcazar*, and *Massacre at Paris*.[62] It is striking that in its earliest instantiations, revenge tragedy was also associated with the Rose and, possibly, the Curtain: in 1592 *The Spanish Tragedy* was performed by the Lord Strange's Men, who also staged Shakespeare's *Henry VI* plays (presumably in the same theatre, most likely the Curtain), and in 1597 it was revived by the Admiral's Men at, most likely, the Rose.[63] *Titus Andronicus* was first performed at the Rose by Pembroke's or Sussex's Men in 1594. Performed outdoors, in open amphitheatres like the Rose and the Curtain, these plays' very noisiness may have served as an advertisement to the men and women who passed by the playhouses' walls that a particular type of play was being performed – a specific theatrical form, but one that nonetheless cuts across twenty-first-century generic categories. Simply by showing up at a particular theatre, individuals could be said to have chosen to hear a specific kind of play – noisy, bombastic and positively saturated with sound.

It is therefore worth asking why such productions may have appealed to audiences in sixteenth-century London. Since this feature was so central to the formal development of revenge tragedy, to tackle this question is also to hunt for reasons for that popular genre's longevity. Revenge tragedies born out of the tradition that *The Spanish Tragedy*, *3 Henry VI* and *Titus Andronicus* helped develop invite theatregoers to contemplate the risks of their own theatrical audition, even as they also direct that violence into the ears of someone else, and surely this helped contribute to the form's appeal. But in a culture that imagined sound as a kind of force, capable of producing profound physiological changes in its hearers, what would it mean to immerse the body in spaces so saturated with it? For Bruce R. Smith, the appeal of the public playhouse experience, regardless of the kind of play being performed, is that it 'engendered, through sound, a subjectivity that was far more exciting – and far more liberating – than those created by oratory, conversation, and liturgy by themselves'.[64] My own interpretation is less rosy, and more formally specific, but there must have been something particularly pleasurable about hearing loud, bombastic plays if they were to draw the kinds of crowds that made them commercially viable. Late-sixteenth-century theatre's sonic assaults may have entailed, for some, an exhilarating obliteration of subjectivity (or, in Cynthia Marshall's more explicitly psychoanalytic terms, the *jouissance* of self-shattering); for others, they could have done just the opposite, helping to restore a sense of control over how and what one heard in an at times disturbingly noisy city.[65] For Shakespeare at least, it is this multiplicity of responses that seems, in fact, to be the point, as the Roman lord who speaks at the end of *Titus* reminds us. Regardless of how these sounds may have felt to individual theatregoers, what emerges from these plays collectively is a model of the theatre itself as physically transformative, its effects produced largely by ear – an early modern theory of performance that seems to have had lasting appeal and power. The battle plays of the 1580s, and the later revenge tragedies they helped to shape, modelled a form of theatrical reception that would remain viable up until the theatres were closed down in 1642. In the process, they helped to introduce and keep current an understanding of theatrical audition as immersive and effective. It is to the ways in which this theory of performance, and the theatrical sound and styles of reception associated with it, evolved over the next several decades that I turn in the following chapters, which track how such thinking was challenged, recuperated and revived during the first half of the seventeenth century.

Notes

1. For early descriptions of the genre, see Churchill, *Richard the Third up to Shakespeare* and Bowers, *Elizabethan Revenge Tragedy*. Linda Woodbridge argues for a shift in focus from revenge tragedy as a genre to vengeance as a motif in *English Revenge Drama*. See also Pollard, 'Revenge Tragedy'.
2. Dessen, 'Robert Greene and the Theatrical Vocabulary of the Early 1590s'.
3. Peele, *David and Bethsabe*, in *The Dramatic Works of George Peele*, ll. 1377–9.
4. Nashe's complaints about these authors' dependence on Seneca, their use of translations and their insistence on 'thrust[ing] *Elisium* into hell' all seem to point to plays like Thomas Kyd's *The Spanish Tragedy* (and quite possibly to *The Spanish Tragedy* specifically), while his glancing reference to 'the Kidde in *Aesop*' also suggests he has Kyd in mind (**3r).
5. The quote appears in the prefatory letter to Greene's *Perimedes the Blackesmith*, A3r.
6. This protectiveness contrasts sharply with Ben Jonson's better-known dismissal of the same sound in *Timber or Discoveries*, in *Ben Jonson*, ed. Herford, Simpson and Simpson, vol. 8, p. 587.
7. Citations to *Tamburlaine* are taken from *Tamburlaine, Parts One and Two*, ed. Anthony B. Dawson.
8. On Tamburlaine's oratorical power, see Altman, *The Tudor Play of Mind*; Rebhorn, *The Emperor of Men's Minds*; and Cartwright, *Theatre and Humanism*.
9. This is not to say that all theatregoers heard, and responded to, Tamburlaine's oratory in the way the Prologue anticipates they will. See Thomas Cartelli's *Marlowe, Shakespeare, and the Economy of Theatrical Experience*.
10. See Berek, '*Tamburlaine*'s Weak Sons'.
11. 5.5.1. This and subsequent citations to *3 Henry VI* are from Shakespeare, *King Henry VI, Part 3*, The Arden Shakespeare, Third Series, ed. Cox and Rasmussen.
12. *Richard III*, ed. Siemon, 1.1.7–8.
13. Act Four, p. 50. Citations to *Alphonsus* are taken from *The Dramatic Works of Robert Greene*, vol. 2. The text is not lineated; I provide act and page numbers.
14. Lodge, *The Wounds of Civil War*, 4.1.46–7.
15. For example, the comedies of John Lyly.
16. *Alphonsus, King of Aragon*, in *The Dramatic Works of Robert Greene*, Act 2, p. 9.
17. Lodge, *A Looking-Glass for London and England*; Michie, *A Critical*

Edition of *The True Chronicle History of King Leir and his Three Daughters*.
18. This survey only includes plays performed in the commercial playhouses, both public and private. It does not include plays we know were performed only at court (with the possible exception of *Fedele and Fortunio*) or academic drama.
19. *The First Part of King Henry VI*, ed. Cairncross.
20. *James the Fourth*, in *The Dramatic Works of Robert Greene*, vol. 2, Act 5, p. 152. The text is not lineated or divided into scenes.
21. On this point see Bruce R. Smith, *The Acoustic World of Early Modern England*; and Gina Bloom, *Voice in Motion*.
22. John Banister's *The Historie of Man* explains that the fleshy outer ear is cupped around the 'hole of hearyng' in order 'to dilate, and keepe open the same continually, to the perpetuall promptitude of hearyng' (sig. Mii^v). The phrase is also found throughout Helkiah Crooke's description of hearing and the ear in *Microcosmographia, A Description of the Body of Man* (1616); in Thomas Vicary's *Anatomie of Mans Body*, at p. 35; and in Ambroise Paré's *Workes*, at p. 172.
23. Crooke, *Microcosmographia* (1616), p. 606.
24. Banister, *The Historie of Man*, sig. Ffi^v.
25. See Baker, *An Introduction to English Legal History*, pp. 507–9.
26. *OED*: 'vehement, a', II.7.
27. Munday, *A Critical Edition of Anthony Munday's Fedele and Fortunio*, ed. Hosley, 2.4.61–3.
28. 'bruit', n. 1, *OED*.
29. Prologue, 9–25. All citations to *The Battle of Alcazar* are taken from *The Stukeley Plays*, ed. Charles Edelman.
30. We know *The Spanish Tragedy* was staged by the Lord Strange's Men in 1592 and 1593, and again by the Admiral's Men in 1597, but it has long been assumed that *The Spanish Tragedy* is a much older play, perhaps first performed as early as 1582. See my fuller discussion below.
31. All citations are to *The Spanish Tragedy* (Arden Early Modern Drama), ed. Calvo and Tronch. See Mazzio, *The Inarticulate Renaissance* and West, 'But this will be a mere confusion'.
32. 'outrage', n. 1b, 1a. The *OED* notes that 'In English' the word was 'often reanalysed as OUT- *prefix* + RAGE *n.*, a notion which affected the sense development'.
33. See Paster, *The Body Embarrassed* and Schoenfeldt, *Bodies and Selves in Early Modern England*.
34. Paster, Rowe and Floyd-Wilson, *Reading the Early Modern Passions*.
35. See Rebhorn, *The Emperor of Men's Minds*.
36. For a different reading of this line, see West, 'But this will be a mere confusion'.
37. Puttenham, *The Art of English Poesy*, ed. Whigham and Rebhorn, at 3.12.246–7.
38. Ellen MacKay makes a similar point, albeit in a different context, when she writes of Sidney's *Apology for Poetry*, 'incredulity is a poor safeguard against theatrical assault'. MacKay, *Persecution, Plague, and Fire*, p. 14.
39. Peacham, *The Garden of Eloquence*, p. 64.

40. I find the existing evidence in favour of an earlier date convincing and add to it a contemporary reference found in Thomas Lodge's *A Looking-Glass for London and England* (1587–91), which closely echoes Act Three, Scene Twelve of *The Spanish Tragedy*. In Lodge's play, a mother, Sami, pleads with the King for justice *against* her son, who has betrayed his parents: 'Iustice, O King, iustice against my sonne' (p. 1101). Her plea, coupled with that son's interruption ('Dread Monarch, this is but a lunacie, / Which griefe and want hath brought the woman to' (pp. 1104–5)), seems inspired by Hieronimo's 'Justice, O justice, justice, gentle king!' and 'Justice, O justice! O my son, my son', as well as by Lorenzo's interruption ('Hieronimo, you are not well-advis'd' (3.12.63, 65, 67)). It is possible, of course, that the influence flowed in the other direction – that Lodge's play shaped Kyd's – but *A Looking-Glass* is built out of borrowings. What is striking about *A Looking-Glass* is the way in which it processes all of this material, taking bits from *The Spanish Tragedy* and incorporating them into what is very much a play of the late 1580s. This suggests to me a resurgent interest in *The Spanish Tragedy*, perhaps coinciding with an early 1590s revival, but a sense overall that Kyd's play was out of step with current theatrical tastes, and that it was therefore most likely first performed towards the beginning of the decade.
41. The work was most likely a collaboration between Robert Greene and Henry Chettle. *Greene's Groatsworth of Wit*, ed. Carroll, pp. 84–5.
42. All citations are from *King Henry VI, Part 3*, The Arden Shakespeare, Third Series, ed. Cox and Rasmussen. In 1595, *The True Tragedy of Richard Duke of York and the Good King Henry the Sixth* appeared in octavo format; the play was printed in quarto in 1600 and again (with changes) in 1619. It is unclear whether *The True Tragedy*, which is significantly shorter than the 1623 Folio's *The third part of Henry the sixt*, and which contains more stage directions (among other important differences), represents an earlier version of the Folio play. The Octavo has been assumed, on the one hand, to reflect an early draft of Shakespeare's play or possibly a play written by someone else that Shakespeare later revised; it has also been thought to be a memorial reconstruction or a printed text produced from a prompt book of the same play (more or less) represented in F. Whatever O's relationship to F, F is generally considered to have been produced from Shakespeare's 'foul papers'. I follow the Arden 3 editors, Cox and Rasmussen, in using the 1623 Folio text with frequent reference to the Octavo. While the argument I am advancing about 3 Henry VI in this chapter is intimately tied to the moment of its first performance (itself a matter of much debate), the claims I am making about the play can be applied to both the O and F texts. Randall Martin claims, however, that F represents a revision by Shakespeare of his own earlier play, and states that Shakespeare's revision turns the play into a more reflective, anti-war production by 'toning down the sound and the fury' of the first play. Whatever the exact relationship between O and F, the Octavo text is clearly a product of its late-sixteenth-century theatrical moment, participating in the fashion for noise and bombast discussed above. See *Henry VI, Part Three*, ed. Martin, p. 37.
43. The debate is usefully summarised by Cox and Rasmussen (pp. 44–9). I take their lead in assuming that the work is more likely collaborative than

44. Cox and Rasmussen point out that of Shakespeare's works, *Henry VI, Part 3* is 'second only to *Tit[us]* in the number of words with the root venge' (p. 190, n. 55).
45. When York, captured by the Lancastrians, tells Clifford and Northumberland, 'I dare your quenchless fury to more rage; / I am your butt and I abide your shot', the 'shot' he refers to could be gunfire, but it could also be the braving insults he rightly assumes are coming (1.4.28–9).
46. According to Dent, the 'croaking raven (screeching owl) bodes misfortune'. Dent, *Shakespeare's Proverbial Language: An Index*, p. 33. Quoted by the Arden 3 editors on p. 258, fn 56.
47. Among the Arden 3 editors, the consensus is that *2 Henry VI* was staged first, followed by *3 Henry VI*, and finally *Henry VI, Part 1*. See *Henry VI Part 1*, Arden 3, ed. Burns; *Henry VI Part 2*, Arden 3, ed. Knowles; and Cox and Rasmussen. On the sequencing of Shakespeare's *Henry VI* plays in general, and the association of *The First Part of the Contention* with Pembroke's Men (as an adaptation of the *2 Henry VI* Folio text, originally written for Strange's Men), see Manley, 'From Strange's Men to Pembroke's Men: *2 Henry VI* and *The First Part of the Contention*'.
48. Jonson, *Bartholomew Fair*, New Mermaids, Ind. 96–9.
49. All citations to *Titus* are taken from Shakespeare, *Titus Andronicus*, The Arden Shakespeare, 3rd Series, ed. Bate.
50. See Beaver, 'The Great Deer Massacre' and *Hunting and the Politics of Violence before the English Civil War*.
51. See 'Dido's Ear: Tragedy and the Politics of Response'.
52. On the association between the devouring pit and the womb, see Roberts, *The Shakespearean Wild*, pp. 28–38; Wynne-Davies, 'The Swallowing Womb'; and Kahn, *Roman Shakespeare: Warriors, Wounds, and Women*. The central role feminist scholars have played in revitalising the critical history of (and enthusiasm for) this play is elegantly summarised by Deborah Willis in 'The Gnawing Vulture'.
53. Kendall, '"Lend me thy hand": Metaphor and Mayhem in *Titus Andronicus*', p. 299. Scholarship on the relationship between the body, language and violence in this play is extensive, but it has tended to focus on the written word and especially on the 'central emblem' of 'the mute Lavinia', who also becomes a text to be read. See Mary Laughlin Fawcett, whom I quote here, 'Arms/Words/Tears', p. 265.
54. In focusing on the ways in which speech becomes weaponised in this play, I am both drawing on and departing from a critical tradition highlighting *Titus*'s interest in decidedly literary subjects—for example, the limits and excesses of rhetoric, metaphor, imitation or emulation. See Tricomi, 'The Aesthetics of Mutilation in *Titus Andronicus*'.
55. Bruce R. Smith argues in *Phenomenal Shakespeare*, pp. 48–9 that gesture comes after language in classical rhetoric. See also McNeill, *Gesture and Thought* and Bremmer and Roodenberg, *A Cultural History of Gesture*.
56. This last definition is provided by the OED: 'action', n. 17.

57. Gurr, *The Shakespearean Stage*, p. 97; see also Neill, '"Amphitheaters in the body"', p. 33.
58. Jonathan Bate attributes the second half of this speech to Marcus, although, as he points out, Q1 attributes the speech in its entirety to the Roman lord (and although Bate's edition takes Q1 as 'unusually close to a play as Shakespeare wrote it and as it was first performed' (p. 98)). While the case for the change in attribution is compelling, I follow Q1 in assigning the speech to the Roman lord (and in leaving Lucius, rather than Marcus, as his addressee). Cf. the Oxford World's Classics edition, which follows Capell in assigning the *entire* speech to Marcus. *Titus Andronicus*, ed. Waith.
59. On the dating of this play, which was first printed in 1599, see Charles D. Cannon's Introduction, in *A Warning for Fair Women*, pp. 43–8.
60. Cannon, *A Warning for Fair Women*, Ind. 1 SD. All subsequent citations are to this edition.
61. The 'ensign' that 'disturbs our stage' refers to History's flag, though the term could also mean 'a rallying or battle-cry' (which, given Tragedy's other complaints, may be an intended pun).
62. We don't know about the location of *Alphonsus* or *Locrine*.
63. See Manley, 'From Strange's Men to Pembroke's Men' and Gurr, *Playgoing in Shakespeare's London*.
64. Smith, *Acoustic World*, p. 270.
65. Marshall, *The Shattering of the Self*.

Chapter 3

'Sprinkled Among your Ears': Ben Jonson, John Marston and the Cultivation of the Listening Connoisseur

Introduction

Sometime before 1616, Ben Jonson thoroughly revised his *Every Man in His Humour*, which had first been performed in 1598.[1] In addition to editing the dialogue, changing the play's setting from Italy to England, and Anglicising the names of his characters, Jonson added a lengthy new prologue that pays theatregoers a backhanded compliment: applaud my play, Jonson writes, and 'there's hope left then, / You, that have so grac'd monsters, may like men' (Prologue, ll. 29–30).[2] The monsters referred to here are the wildly popular, larger-than-life creations of the previous century still stalking the Jacobean stage, most notably Christopher Marlowe's Tamburlaine and Hieronimo of Thomas Kyd's *The Spanish Tragedy*. Instead of such absurdly fantastic 'monsters', Jonson promises to present London's real-life ones: its fools, fops and most of its women.[3] Though many of Jonson's complaints about contemporary theatre are conventional, the playwright saves much of his vitriol for a surprising subject: sound effects. Unlike other productions, *Every Man In* features no 'nimble squib', or firecracker, 'to make afear'd / The gentlewomen':

> . . . nor rolled bullet heard
> To say, it thunders; nor tempestuous drum
> Rumbles, to tell you when the storm doth come;
> But deeds, and language, such as men do use:
> And persons, such as Comedy would choose,
> When she would show an image of the times. (Prologue, ll. 17–23)

Brash sound effects (a 'rolled bullet' signifying thunder, or a rumbling drum mimicking a tempest) are here to be replaced with a new set of noises, including, most importantly, a new kind of speech: 'language such as men do use' rather than 'some few foot-and-half-foot words'

(Prologue, ll. 21, 10). It is this aural difference that Jonson insists will distinguish his *Every Man In* from the supposedly 'monstrous' productions on offer elsewhere. By replacing antiquated language and booming sound effects with contemporary speech, Jonson promises his audiences an altogether new theatrical sound.[4]

I open with Jonson's 1616 Prologue because it demonstrates just how fully poetic style, sound and dramatic form were associated in the playwright's thinking. Consider the Prologue's jab at Shakespeare's *Henry VI* plays, in which actors 'with three rusty swords, / And help of some few foot-and-half-foot words, / Fight over York and Lancaster's long jars' (ll. 9–11). It is not just that these plays condense many years into a brief span of theatrical time, so as to 'make a child, now swaddled, to proceed / Man, and then shoot up . . . past threescore years'; it is that they do so with so much clatter. To call York and Lancaster's battles 'jars' instead of wars is to emphasise the clang of those players' 'rusty swords' in performance.[5] The Prologue's criticism of these 'monstrous' plays' formal, structural failings, such as the licences that they take with place and time, are of a piece with its criticism of their 'jarring' sounds (ll. 7–9). According to the poetic theory that is here being outlined by negative example, all of these are formal faults: the failure to contain the action to a single day, or place; the reliance on sound effects; the use of bombast.

Throughout his career, Jonson would continue to distinguish his own poetic style (and, by extension, the plays in which he deployed it) from others' in similarly aural terms. He insists in his *Discoveries* that the 'true artificer will not run away from nature', but

> speak to the capacity of his hearers. And though his language differ from the vulgar somewhat, it shall not fly from all humanity, with the Tamerlanes, and Tamer-chams of the late age, which had nothing in them but the scenical strutting, and furious vociferation, to warrant them to ignorant gapers.[6]

Sliding back and forth, as he does throughout the *Discoveries*, between readers and hearers, spectators and audiences, Jonson does not dissociate himself from the stage altogether but from a particular dramatic sound and mode of reception: the furiously and vociferously uttered speeches of a Tamburlaine, or Tamer-cham, and the open-mouthed, indiscriminate reception of 'ignorant gapers' whose manner of hearing those speeches are assumed to anticipate. For Jonson, this is an ethical as well as an aesthetic distinction, since the good poet 'doth inspire his readers' and 'reign in men's affections', writing lines that 'invade, and break in upon them' until he 'makes their minds like the thing he writes' – in other words, until he makes them better (p. 587). But it is also a practically and competitively useful one. Whenever the 1616 Prologue was actually written, it recalls an earlier moment in English theatre history, when Ben Jonson and other, similarly minded playwrights were positioning themselves as having introduced to London's stages a new dramatic mode. Boasting in prologues, inductions and epilogues that their plays sounded different from other popular theatrical productions – and increasingly, I will show, from revenge tragedies in particular – these playwrights insisted that audiences listen to their turn-of-the-century comedies in a new way. The self-consciously sophisticated listening skills their plays modelled and encouraged promised a kind of social distinction, as well as the possibility of selective insulation against the material, physical threat sound embodied in London's playhouses and outside them, in the rapidly expanding, increasingly noisy city of London.[7] As much an effective competitive strategy as an accurate reflection of differences in sound, poetic style and reception, this approach nonetheless celebrated conscious, selective auditory reception in ways that would have lasting impact on the period's drama.

'Will he be Poisoned with a Simile?': Humoral Hearing and Selective Reception in *Every Man in His Humour*

> Besides, hammers are beating in one place, tubs hopping in another, pots clinking in a third, water-tankards running at tilt in a fourth: here are porters sweating under burdens, there merchants-men bearing bags of money, Chapmen (as if they were at leap frog) skip out of one shop into another: tradesmen (as if they were dancing galliards) are lusty at legs and never stand still: all are as busy as country attorneys at an assizes.[8]
>
> Thomas Dekker, *The Seven Deadly Sins of London* (London, 1606)

Late-sixteenth-century London must have seemed astonishingly loud, particularly to those who were unaccustomed to life in the city. As Bruce R. Smith puts it, the city was 'full of sound', alive with the noises of the people who lived, worked and moved within it.[9] The loudest of London's noises would have been produced by its parish bells (and, more occasionally, by cannon fire and shots of ordnance), but these were just part of a richly varied acoustic field filled with the sounds of trade and manufacturing, of commerce and (as Smith reminds us) of so very many people talking.[10] In 1600, London's population reached roughly 200,000, quadrupling its 1550 total of 55,000. This extraordinary growth seems all the more significant when we compare London's size with that of England's second- and third-largest cities, Norwich (15,000) and Bristol and York (12,000 each).[11] The din heard within this 'City amongst so many people', as Thomas Dekker put it in 1606, was both a sign of the city's vibrancy and a constant oppressive presence, one that could be as materially felt as the press of people who made it: 'in every street, carts and Coaches make such a thundering as if the world ran upon wheels: at every corner, men, women, and children meet in such shoals, that posts are set up ... to strengthen the houses, lest with jostling one another they should shoulder them down'.[12]

Set largely in Florence, Jonson's *Every Man in His Humour* is nonetheless richly shaded with local London colour. The play includes references to the London book trade and its taverns, and it is filled, if not exactly with 'language such as men do use', then at least with language that approximates everyday speech.[13] Much of the play is written in prose, and it is through these speeches, rather than through sound effects, that the sounds of the city are brought onstage.[14] Jonson uses language to create a highly stylised urban cacophony. His Florence is filled with fools, each of whom has a particular verbal tick: Stephano, a country gentleman who longs to be a fashionable city wit, affects both melancholic and irascible speech. Matheo, a would-be love poet who tries to pass off verses by Christopher Marlowe and Samuel Daniel as his own, frequently refers to his prized pilfered poems as 'a toy' and offers anyone who will listen access to his 'study' (1.3.144–5). And the Falstaff-like braggart Bobadilla pretends to be a brave and quarrelsome soldier, peppering his speeches with grandly colourful oaths (the waterbearer Cob, in whose house Bobadilla has peremptorily taken up residence, says admiringly of him, 'Oh, I have a guest ... doth swear the best of any man christen'd: By Phoebus, by the life of Pharaoh, by the body of me ... such dainty oaths' (1.3.71–4)). The fools' verbal quirks have been analysed by critics like Jonas Barish and Lorna Hutson, who have linked each to a rhetorical or literary crime the playwright is, through them, indicting, but the quirks also serve as aural cues for particular urban types that would become staples of Jonsonsian city comedy: the pretend wit, the roaring braggart, the country gull.[15]

Appreciating the stylised noise these fools produce, both individually and collectively, becomes the business of Jonson's comedy – both for the gentlemen wits, Lorenzo Junior and Prospero, whose friendship is at its centre, and for Jonson's audience. At the start of the play, Prospero boasts in a letter to his friend, 'I can show thee two of the most perfect, rare, and absolute true gulls that ever thou saw'st' (1.1.155–6). The boast inspires Lorenzo Junior to bring his cousin, Stephano, along to 'furnish our feast with one gull more toward a mess' (1.2.69–70). Despite Prospero's emphasis on the visual (or, for that matter, Lorenzo Junior's on the gustatory), it seems these fools are best appreciated by ear: 'You speak very well sir', Lorenzo Junior says approvingly of his cousin (1.1.93). And Prospero, on introducing Lorenzo to Matheo and Bobadilla, says, 'I pray thee, be acquainted with my two *zanies* here. Thou wilt take exceeding pleasure in them if thou hear'st them once' (2.3.53–4, emphasis original).

Each of these 'zanies' is sought out and collected by the gentlemen wits for his signature style of speaking. But it becomes increasingly clear over the course of the play that, if the fools are going to perform as desired, then they must be goaded, or 'humoured', into producing just the right sounds. *Every Man In* participates in a fashion for humoral comedies spawned by George Chapman's staggeringly successful *An Humorous Day's Mirth*, which was first performed in 1597. Drawing on Galenic medical tradition, which held that the human body was composed of four substances (choler, melancholy, phlegm and blood) that needed to be kept in balance in order to maintain physical and emotional health, humoral comedies feature characters affected by such imbalances and characters who affect them. Despite the centrality of Galenic humoral theory to much recent early modern literary criticism, relatively little has been written about the humoral imbalances in these plays, probably because they have been understood as largely figurative.[16] In Jonson's play, the production of these imbalances is both registered and encouraged by the circulation of speech as much as, if not more than, it is by the humours themselves. The two processes seem to be analogous. Before bringing Stephano along to meet his friend, Lorenzo muses, 'Now, if I can but hold up this humor in him as it is begun, *cazzo* for Florence! Match him an' she can' (1.2.118–20). Helping Stephano 'hold up' his humour (an affected melancholy) requires lavishing him with false praise ('You speak very well, sir'), which in turn inspires the kind of speech Lorenzo wants his friend to hear (1.2.93). 'I will be more melancholy and gentlemanlike than I have been', Stephano promises (1.2.115–16).

Like finely skilled musicians, Prospero and Lorenzo Junior play their gulls as instruments, causing them to produce the foolish note, or notes, desired. It is a metaphor the wits themselves often use. In response to Prospero's initially sceptical reception of Stephano ('But what strange piece of silence is this? The sign of the Dumb Man?'), Lorenzo explains reassuringly, 'Oh, sir, a kinsman of mine; one that may make our music the fuller, an' he please; he hath his humor, sir' (2.3.55–7, ll. 58–60). Since it is in his ability to produce 'humorous' speech for their consumption that, according to the wits, Stephano's value lies, his silence seems initially to render him useless. But once he starts speaking, he produces a strain of speech in concert with Matheo and Bobadilla's that sends the wits into rhapsodies: 'Oh, it's a precious good fool!' Prospero declares; 'I can compare him to nothing more happily than a barber's virginals; for everyone may play upon him' (2.3.192–5). Like a musical instrument, a virginal, Stephano is played upon to produce a desired sound, the affected language of the melancholic gentleman.[17] But though 'everyone may play upon' Stephano, it is Prospero and Lorenzo who show themselves to be the proficients. Both the production and the enjoyment of this 'music' distinguish the gentlemen-players from their instruments while simultaneously helping to cement the men's homoerotic bond (a point which is underscored by the metaphor of the virginal). Stephano becomes a conduit physically linking the two friends in a way that helps to consummate Prospero's relationship with Lorenzo Junior, whom he has earlier termed his 'ingle' (1.1.139).[18] The 1616 revision of *Every Man In*, from which the term 'ingle' is expunged, extends the instrumental metaphors in this scene to the other fools as well, making the physicality of the wits' humouring even more explicit. Wellbred (Prospero) introduces his fools to Edward (Lorenzo Junior) as 'my wind instruments', and offers to 'wind 'em up' (3.1.52). It is tempting to read this addition, in which Wellbred is imagined as blowing into Matthew and Bobadil's bodies, as being necessitated by the loss of the play's more explicitly homoerotic terms.

The physicality of this humouring process is further suggested by the ways in which *Every Man In*'s truly 'humorous' characters are affected by what they hear. Thorello, the jealous husband with whom Prospero, his brother-in-law, has taken up residence, is stirred involuntarily, even dangerously, by his houseguest's speech. When Thorello's wife, Bianca, chastises Prospero for one of his pranks, Prospero waves away her concern by pointing out that it caused no serious harm. But it might have, Bianca insists. Prospero scoffs, 'Might? So might the good warm clothes your husband wears be poison'd, for anything he knows; or the wholesome wine he drunk even now at the table' (4.3.16–18). The listening Thorello suddenly begins to feel the effects of this imaginary poison: 'Oh, I am sick at heart! I burn, I burn' (4.3.25–6). At this, Prospero is amazed: 'Oh, strange humour! My very breath hath poison'd him' (4.3.27–8). Prospero's words (his 'very breath') produce bodily effects Thorello can sense – he truly feels 'sick at heart' as a result of what he has heard. It is an unintentional replication of the kind of humouring work that Prospero and Lorenzo consciously perform in the play's opening acts, on their instrumental fools, and it is of a piece with that process. For Prospero, who can sample a variety of different kinds of speech without apparent risk of contamination or transformation, his brother-in-law's susceptibility is cause for frustration, even disgust.

What we have, then, are two seemingly incompatible models of listening, and two seemingly incompatible ways of thinking about speech, all coexisting in the same play. Hearing is an involuntary, corporeally affective process. It subjects individuals to physiological transformations, causing them to produce 'humorous' speech (in every sense) which in turn exposes them to ridicule. But hearing is also the voluntary act of a privileged subject who can be entertained, rather than materially altered, by what he hears. Lorenzo and Prospero not only conduct and cause fools to produce ridiculous speech, they also listen to them critically, judging the performances' artistic merit: 'Oh rare! Your cousin's discourse is simply suited, all in oaths', Prospero applauds (3.2.147–8). A similar, and I think related, confusion can be found in early modern anatomical texts, which routinely describe the human ear in paradoxical terms. As I argued in Chapter 2, the ear is an 'always open' orifice, but it is also described, often in the same texts if not within the very same passage, as an elaborately constructed intruder defence system. Hearing is both a sense over which one has no control and a sense that the body is actually designed to indulge in selectively. The pinna, for example (a part of the 'outward ear'), frames what is commonly referred to as 'the hole of hearing', or auditory passage, which is 'always open' or 'continually open'.[19] Its fin-like shape both captures sounds that would otherwise elude the ear and prevents unwanted matter from entering the body.[20] Yet the pinna also refracts the air 'least it should enter into the Eare too cold', and 'if it were not for these breaches', Crooke adds, 'many violent sounds would suddenly rush into the eare to the great offence of the Hearing' (p. 576). Drawing sound in, keeping it and other matter out, the pinna is part funnel, part door. The simultaneity with which these paradoxical functions are performed is linguistically mimicked in the anatomist Alexander Read's jumbled two-sentence description of them in his *Manuall of the Anatomy* (London, 1638):

> The outward eare is alwayes open, because we have ever need of this sense. It is a beauty to the head, it is a defence to the braine, by moderating the sounds, that they may gently move the tympanum, and it gathereth the sounds dispersed in the ayre. (pp. 449–50)

An always-open defence that both moderates and gathers sounds, the pinna, or outward ear, performs seemingly contradictory functions. Sound must enter the body in order to be heard, and so the pinna 'scoops' it up and in, yet sounds that are too 'violent' or 'cold' must be, and somehow are, kept out of the hole of hearing.[21] Always open to receive sounds, the ear also moderates the sounds it receives. Like the pinna, the auditory passage focuses some sounds while simultaneously diffusing others. Read writes that the auditory canal 'hath turnings to hinder the violent rushing in of any thing to the *tympanum*. It is oblique, that the vehemency of a strong sound might bee moderat' (p. 451). Without such moderation, the tympanum and even the brain would be vulnerable.

It is not that the two models of hearing found in *Every Man in His Humour* perfectly reflect such anatomical theories; rather, it is that collectively all of these texts offer evidence of a larger cultural interest in, and confusion about, sound's potential to affect the listener. Jonson's play, like the books of anatomy discussed above, is informed by this confusion even as it attempts to explain it away. Ultimately, for Jonson, whether one hears involuntarily or chooses to listen, whether one is corporeally affected by speech or able to enjoy it as entertaining, become questions of self-possession. This is the central point of *Every Man In*. Whereas the fools Stephano, Matheo and Bobadilla can be 'humoured' by speech, played upon like instruments by the wittier Prospero and Lorenzo, not every listening individual is so vulnerable. The difference lies in how specific characters listen, which reveals in turn the relative control they have over their own bodies. Prospero and Lorenzo engage in a kind of selective hearing that physically insulates them from the effects that sound – *any* sound – may have on the body. To listen to Stephano is not, for Prospero and Lorenzo, to risk physical transformation any more than it is to risk a slide into insipidity. It is to transfer even the physicality of their own desire onto another body. Fools, by contrast, hear involuntarily and indiscriminately, and their bodies are constantly being worked upon and violated as a result: anyone may play upon them. Prospero's comparison of Stephano to a 'virginal' emphasises the physicality of this vulnerability and the potential for violation it produces. As the waterbearer Cob complains about Matheo, whose verses he finds insufferable, 't'will make a man burst to hear him' (1.3.67).

The problem is that these bodily distinctions cannot easily be mapped onto social ones. So that, while the waterbearer Cob's 'bursting' reception may differ markedly from Lorenzo and Prospero's, it has much in common with that of their relatives, Thorello and Stephano. This is not just a problem as far as the wits are concerned, but one that troubles nearly everyone to whom these overly susceptible hearers are related. When in response to a serving man's perceived slight, Stephano becomes irascible, his uncle (Lorenzo's father) demands,

> What would you do? You peremptory ass,
> An you'll not be quiet, get you hence!
> You see the gentleman contains himself
> In modest limits, giving no reply
> To your unseasoned, rude comparatives.

> Yet you'll demean yourself without respect
> Either of duty or humanity. (1.1.103–9)

While the serving man, hearing Stephano's insults, 'contains himself' against them, 'giving no reply', Stephano can 'not be quiet'. He mishears an insult where there is none and is thus compelled to speak. Lorenzo Senior's outrage is increased by the fact that the serving man is able to do what his own nephew is unable to do (give no reply when provoked, let alone when unprovoked). In other words, Stephano's inability to contain himself, to be unaffected by what he hears and give no reply, undercuts his status as a gentleman.[22] 'I am ashamed', Lorenzo Senior concludes, 'Thou hast a kinsman's interest in me' (ll. 110–11). Something similar is at risk for Thorello, whose susceptibility to Prospero's 'breath' I discussed above, and his choleric brother-in-law Giulliano, since both are humoured by sounds they should instead find entertaining. Hearing Bobadilla, who has visited Thorello's house, speak in loftily inflated, pompous language, Giulliano rants: 'S'blood, an' I swallow this, I'll ne'er draw my sword in the sight of man again, while I live' (1.4.121–3). Thorello warns him not to be so physically affected, to control his body's response to Bobadilla's speech and 'not [be] transported / With heady rashness or devouring choler' (ll. 136–7). Yet Giulliano is incapable of following this advice. Unable to 'swallow' Bobadilla's words without his choler in turn devouring him, Giulliano is as vulnerable to being 'played upon' as Stephano, Matheo and Bobadilla. It is a physical and a critical failing, one that disqualifies him from appreciating a variety of sounds that the play suggests he should, as a gentleman, be able to enjoy.

These sounds include foolish speech, but they also include the artful and sophisticated language of the poet – and, ultimately, plays like *Every Man In*, which combine both into a single aesthetic production. Prospero's complaint about Thorello's overly violent, physical reaction to his offhand comment about poison ('Oh, strange humour! My very breath hath poison'd him') introduces a debate between Thorello's wife and sister about the physiological effects – or lack thereof – of poetic 'conceits' and 'devices':

> *Hes.* Good brother, be content. What do you mean? The strength of these extreme conceits will kill you.
> *Bia.* Beshrew your heart blood, brother Prospero, for putting such a toy into his head.
> *Pros.* Is a fit simile a toy? Will he be poison'd with a simile? – Brother Thorello, what a strange and vain imagination is this? For shame, be wiser. Of my soul, there's no such matter.
> *Tho.* Am I not sick? How am I then not poisoned? Am I not poisoned? How am I then so sick?

> *Bia.* If you be sick, your own thoughts make you sick.
> *Pros.* His jealousy is the poison he hath taken. (4.3.29–40)

Hearing Prospero's 'fit simile', Thorello does not marvel critically at its construction but instead hears it too literally and too deeply. The chiasmic structure of Thorello's questions ('Am I not sick? How am I then not poisoned? / Am I not poisoned? How am I then so sick?') emphasises the ridiculousness of his response and the literariness of its cause, a simile. Prospero's use of literary-critical language here (calling his own analogy a 'fit simile') encourages consideration of how Jonson's poetic language might affect its offstage listeners, a question that I think is of central interest to *Every Man In*. If fit similes affect their onstage hearers (Prospero, Thorello, Bianca) differently, how might they variously impact the members of Jonson's audience? In a play that is so preoccupied with language's potential to penetrate and affect its listeners, and with privileged hearers' ability to contain themselves against such effects, this question seems crucial. Attending to Jonson's fit similes with an informed, critical ear – in other words, hearing Jonson's play like Prospero and Lorenzo hear everyone and everything around them – lets the audience in on the wits' game and equips them to appreciate what is, according to Jonson at least, an entirely new kind of play. Composed of foolish speech, witticisms, classical references and other poetic strains, *Every Man In* is a carefully constructed mishmash of sounds and styles, a humoral comedy in the fashion of George Chapman's *A Humorous Day's Mirth* (which had just been staged the year before), but also one of the earliest examples of what would later be known as city comedy. For those who can hear *Every Man In* with critical appreciation, membership within an exclusive and privileged community is possible. In their shared enjoyment of these seemingly private jests, audience members and Jonson's wits become linked in an exclusive, even intimate, union.

City Comedy's Musical Speech

> Only vouchsafe me your attention
> And I will give you music worth your ears.
> Ben Jonson, *Every Man out of His Humour*, Ind. ll. 62–3[23]

Jonson's association of certain kinds of dramatic speech with music (likening Stephano to a virginal, for example, on which 'everyone' might play), and his celebration of auditory self-containment, are not peculiar to *Every Man in His Humour*, or even to his writing more generally. We see it in other plays of the period as well, including the

Poets' War plays of John Marston – whose *Tragedies and Comedies*, according to David McPherson, are the only contemporary English plays (excluding closet dramas) that we know to have been in Jonson's library.[24] Satirical comedies written mostly, though importantly not all, for boys' companies performing in private theatres, the so-called Poets' War plays are at least as preoccupied with critically commenting on contemporary theatre practices and conventions as with attacking particular authors.[25] Central to that critique is the question of how plays should sound and be heard. The detached, critical listening celebrated in *Every Man in His Humour* becomes in these plays the necessary complement to their supposedly new theatrical sound. Consider the Prologue to John Marston's *Antonio and Mellida* (first perf. 1599 or 1600), in which the play's 'select and most respected auditors' are told that they will only have 'the pur'st elixed juice of rich conceit' poured in their 'attentive ears' (Prologue ll. 3, 13–14). In these comedies, it is not just fools' speech that wits are imagined as sampling like connoisseurs, but also the dramatic speech of the wits themselves, and even the dramatists' burlesque of older styles. In short, it is the sound of city comedy. This is the 'music', according to the Jonson-like figure Asper in *Every Man out of His Humour* (1599), that is 'worth [the] ears' of a tasteful theatregoing audience.

In order to see how this strategy worked and to better understand how it impacted the theatre of the period, I want to turn briefly to John Marston's *Jack Drum's Entertainment*. First performed in 1600, and featuring a character supposedly modelled on Ben Jonson, Marston's comedy elaborates on many of the same themes outlined above, and shares with Jonson's an emphasis on the importance of listening critically and appreciatively.[26] *Jack Drum* opens with an apology from the Tiring Man: the play cannot be performed, he explains, because its author has 'snatched' the book away from the players. 'One of the Children' in the company then dashes out to declare that the author has far too great a respect for 'this choise selected influence' to risk offending its ears:

> He vowes, if he could draw the musick fro the Spheares
> To entertaine this presence with delight,
> Or could distill the quintessence of heauen
> In rare composed Sceanes, and sprinkle them
> Among your eares, his industry should sweat
> To sweeten your delights: but he was loth,
> Wanting a Prologue, & our selues not perfect,
> To rush upon your eyes without respect:
> Yet if youle pardon his defects and ours,
> Heele give us passage, & you pleasing sceanes,
> And vowes not to torment your listning eares

> With mouldy fopperies of stale Poetry,
> Unpossible drie mustie Fictions. (p. 179)[27]

For all the Prologue's concern with the audience's 'eyes', its emphasis is heavily on the auditory. The harmonious, heavenly sounds the author wishes he could offer his audience, but can't, are contrasted with an outdated poetic style he could offer his audience, but won't. This outdated style is one his audience, or 'influence', is imagined as having come to this particular theatre, and to this particular play, to avoid having to hear. 'Unpossible drie mustie Fictions', like the theatrical 'monsters' derided in Jonson's Prologue to the 1616 *Every Man In*, should be understood as a reference to the period's heroic romance plays and revenge tragedies, as well as to romance more generally.[28] The 'mouldy fopperies of stale Poetry' spoken in such productions have been purged (or so the Prologue promises) from the language of *Jack Drum's Entertainment*. Again, the difference between such genres and Marston's play, as well as between such genres and Jonson's, is primarily aural. Marston's influential audience will be treated to harmoniously 'composed' dramatic speech which, if not as perfectly in tune as the music of the spheres, nevertheless is said to represent an enormous improvement over what can be heard elsewhere.[29]

Marston's claim that his play sounds different from these other productions has some empirical merit. Performed by boy actors who were also choristers, plays like *Jack Drum's Entertainment* were in a very real sense more 'harmonious' than most adult company productions.[30] (In his *Histriomastix*, which may also have been staged by the Children of Paul's, the poet Posthaste urges his companions, 'Let's make up a company of Players, / For we can all *sing and say*. / And so (with practice) soon may learne to play' (1.1.124–6, emphasis added).) Most of the characters in *Jack Drum's Entertainment* sing at least once, and the pages, who were most likely played by the younger or smaller boys in the company, have particularly musical parts. *Jack Drum's* many songs, moreover, are coupled with frequent references to the play's hyper-musicality. Yet Jonson's Prologue to the revised *Every Man in His Humour* makes a similar claim to *Jack Drum's*, though it was performed by adult actors. So, too, does his *Every Man out of His Humour*, which was first performed at the Globe by the Lord Chamberlain's Men in 1599. The different sound is not just a matter of boys' versus men's voices, then, or of indoor versus outdoor theatres' acoustics; nor is it a matter of the plays' relative musicality. Although *Every Man Out* includes musical performances, it does not include as many as are found in Marston's play, and *Every Man In* has far fewer still. Instead, these plays seek to distinguish themselves from contemporary theatre by claiming that their *speeches* are in fact more harmonious and musical than those of other productions.

The genre against which Jonson's (and, to a lesser extent, Marston's) turn-of-the-century satirical comedies repeatedly define themselves, whose lines they represent as unharmonious, clunky and old-fashioned, is revenge tragedy. Though only one of several genres being faulted for its use of mouldy poetry, revenge tragedy is certainly one of, if not the, most often parodied by Jonson. Its biggest fans are his comedies' biggest fools. Consider the following exchange from *Every Man in His Humour*. During a visit to Bobadilla, Matheo engages him in a literary-critical discussion of the merits of Thomas Kyd's *The Spanish Tragedy*. As scholars have pointed out, the gulls' conversation burlesques Lorenzo Junior and Prospero's own literary friendship. Rather than incorporating references to Virgil and other classical authors into their speech, Matheo and Bobadilla draw instead on the literature of the English stage, quoting and ostentatiously praising its literary merits.[31] That the play the men discuss is Kyd's tremendously popular *The Spanish Tragedy* identifies it, in the world of Jonson's comedy, as one of the least literarily subtle and least learned of them all:

> *Bob.* What new book have you there? What? 'Go by, Hieronimo!'?
> *Mat.* Ay, did you ever see it acted? Is't not well penned?
> *Bob.* Well penned? I would fain see all the poets of our time pen such another play as that was. They'll prate and swagger and keep a stir of art and devices when, by Godso, they are the most shallow, pitiful fellows that live upon the face of the earth again.
> *Mat.* Indeed, here are a number of fine speeches in this book: 'Oh eyes, no eyes, but fountains fraught with tears!'; there's a conceit, 'fountains fraught with tears'. 'O life, no life, but lively form of death!' Is't not excellent? 'O world, no world, but mass of public wrongs' – Oh, God's me! – 'Confused and filled with murder and misdeeds.' Is't not simply the best that ever you heard? Ha, how do you like it?
> *Bob.* 'Tis good. (1.3.126–42)

Bobadilla and Matheo's shared critical judgement – that *Go by Hieronimo*, or *The Spanish Tragedy*, is the greatest play of the age – is clearly cued as ill-informed and misguided, even though the play's wild popularity ensures that many in Jonson's audience would have shared their assessment.[32] Above all, the men are interested in the play as performed ('did you ever see it acted?'). Reading aloud, or perhaps even quoting from memory, his favorite lines, Matheo in fact gives a sort of mini-performance of the play, which showcases Kyd's heavy use of 'conceit'.[33] Hardly 'fit similes', according to Jonson, these lines include metaphorical transpositions (eyes become fountains); anaphora (the repeated 'O'); diacope, in which a word is repeated, with only one 'or at least verie few' words between ('O eyes, no eyes'); traductio, in which a single word is repeated several times in a given sentence; and alliteration or even paroemion, in which several words starting with the same letter are grouped together ('fountains fraught'; 'Oh life, no life, but lively ...').[34] In his *Garden of Eloquence*, Henry Peacham notes that traductio and paroemion have the capacity to 'make the oration more pleasant to the eare' (p. 49) and 'delight the eare' (p. 50), but he also warns that their overuse can be 'tedious' and 'wearisome' (p. 49). The problem with Matheo and Bobadilla's reception of Kyd's thickly conceited verse, according to the logic of *Every Man In*, is that they do *not* find its repetition tedious or wearisome, but instead continue to delight in its 'pleasant' sound.

In his *Discoveries*, Jonson complains of poets who have 'no composition at all; but a kind of tuneing, and riming fall'.[35] Such verse 'runs and slides, and *onely makes a sound*' (p. 30, emphasis added). Verse that 'onely makes a sound' (or, as George Puttenham puts it in *The Art of English Poesy*, verse that simply 'recreat[es]' the ear) is both superficial and, somehow, especially dangerous.[36] This seeming contradiction might best be explained by the fact that sound is never 'just' anything in this period, but is instead materialised potential, its very existence evidence of a profound physiological transformation. And yet there is something especially dangerous, because especially seductive, about the sound of spoken verse. For one thing, it is 'easier to bear away and be retained in memory' than prose, 'because' (as Puttenham puts it):

> it is decked and set out with all manner of fresh colors and figures, which maketh that it sooner inveigleth the judgment of man and carrieth his opinion this way and that, whithersoever *the heart by impression of the ear shall be most affectionately bent and directed*. (1.4.98, emphasis added)

Impressed, bent and directed by what the ear hears, the heart can be made passively susceptible to poetry's influence. This imagined 'inveigling' is, of course, all to the good, since for Puttenham, poetry (good poetry) inspires only the right kind of 'opinions' in its hearers. For Puttenham, as indeed for most other early modern English defenders of poetry, it is the sound of verse that captures and excites the attention and, in turn, inspires ethical action. But the very power of poetry's sounds to seduce 'by impression of the ear' is what, in Jonson's formulation especially, makes it so dangerous. Of bad poets, or 'Womens-Poets ... as you have womens-Taylors', Jonson complains that *'They write a verse, as smooth, as soft, as creame; / In which there is no torrent, nor scarce streame*. You may sound these wits, and find the depth of them, with your middle finger.'[37] Smooth and soft as cream, shallow in depth but also sweetly seductive, these are the kinds of speeches Matheo and Bobadilla most admire. For Jonson, this is a mark of their unsophisticated literary and theatrical tastes, but it is also a sign of their susceptibility to such language, an ethical, social and physical failing that this play's gallant wits are assumed not to share.

Kyd's lines, which are dense with Puttenham's 'auricular figures', and which Matheo and Bobadilla judge 'simply the best that ever [they] heard', are the sort of smooth, soft and seductive sounds enjoyed by those who (as Francis Bacon would later put it) have 'stay[ed] too long at the theater' – in other words, by those who have allowed themselves to be seduced by poetry's sensorial beauty without applying the necessary judgement or suspicion.[38] If for Bacon it is not good to stay too long at the theatre, then for Jonson it is not good to stay too long at the *wrong* theatre – or at theatres performing the wrong kinds of dramatic productions. As Matheo and Bobadilla's mini-performance suggests, according to Jonson, such productions are in the style, sound and, I would argue, the form of Kyd's *The Spanish Tragedy*. This is not a stray reference. Jonson also stages a condensed, burlesqued production of *The Spanish Tragedy* in the midst of *Poetaster*, a Poets' War play performed at Blackfriars by the Children of the Chapel in 1601. Tucca, a gruff and disbanded soldier, complains that today's players perform nothing 'but humours, revels, and satires that gird and fart at the time'. The player Histrio protests, 'No, I assure you, captain, not we. They are on the other side of [the] Tiber' (3.4.162–5).[39] The exchange lurches the play's action out of ancient Rome into early modern London, and Tucca's taste allies him with audiences who prefer the old-fashioned popular productions still being staged in London's outdoor, open amphitheatres. What follows is a series of impromptu parodic performances by Tucca's two servants, or Pyrghi, of some of the period's most popular productions and most familiar dramatic tropes. Chief among these is Kyd's *The Spanish Tragedy*, as well as revenge tragedy in general. The first production to be mimicked employs the sort of conceits Matheo and Bobadilla most admire in *Every Man In*.[40] Next to be burlesqued is an actual scene from *The Spanish Tragedy*, the stylised exchange between Balthazar and Bel-Imperia:

> TUCC. In an amorous vaine now, sirrah, peace.
> 1. PYR. *O, shee is wilder, and more hard, withall,*
> *Then beast, or bird, or tree, or stonie wall.*
> *Yet might shee loue me to upreare her state:*
> *I, but perhaps, shee hopes some nobler mate.*

Yet might shee loue me, to content her sire:
I, but her reason masters her desire.
Yet might shee loue me as her beauties thrall:
I, but I feare, shee cannot loue at all. (3.4.214–22)

The emphasis here is less on the theme of revenge than on the way this play's poetry sounds: highly stylised, with each rhyming couplet full of 'auricular figures'. Tucca next directs his servants in a general revenge tragedy burlesque: 'the ghost, boys' (ll. 199).[41] The servant-as-ghost's Latin call for revenge ('Vindicta!') and his companion's response ('Timoria!') immediately evoke the Seneccan revenge tradition. From this parody of the genre more generally, the servants then shift to a burlesque of *The Spanish Tragedy* specifically and, I think, of a second revenge play that has since been lost:

> TUCC. Now, thunder, sirrah, you, the rumbling plaier.
> 2. PYR. I, but some bodie must crie (*murder*) then, in a small voice.
> TUCC. Your fellow-sharer, there, shall do't; Crie, sirrah, crie.
> 1. PYR. *Murder, murder.*
> 2. PYR. *Who calls out murder? lady, was it you?...*
> TUCC. Sirrah, boy, brace your drumme a little straighter and doe the t'tother fellow there, hee in the – what sha' call him – and yet, stay too.
> 2. PYR. *Nay, and thou dalliest, then I am thy foe,*
> *And feare shall force, what friendship cannot win;*
> *Thy death shall burie what thy life conceales,*
> *Villaine! thou diest, for more respecting her –*
> 1. PYR. *O, stay my Lord.*
> 2. PYR. *Then me: yet speake the truth, and I will guerdon thee:*
> *But if thou dally once againe, thou diest.* (ll. 236–54)

The specific scene Tucca concludes this vignette by requesting – that which begins 'yet stay' – is lifted from *The Spanish Tragedy*. (The 'tother fellow' who speaks these lines is Lorenzo, Kyd's Machiavellian villain; his victim is the servant Pedringano.) The line 'Who calls out murder? lady, was it you?' is more difficult to trace. It appears in George Chapman's *The Blind Beggar of Alexandria*, which was first performed in 1596, and would later be quoted again in the comedy *Eastward Ho!* co-authored by Jonson, Marston and Chapman for performance in 1605. Like 'Go by, Hieronimo', another oft-quoted line, it seems to have become synecdochic for an entire group of plays by the close of the sixteenth century – the formal category we now call revenge tragedy.[42]

This lengthy inset performance does more than mock thickly conceited poetry. It also mocks the way that poetry sounds, or, to be more precise, the way it is pronounced. This is key. To his critique of revenge tragedy's supposed overuse of specific auricular figures, Jonson adds an attack on the noisiness, or the thunderous delivery, of its speeches – an effect that I have been arguing was central not only to later revenge tragedies, but also to the battle plays that helped give shape to revenge tragedy as a dramatic form. In other words, Jonson's critique is not just one of poetic style, or even of sense, but of poetic sound, which is here being mapped onto formal contests. In *Poetaster*, Tucca directs his servant to assume the part of 'the rumbling plaier'. Well-versed in theatrical conventions and the technologies of performance, the servant reminds Tucca that though he may speak in a rumbling voice, somebody else must pitch his voice a little higher to play the lady: 'but some bodie must cry (*murder*) then, in a small voice.' In order to assume the role of Lorenzo, the servant must once again change his tone, or 'brace [his] drum a little straighter' (3.4.236–44). All of these references to tone, pitch and the physical requirements of their production emphasise the fact that certain plays were expected to sound a certain way. The actors' pronunciation of revenge tragedy's lines, then, appears to have been as familiar to early modern audiences as some of the more famous lines themselves.[43]

I attend to these scenes in order to demonstrate three points. First, that revenge tragedy's most familiar 'auricular figures' and the manner in which they were pronounced or sounded in performance were pointed to by Jonson and Marston (and, to a lesser extent, Chapman) as an example of how theatre should *not* sound, or should no longer sound. Second, that in mocking revenge tragedy, these authors nevertheless reveal their own deep knowledge of the genre and its most popular productions. (That Jonson had at least some appreciation for revenge tragedy seems clear: in 1602, he received payment from Philip Henslowe for revising *The Spanish Tragedy*;[44] he also wrote an epigram praising Admiral's Men actor Edward Alleyn.[45] Marston, for his part, wrote a revenge play as a sequel to his *Antonio and Mellida*.[46]) And third, that in order for these parodies to work, the audiences being complimented by Marston and Jonson for eschewing such noisy, unharmonious productions must have been quite familiar with the plays they were supposedly avoiding so fastidiously.[47] This is perhaps an obvious point, but it matters for thinking about how these genres took shape in competition and collaboration with one another. If a key difference between satirical city comedy and revenge tragedy lies in how these plays sound, and if Jonson's plays demand of their audience a self-consciously new style of listening to complement that sound, then audiences must have been thought capable of practising both styles of listening all but simultaneously.

My emphasis thus far has been on scenes of failed listening: Thorello and Stephano's overly susceptible reception, Bobadilla and Matheo's seduction by conceits as 'soft as cream'. But Jonson's comedies also offer more positive models. In Act Two of *Every Man In*, when Lorenzo and Prospero listen to the foolish consort they have brought Stephano, Bobadilla and Matheo together to produce, they demonstrate a much more idealised auditory practice of critical audition. At Prospero's humouring cue ('Signior Bobadilla, why muse you so?'), the braggart Bobadilla pipes up (2.3.102). Out bursts his signature refrain, a lengthy, boastful account of battles he probably never saw: 'Faith, sir', Bobadilla begins, 'I was thinking of a most honorable piece of service was performed – tomorrow being Saint Mark's day – shall be some ten years' (ll. 104–6). Looping his way through over-the-top descriptions of different campaigns (the 'beleaguring of Ghibeletto'; the 'taking in of Tortosa'), Bobadilla provides a colourful account of courageous services supposedly rendered (ll. 109, 113–14):

> *Bob.* Observe me judicially, sweet signior: they had planted me a demiculverin, just in the mouth of the breach; now, sir, as we were to ascend, their master gunner – a man of no mean skill and courage, you must think – confronts me with his linstock ready to give fire. I, spying his intendment, discharged my petronel in his bosom, and with this instrument, my poor rapier, ran violently upon the Moors that guarded the ordnance and put them pell-mell to the sword. (ll. 130–7)

Listening carefully to Bobadilla's description, Prospero is able to ask: 'To the sword? To the rapier, signior' (l. 138). Bobadilla's preference for the more fashionable 'rapier' ('my poor rapier') clashes with his use of the proverb 'to the sword' – an inconsistency Prospero seizes upon in order to make a joke about Bobadilla's pretentiousness. His aural attention to the minutiae of Bobadilla's speech is a skill that serves him well as a wit, as it enables him to use the gulls' own words against them and, ultimately, perform verbal tricks of his own.

Every Man In implies that an ideal theatregoer should be able to catch, as Prospero does, the subtle inconsistencies of speech as well as the literary and theatrical references Jonson's play includes. Such a model of listening would enable certain audience members to hear what others, including the fools on stage, might miss, and consequently provide them with the opportunity to demonstrate their own superior understanding. Consider the following exchange between Stephano and Lorenzo Junior:

> *Lo.iu.* You speak very well, sir.
> *Step.* Nay, not so neither, but I speak to serve my turn.

Lo.iu. Your turn? Why, cousin, a gentleman of so fair sort as you are, of so true carriage, so special good parts ... Nay, more, a man so graced, gilded, or rather, to use a more fit metaphor, tinfoiled by nature? Not that you have a leaden constitution, coz ... but for your luster only, which reflects as bright to the world as an old ale-wife's pewter again' a good time ... Cousin, what think you of this?
Step. Marry, I do think of it, and I will be more melancholy, and gentleman-like than I have been, I do ensure you. (1.2.93–117)

Humouring his cousin, Lorenzo also mocks him in the process, yet Stephano does not hear the underlying meaning. Jonson's audience, of course, is expected to do better, noticing that Lorenzo's adjectives become increasingly insulting (as he shifts from 'graced' to 'gilded' to 'tinfoiled'). Catching these barbs would probably be easier than catching Bobadilla's inconsistent weaponry, but both scenes work according to the same principle: wits hear things others miss, including classical allusions, the fitness of similes and (in this case) jokes made at others' expense. The social significance of this skill is what matters, enabling those who practise it well to accumulate and display their possession of cultural capital in a city undergoing enormous socio-economic change. Lorna Hutson has called *Every Man in His Humour* the first play 'to make a hero of the glamour and social power of masculine conversation'.[48] If masculine conversation is the glamorous, eroticised commodity in this play, then listening is the skill one must learn to participate in its exchange. Listening well identifies individuals as worthy of joining the same witty club to which Lorenzo and Prospero belong, laughing with them while the gulls onstage (and off) remain silent.[49] By catching the double meanings of 'fit similes' (and understanding, as a result, why they are so 'fit'), listeners find the humour in language rather than risk being humoured by it, so that a 'fit simile' produces no physical effect but laughter.

Auditory Training, Taste and Selective Reception

Informed critical perception, which is depicted in these plays as a valuable, socially desirable skill, is determined largely by culture: getting Jonson's jokes about *The Spanish Tragedy*, for example, requires a familiarity with the play being ridiculed, while recognising his quotations from the *Aeneid* requires at least a passing knowledge of Virgil. Catching all of these references could be – and, I will argue in this section, is in fact *meant* to be – difficult. The individual poetic strains of Jonson and Marston's turn-of-the-century plays, including their fit similes, fools' musical consorts, classical references and ridiculing remarks about other kinds of contemporary English drama, do not always fit together well. Instead, these disparate strains cohere into productions that can seem disjointed or patchy, rather than harmoniously whole. While Jonson's later comedies, like *Epicoene* and *The Alchemist*, have long been considered 'pattern[s]' of 'perfect' plotting, his earlier plays' patchiness has irked some critics, who have commented on how difficult their plots can be to remember. This is perhaps especially true of *Every Man In* and its sequel, *Every Man out of His Humour*.[50] Marston's *Jack Drum's Entertainment*, too, is a patchwork of parts: its romance plot is spoken in highly stylised verse that clashes with the everyday prose of the ordinary or tavern, which the play also includes.[51] Something similar can be said of his *Histriomastix*, which combines speeches by Grammar, Logic and Rhetoric (as well as Fury, Envy and Hypocrisy) with others by characters who would become familiar in seventeenth-century city comedy: acquisitive merchants' wives, pedants, gallants. All of this material is yoked together in the service of a moral allegory about civic unrest, war and peace.

Rather than reading such patchiness as evidence of the plays' limitations, or dismissing it as unimportant, I want to suggest that it serves a purpose by challenging and in fact training theatregoers to hear commercial drama adeptly. *Every Man Out* is written, according to Asper, for 'Attentive auditors, / Such as will join their profit with their pleasure' (Ind., ll. 199–200). Such listeners are formed as well as solicited by these productions.

An analogous challenge – one that I think helps to illuminate the theory and practice of critical audition in Jonson and Marston's plays – was posed by polyphonic music, which was receiving new attention at the close of the sixteenth century. In England, as well as on the Continent, polyphony had been part of religious ceremony and practice for centuries, but a fashion for madrigals (both imported from Italy and 'Englished', or translated, for print in London) suddenly increased the presence of secular polyphonic vocal music in print and performance in the 1590s.[52] A musical effect created, according to the composer and musician Thomas Morley, through 'the whole harmony of many voices', polyphony combines competing melodic strains into a single composition.[53] Even those who emphasise polyphony's beauty tend to admit how hard it can be to hear. The composer Johannes Tinctoris wrote as early as the fifteenth century that the best singers 'sing ... praise to our God with *diverse* (but not *adverse*) voices'; and Jacques of Liege complained that even 'judicious men' could not tell 'what language such singers were using' when hearing such compositions.⁵⁴

Jonson's and Marston's turn-of-the-century comedies frequently draw on musical theory, practice and vocabulary in ways that suggest related processes of composition and reception. Partly, this stems from ancient associations between music and poetry, beginning with the myth of Orpheus (which Puttenham and countless other early modern rhetoricians cite as originary to the art of poetry). But there is also, I think, a more practical set of associations at work. As a student at Westminster, Jonson would have been taught that speaking, like singing, required vocal control, and he would have received musical training for the express purpose of improving his oratorical skills.⁵⁵ English rhetorical manuals and grammar books often insist that the English language has a particularly musical quality, moreover, that makes it ideally suited to poetic composition. While 'all the beauty of [the ancients'] poesy' depends on 'their feet' or 'measures', Puttenham writes, in English 'we have instead thereof twenty other curious points in that skill more than they ever had, by reason of our rhyme and tunable concords or symphony, which they never observed' (pp. 95–6). What gives English verse its beauty, in other words, is not its 'measures', or feet (quantification), but its sound: its 'rhyme' and 'tunable concords or symphony'. Elsewhere, Puttenham insists that verse is 'more delicate to the ear than prose is, because it is more current and slipper upon the tongue, and withal tunable and melodious, as a kind of music, and therefore may be termed a musical speech or utterance' (p. 98). What differentiates verse, and particularly English verse, from prose is its 'tunable' and 'melodious' quality: it is, quite simply, 'musical speech'. In his *English Grammar* (1640), Jonson suggests that even prose might have tunable, musical qualities. He defines a 'word' as 'a part of speech, or note, whereby a thing is known, or called; and consisteth of one or more syllables', and writes that in English, 'All our vowels are sounded doubtfully. In quantity, (which is time) long or short. Or, in accent (which is tune) sharp or flat.'⁵⁶ The task here, for Puttenham and Jonson alike, is either to suggest that English can be made to sound and scan like Latin or to obviate the need for it to do so. But words like 'note', 'tune', 'sharp' and 'flat' link spoken English to music in ways that suggest *all* English, not just English composed into verse, might be called 'musical speech'.⁵⁷

Such thinking gives new meaning to the musical metaphors in Jonson's plays, including both *Every Man In* and its sequel, *Every Man Out*. When Saviolina, a lady of the court with a reputation for verbal dexterity, asks her suitor, Fastidious Briske, to play 'upon the viol de gamba', he demurs, 'It's miserably out of tune.' This leads the cynic Macilente to mutter, 'It makes good harmony with her wit' (3.3.92–5). The joke, of course, is that both Saviolina's wit and the instrument are 'out of tune'. Macilente continues, 'Are these the admirable lady-wits, that having so good a plainsong, can run no better division upon it?' (ll. 141–2). 'Division' is defined by the *OED* as a 'rapid melodic passage' or 'florid phrase or piece of melody, a run; esp[ecially] as a variation on ... a theme or "plain song"'.[58] According to Macilente, the 'plainsong' in this scene (Fastidious's foolish speech) deserves a better division, or wittier accompaniment, than Saviolina can supply – one which he himself is more than happy to offer through *sotto voce* asides. It is not just that this scene likens speech to music, but that it likens speech to elements of a particular *kind* of music. 'Descant' is, according to Thomas Morley, a feature peculiar to vocal music in multiple parts. His *a Plain & Easy Introduction to Practical Music* (1597) defines it as follows:

> The name of Descant is usurped of the musicians in divers significations; sometime they take it for the whole harmony of many voices; others sometime for one of the voices or parts, and that is when the whole song is not passing three voices; *last of all they take it for singing a part extempore upon a plainsong, in which sense we commonly use it; so that when a man talketh of a Descanter it must be understood of one that can, extempore, sing a part upon a plainsong.*[59]

This is, essentially, what Macilente does – he descants upon Saviolina's and Fastidius's remarks. Like a singer who forms a line of melody 'extempore', a true wit, Jonson's play suggests, can instantly compose a spoken 'descant', or 'division', that builds on and complements another's speech. The wit's, like the singer's, part is to 'compose' a fit musical-poetic accompaniment to another's words.

Marston's *Jack Drum* similarly blends musical and poetic terms, as well as music and poetry. Songs figure prominently in Marston's play, and music is represented as having vital physical and emotional effects on its onstage listeners: music has the conventional romantic power to seduce and to charm as well as the medicinal power to cure illness.[60] When word reaches Katherine that her beloved, Pasquil, has been killed, she flees to the forest, where she stumbles into him, still very much alive. Their happy reunion is interrupted, however, by the lecherous usurer Mammon, who (furious at Katherine's continued rejection of him) poisons her and horribly disfigures her face. The mortified Katherine tells Pasquil to leave her forever, and the shock drives Pasquil mad. Katherine's father is then advised to restore Pasquil's wits with music:

> Let Musicke sound, for I haue often heard
> It hath such sweet agreement with our soules,

That it corrects vaine humours, and recalls
His stragling fancies to faire vnion.

Ned Planet, a wit and a friend of Brabant, agrees:

Why the soule of man is nought but simphonies,
A sound of disagreeing parts, yet fair vnite
By heauens hand, diuine by reasons light. (p. 235)

Katherine's father orders his servants to 'Sound Musicke, then pray it take good effect.' It does: the stage direction indicates 'The Musicke soundes, and Pasquils Eye is fixt upon Catherine [sic]', who has been standing off to the side unseen, her beauty miraculously restored (p. 236). Planet's choice of word in this passage, 'simphonies', is significant in its unification of musical with verbal, or poetic, harmony.[61] Our modern sense of 'symphony' is of course anachronistic to 1600, yet the familiar understanding of an ordered musical whole composed of disparate, individual parts complements definitions current in the period.[62] 'Simphonies' were well-balanced but not necessarily harmonious compositions of individual musical strands.[63] In fact, the central feature of Ned Planet's 'simphonies' is their *un*-harmonious quality, being composed 'of disagreeing parts'. Metaphorically linking man's soul to musical and poetic 'symphonies', Marston actually emphasises their shared polyphonic quality: man's soul is a collection of musical strands which are brought into tune by 'heaven's hand', or through musical (or poetic) application.

In the end, Marston's and Jonson's plays both draw attention, through their combination of 'disagreeing parts' 'fair unite', to the act of poetic composition itself. It is not really 'Macilente', after all, who composes extempore descants in *Every Man out of His Humour*, but Ben Jonson; while it is John Marston who composes *Jack Drum*'s competing strains into a united whole.[64] And yet, if it is the dramatists, or perhaps the actors, who 'compose' these disparate parts into a not-altogether-harmonious production, it is the offstage listener who must do the equally important work of making sense of them in reception – and this work is not necessarily easy. It is here that the network of associations being drawn in these plays between music, particularly polyphonic music, and dramatic production become most significant: they help to underline the *work* that is entailed in making sense of complex sonic material. For many of the sixteenth-century writers who complained about polyphony, in fact, it is the listeners' difficulty hearing it that is polyphony's defining feature. In 1572, the Florentine scholar Girolamo Mei (a proponent of the supposed 'return' to the monophonic style of ancient Greece) railed in a letter to Vincenzo Galilei against composers who 'distract the mind with diverse and, if necessary, contrary parts'.[65] At issue is not just the songs' combination of competing musical strains (the 'various melodies in several modes in low, high, and intermediate pitch, sung together at one time'), but also differences in tempo between discrete parts.[66] As Mei puts it, 'often the soprano hardly moves, while the tenor flies, and the bass goes strolling in slipper-socks, or, indeed, the other way around'.[67] The complexity of these musical structures may be technically impressive, but it makes them difficult to appreciate, let alone enjoy: there is just too much going on.

A musically inflected, and especially a polyphonic, understanding of dramatic production and reception would help to explain why Marston's play includes the very 'mouldy fopperies of stale Poetry, / Unpossible drie mustie Fictions' its prologue dismisses. Consider the following exchange between Pasquil and Katherine in the play's final scene:

> *Pas.* Deare Katherine, the life of Pasquils hopes.
> *Ka.* Deare Pasquil, the life of Katherines hopes.
> *Pas.* Once more let me imbrace the constant's one
> That e're was tearmde her Sexe perfection.
> *Kathe.* Once more let me be valued worth his loue,
> In decking of whose soule, the graces stroue.
> *Pas.* Spight hath ourspent it selfe, and thus at last,
> *Both speake.*
> We clip with joyful arme each others wast. (p. 236)

Pasquil and Katherine articulate their reunion in perfectly parallel, chiasmic verse. Their duet culminates in a single line of poetry spoken in unison, which prefigures the spiritual union the speakers' souls will achieve in marriage.[68] Yet this passage is out of tune with much of Marston's play. Though the exchange complements other segments of dialogue spoken by Pasquil and Katherine, which employ similar conceits and figures (for example, anaphora and epistrophe), it contrasts sharply with the witty, largely prose exchanges that fill out the rest of *Jack Drum*.[69] Of course, combining verse and prose in a single play is not the exception, but the rule in early modern English drama, as is incorporating elements from different genres: indeed, for Sidney, this is English theatre's defining feature, its 'mingling kings and clowns'.[70] But *Jack Drum*, much like Marston's *Histriomastix*, does not suborn one plot to another; instead, it moves between the worlds of romance and city comedy, of the court and the ordinary, in equal measure, at times knitting them together. The Pasquil and Katherine sections could be, and have been, understood as parodic, a burlesque of adult company plays; but we might also say that they complement the play's other 'parts' by throwing them into stark, polyphonic relief.[71] This is the dramatic sound, or set of sounds, that together produce the 'rare composed scenes' promised by the Prologue – a composition fit, in both its variety and its attendant difficulty, for the consumption of 'this choise selected influence'.

As Marston does in *Jack Drum*, in *Every Man out of His Humour* Jonson blends romantic verse with prose, but he further signals the disjunction between the two by having one of his characters comment on its unsuitability. When the knight Puntarvolo addresses his wife in lines that are noticeably thick with poetic conceit, the eavesdropping Fastidious Briske cries out incredulously, 'How? In verse?' (2.1.311).[72] As Carlo Buffone explains, the speech is 'a project, a designment of his own, a thing studied and rehearsed as ordinarily at his coming from hawking or hunting as a jig after a play' (ll. 223–5). In short, it is a carefully scripted performance. Puntarvolo continues:

> Stay! Mine eyes hath (on the instant) through the bounty of the window received the form of a nymph. I will step forward three paces; of the which I will barely retire one, and (after some little flexure of the knee), with an erected grace salute her: one, two, and three. – Sweet lady, God save you . . . What call you the lord of the castle, sweet face? (ll. 196–216)

The artificiality of this speech is emphasised by Puntarvolo's carefully synchronised accompanying gestures – three strides forward, one back and a slight bending of the knee. Watching, listening to and commenting on the couple's romantic exchange are three distinct groups, and the critical comments each of these onstage audiences make signal the performance's artificiality while at the same time providing us with an example of one of the dramatic techniques that make Jonson's 'music' potentially difficult to follow.[73] Rather than adjusting their ears from one style of poetry to another – from the stylised language of romance, say, to the everyday speech of the ordinary – playgoers must focus their ears on competing layers of dialogue as they are spoken within a single scene. These speeches are complexly interwoven, and so the playgoer's attention must shift from one set of eavesdroppers to the conversation being overheard, then to a second set of eavesdroppers, and then back again to the first group.

Jonson employs this approach throughout *Every Man out of His Humour*, but he does so most dizzyingly in Act Three, Scene One, which is set in St Paul's. As in Jonson's later comedy, *Bartholomew Fair*, the staging in this scene is 'tidal' (to borrow Peter Barnes's term).[74] Nearly the entire cast makes an appearance, walking up and down Paul's Walk in order to parade various performed identities: a poor gallant plays a proud, wealthy soldier, and two fools try to sound like scholars to all within earshot. The scene has been likened to a carefully choreographed dance, one which conveys multiple perspectives to the theatregoing audience, and in the process makes the play seem more realistic.[75] Its peculiar effect, however, is at least as aural as it is visual. The stage directions indicate that groups of speakers form, disperse and blend into one another throughout this scene. As they do so, the focus shifts from one part of the stage to another, and from one conversational set to another, and Jonson's audience members must shift their attention accordingly.

Without any physical cues to suggest where we are (Cordatus, one half of Jonson's two-man chorus, asks, 'we must desire you to presuppose the stage the middle aisle in Paul's'), it is the movement of the actors and the choreographed cacophony they produce in performance that sets this scene (3.1.2–3). The act opens with Jonson's chorus commenting on the entrance of Cavalier Shift, who walks the stage alone, waiting for someone to answer the advertisements he has posted. Next enters Orange, who speaks briefly with Shift before leaving him to talk to the newly entered Clove. As Clove and Orange, incidental characters included only in this scene, pace Paul's, and as Shift walks the aisle alone, Puntarvolo and Carlo Buffone enter.[76] A stage direction then indicates, 'They go to look upon the bills. / Enter Fastidious, Deliro, and Macilente' (l. 90 SD). Carlo and Puntarvolo then speak together, probably shifting their position from the centre to the side of the stage, as Fastidious and his two companions take their place. Their conversation in turn becomes the focus of the scene. Once this conversation ends, Puntarvolo, who presumably still stands off to the side of the stage, begins reading aloud from Shift's posted bills.[77] At times the discussions, as well as the speakers, briefly merge: Puntarvolo's complaint about Sogliardo's ridiculous coat of arms is interrupted, for example, as he pauses to greet Fastidious Briske: 'It is the most vile, foolish, absurd, palpable, and ridiculous escutcheon that ever this eye survised. – Save you, Monsieur Fastidious' (ll. 230–2). As the stage direction indicates, 'They salute as they meet in the walk' (3.1.232 SD). Later, the groups combine and split again, this time into pairs ('Here they shift, Fast. mixes with Punt. Car. and Sogli. Deli. and Macilente, Cloue and Orenge, foure couple'). As conversational groups collect, disperse, reform and realign, the dialogue they produce becomes increasingly complex. Different actors, like different instruments, sound out their parts on cue, performing a sonically and spatially sophisticated production.

In the complexity of its choreography, this scene differs from other, roughly contemporary scenes of urban life on the early modern stage – for example, Laxton, Goshawk and Greenwit's movement between three different shops in *The Roaring Girl*, during which the focus remains primarily on the men's conversation as they make their way across the stage. Designedly more difficult to follow, Jonson's Paul's Walk scene replicates the numerous competing exchanges one would have been likely to have heard in Paul's, even as it also gestures to its artificiality as a performance. In 1633, John Earle described Paul's Walk as 'a heap of stones and men, with a vast confusion of Languages, and were the Steeple not sanctified, nothing liker *Babel*'.[78] It is this site's notorious noisiness that Jonson's experimental techniques seem intended to replicate – both in performance and, possibly, in print. Unlike the 1616 Folio, which shifts the stage directions to the margins (see Figure 3.1), all three of the first quartos of *Every Man Out* embed these into the body of the text itself, using braces to indicate the simultaneity, or near-simultaneity, of speech and action (see Figure 3.2).[79] The page reproduced here, which was printed for William Holme by Peter Short and Adam Islip, seems especially busy. Its braces are more ornate than those used by Islip alone (or, for that matter, for Nicholas Linge's edition, which may in fact have appeared much later), and it is much more crowded: this quarto is a full sheet (eight pages) shorter than the one Short produced with Islip.[80] Short's involvement in this edition is also interesting as he was one of the most prolific printers of music in the years just before Jonson's play was published. In 1597, he produced no fewer than seven volumes of music, an output that the musicologist Jeremy L. Smith calls 'extraordinary'.[81] In addition to Morley's *Plain & Easy Introduction*, Short was also responsible for two collections of Morley's songs: the English *Canzonets, or little short aers to five and six voices*, and *Canzonets, or little short songs to four voices*. Both were published in partbook format, meaning as a set of four or five books, each of which contains only one or two voice parts (cantus, altus, tenor/sextus, bassus and quintus). That same year, Short printed John Dowland's *The First Booke of Songes or Ayres* in table-book format, a layout combining all four voice parts onto a single facing page, with each part oriented in a different direction (see Figure 3.3). Designed to allow singers to stand around a shared, open book, orienting themselves towards their respective parts, table-books differ from partbooks in both their form and function. The table-book is a visually kinetic and, according to Richard Wistreich, especially sociable form of music book printing, which anticipates a collective, communal singing experience. In its spatialisation of sound, and its orientation of different voice parts onto different sections of the page (and presumably into different positions around a table), the polyphonic *First Booke of Songes or Ayres* recalls Giovanni Mei's complaints about sopranos who 'hardly move[], while the tenor flies, and the bass goes strolling in

124   *Euery Man out of his Humour.*

or rather *diamondizing* of your *subiect*, you shall perceiue the *Hipothesi*, or *Galaxia*, (whereof the *Meteors* long since had their *initiall inceptions* and *notions*) to be meerely *Pithagoricall*, *Mathematicall*, and *Aristocraticall*— For looke you, sir, there is euer a kinde of *concinnitie* and *species*— Let vs turne to our former discourse, for they marke vs not.

FAST. Masse, yonder's the knight PVNTARVOLO.
DELI. And my cousin SOGLIARDO, me thinkes.
MACI. I, and his familiar that haunts him, the deuill with a shining face.

Sogliardo, Puntaruolo, Carlo, walke.

DELI. Let 'hem alone, obserue 'hem not.
SOGL. Nay, I will haue him, I am resolute for that. By this parchment, gentlemen, I haue beene so toil'd among the Harrots yonder, you will not beleeue, they doe speake i' the strangest language, and giue a man the hardest termes for his money, that euer you knew.
CARL. But ha' you armes? ha' your armes?
SOGL. Yfaith, I thanke god, I can write my selfe gentleman now, here's my pattent, it cost me thirtie pound, by this breath.
PVNT. A very faire coat, well charg'd, and full of armorie.
SOGL. Nay, it has as much varietie of colours in it, as you haue seene a coat haue, how like you the crest, sir?
PVNT. I vnderstand it not well, what is't?
SOGL. Mary, sir, it is your *Bore* without a head *Rampant*.
PVNT. A Bore without a head, that's very rare!
CARL. I, and rampant too: troth, I commend the Heralds wit, hee has decyphered him well: A Swine without a head, without braine, wit, any thing indeed, ramping to gentilitie. You can blazon the rest, signior, can you not?
SOGL. O, I, I haue it in writing here of purpose, it cost me two shillings the tricking.
CARL. Let's heare, let's heare.
PVNT. It is the most vile, foolish, absurd, palpable, & ridiculous escutcheon, that euer this eye suruis'd. Saue you, good monsieur FASTIDIVS.

They salute as they meet in the walke.

CARL. Silence, good knight: on, on.
SOGL. GYRONY, of eight *peeces*; AZVRE and GVLES, betweene three *plates*; a CHEVRON, *engrailed checkey*, OR, VERT, and ERMINES; on a *cheefe* ARGENT betweene two ANN'LETS, *sables*; a Bores head, PROPER.
CARL. How's that? on a *cheefe* ARGENT?
SOGL. On a *cheefe* ARGENT, a Bores head, PROPER betweene two ANN'LETS *sables*.

Here they shift. Fastidius mixes with Puntaruolo Carlo, and Sogliardo, Deliro, and Macilente, Cloue and Orange, sou couple.

CARL. S'lud, it's a Hogs-cheeke, and puddings in a pewter field this.
SOGL. How like you 'hem, signior?
PVNT. Let the word bee, *Not without mustard*; your crest is very rare, sir.
CARL. A frying pan to the crest had had no fellow.

FAST.

Figure 3.1 The Paul's Walk scene as it appears in the Folio text of *Every Man out of His Humour*. Ben Jonson, *The Workes of Beniamin Jonson* (London, 1616), p. 124. STC 14752. RB 600687, The Huntington Library, San Marino, California.

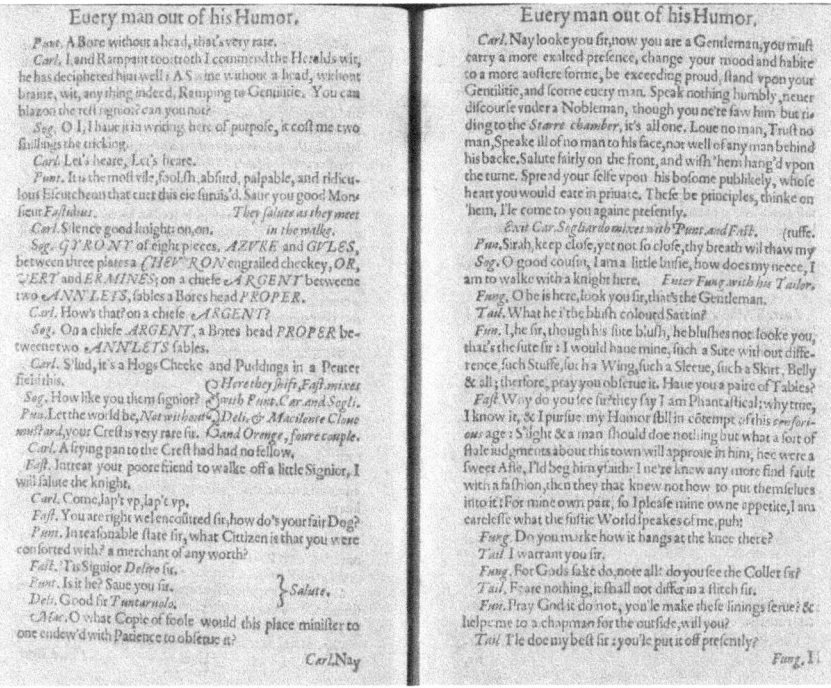

Figure 3.2 The Paul's Walk scene as represented in one of the play's earliest quartos. *Every Man out of His Humour* (London: printed by Peter Short or by Peter Short and Adam Islip for William Holme, 1600), sig. H3ᵛ. © Victoria and Albert Museum, London.

slipper-socks'. Table-books like Dowland's visually replicate the sonic complexity of vocal polyphony, and they also give some sense of the precarity of its order. Beautifully, meticulously arranged on the printed page, these songs are also, when viewed a bit differently, a jumble of notes, the precision of which threatens to become lost.

The Paul's Walk scene in *Every Man out of His Humour* seems to draw on such thinking, at least indirectly. Jonson's playbook looks nothing like a table-book of polyphonic music, but in its kinetic energy, its noisiness, and in the sense it communicates (both in print and performance) of barely contained, carefully choreographed chaos, the two have something in common. In fact, there is good reason to assume that Jonson and Marston, as well as other dramatists, actors and the audiences for whom they performed, would have been newly drawn to polyphony as a metaphor for conceptualising poetic composition and reception at the close of the sixteenth century. From 1587 to 1593 more music books appeared in print in England than in all the past eighty years combined. Although books of the metrical psalms

Figure 3.3   John Dowland, *The First Booke of Songes or Ayres* (London, 1597), sig. D2ᵛ-Eʳ. RB 59102 The Huntington Library, San Marino, California.

'Sprinkled Among your Ears' 93

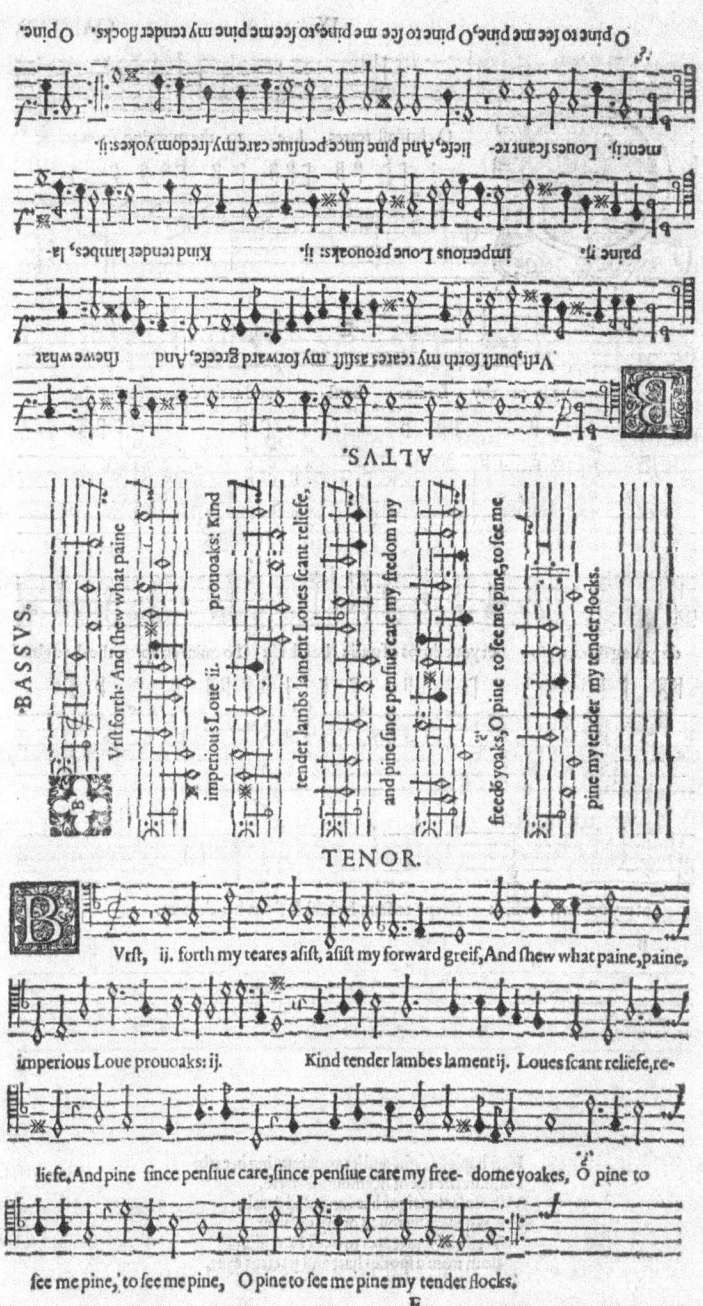

had been printed steadily throughout the sixteenth century, these were monophonic rather than polyphonic, and in both their material, printed form and in their musical content they were markedly different from the partbooks and table-books of madrigals that began appearing in such large numbers in the 1580s and 1590s.[82] After a thirteen-year hiatus, during which no polyphonic music whatsoever was published in England, the 1590s saw a profusion of such books, and consequently the wider dissemination of polyphonic music theory and practice. For dramatists like Jonson and Marston, who repeatedly stressed their poetry's musicality, and who were so attuned to musical metaphors, this new material may have seemed particularly resonant. Certainly Jonson's humours plays, which stress the importance of conscious listening, and which represent theatrical audition as challenging, celebrate something like polyphony's demands on the listener. In *Every Man Out*'s Paul's Walk scene, audience members are faced with a similar set of challenges to those complained of by polyphony's detractors. But they are also urged to keep up, practising the critical listening skills represented and taught in Jonson's and Marston's plays under pressure and at great speed. The Chorus is there to help them along: 'lose not yourself', Cordatus later urges Mitis, 'for now the epitasis, or busy part of our subject, is in action' (3.2.165–6). Concentrate on the play, in other words; it is about to get complicated. *Every Man Out*'s difficulty may therefore have been part of what Jonson assumed would have made the play pleasurable. Those able to keep up with its dramatic polyphony – a complex composition of what Puttenham called 'musical speech' and Dowland called 'speaking harmony' – could relish having accomplished a difficult task, one that *Every Man Out*, *Jack Drum* and *Every Man In* distinctly value.[83]

Hearing in 'the Eares Brothell'

The successful practice of this auditory skill, I want to conclude by suggesting, may have had just as much value outside the theatre as within it, and particularly in the very spaces that *Every Man Out* was among the first plays to represent onstage.[84] The notorious noisiness of Paul's Walk, which I have been arguing Jonson's comedy seeks to replicate (albeit in a highly stylised fashion), would have presented a similar set of challenges to the people who went there to conduct business, to gossip or simply to look around. How were individuals to hear with intent and precision in a space that sounded, as Earle put it, 'nothing liker Babel'?

> The noyse in it is like that of Bees, a strange humming of buzze-mixt of walking tongues and feete: It is a kinde of still roare or loud whisper. It is the great Exchange of all discourse, and no business whatsoever but is here stirring and a foote . . . It is the eares Brothell, and satisfies their lust, and ytch.[85]

The constant drone or hum that Earle hears as the product of so many tongues and feet is described as both seductive and oppressive. It seems to be the main draw of the space, both for tourists and locals alike, a quality that it shares with certain other well-known sites of entertainment. ('It is the other expence of the day', Earle adds, 'after Playes, Taverne, and a Bawdy-House' (sig. L8^v).) If Paul's Walk reminds Earle of the insalubrious pleasures offered in these other spaces, it also reminds him (as the above quote suggests) of the Royal Exchange, where business was similarly conducted with a great noise of tongues and feet. In fact, the same could be said of many of the other spaces which would become so central to seventeenth-century city comedy: London's fairs and marketplaces, its shops and its streets. It is in these spaces that the city must often have seemed its loudest, simply by virtue of the number of people present. And the challenges such sites would have presented to hearers must have seemed similar to those staged in Jonson's and Marston's plays.

The fictional representation of this city, and the ideological construction of it in which those fictions played such a vital role, would therefore have been bound up from the beginning in thinking about sound and its reception.[86] London's playhouses not only represented some of the more culturally significant sites in the city's soundscape; they were also, of course, a vibrant part of it. The selective listening skills celebrated and taught by Jonson's and Marston's turn-of-the-century city comedies may have helped individuals to manage the city's sounds more effectively both within and outside the playhouse walls. By training theatregoers to tune in to certain sounds and tune out others, and to make sense of auditory excess, these plays promised to provide early modern men and women with valuable new strategies for handling London's aural onslaught. In short, they marketed themselves as offering playgoers a vital urban skill, the successful practice of which (according to the plays' own logic) identified them as belonging to a small and privileged community of urbane gentlemen-wits.

For Jonson, the successful cultivation, performance and display of this skill would come to be subjects of increasingly intensified attention and interest as he experimented, again and again, with the dramatic form he had such a hand in inventing for the English stage. His Lorenzo Junior and Prospero are the dramatic progenitors of a large homosocial fraternity of wits, including Clerimont, Truewit and Dauphine in *Epicoene*, and Quarlous and Winwife in *Bartholomew Fair*, to name just a few; and they share with their heirs a talent for sampling sounds selectively and with purpose, as well as with taste. It is a skillset we can already see taking shape in Jonson's and Marston's late-sixteenth-century plays (which Jonson, in the induction to *Every Man Out*, labelled 'satirical comedy'), but we can also see it continuing to structure Jonson's and other dramatists' work in the years and decades that followed. The following chapters trace the impact of this thinking on the production and reception of early modern drama, through Shakespeare's targeted, critical response to Jonson in *Hamlet* up through the final decade of the commercial theatres' operation.

Notes

1. For a summary of the debate over when the play was revised, see Robert Miola's introduction to *Every Man in His Humour*, pp. 1–3. On the play's relative popularity, see Riggs, *Ben Jonson*.
2. Citations from the revised *Every Man in His Humour* are taken from *Every Man in His Humour: A Parallel-Text Edition of the 1601 Quarto and the 1616 Folio*, ed. Lever. It is possible that this prologue was performed when the play, which was first staged in 1598 by the Lord Chamberlain's Men, was revived for court performance in February 1605.
3. That Jonson's prologue claims his play introduces a new realism to the early modern stage is a verity of Jonson criticism. See Watson, *Ben Jonson's Parodic Strategy*, pp. 17–46.
4. The 'newness' of this sound is also discussed by Natasha Korda in *Labors Lost*, pp. 144–73.
5. OED, 2nd edn., 'jars, n' I.1: 'A harsh inharmonious sound or combination of sounds; †*spec.* in *Music*, A discord'; cf. 2.5, 'Discord, want of harmony, disagreement; a divergence or conflict of opinions.'
6. *Timber or Discoveries*, in *Ben Jonson*, ed. Herford, Simpson and Simpson, vol. 8, p. 587.
7. As my terms here suggest, I am drawing on the work of Pierre Bourdieu in *Distinction: A Social Critique of the Judgement of Taste*.
8. Dekker, *The Seven Deadly Sins of London*, p. 50. I have modernised the spelling in this edition.
9. Bruce R. Smith, *The Acoustic World of Early Modern England*, p. 52.
10. Ibid., pp. 49–71.
11. See Sacks and Lynch, 'Ports 1540–1700'. Jean Howard opens her *Theater of a City* with a discussion of these numbers, pointing out the role such massive growth played in impressing visitors and newcomers to London.
12. Dekker, *The Seven Deadly Sins of London*, p. 50.
13. Matheo swears he composed the verses he (falsely) presents as his own 'extempore' at 'the Mitre' with Bobadilla as a witness (3.4.92, 97); and in

Act Four, Scene One, Peto tells Musco, 'We'll go to the Mermaid' for 'a cup of neat wine' (4.1.72–3). All citations to the original, unrevised version of *Every Man in His Humour* will be taken from *Every Man in His Humour*, ed. Miola.

14. No songs, sound effects or musical flourishes are explicitly called for in the text, although of course these could have been added during performance. Apart from the several fights that break out in this play, and the 'great cry' these elicit from 'the women' (including, most gruesomely, when 'Cob beats his wife' (5.2.85 SD)), it is language that makes up the acoustic world of Jonson's play (3.4.150 SD).
15. Barish, *Ben Jonson and the Language of Prose Comedy*; Hutson, 'Liking Men'.
16. Richard Allen Cave writes that to 'categorize the characters of the play in terms of the mental and emotional disorders which were said to derive from particular forms of imbalance within the disposition of humours is to risk reducing them to precise and predictable types' (p. 1). See Cave, 'Ben Jonson's *Every Man in His Humour*: A Case Study'. Scholarship on humoral theory and early modern literature begins with Gail Kern Paster's *The Body Embarrassed* and Michael Schoenfeldt's *Bodies and Selves in Early Modern England*.
17. Defined by the *OED* as 'A keyed musical instrument (common in England in the sixteenth and seventeenth centuries), resembling a spinet, but set in a box or case without legs' *OED*, 2nd edn., 'virginal, n' 1a.
18. On the homoeroticism of Lorenzo Junior and Prospero's friendship (or, as they are named in the 1616 revision, Edward Knowell and Wellbred), see Lorna Hutson, 'Liking Men' and DiGangi, *The Homoerotics of Early Modern Drama*.
19. Both phrases appear frequently in early modern anatomy texts. See my discussion in Chapter 2, pp. 28–30 and p. 58, n. 22.
20. Helkiah Crooke's description is representative: through the pinna, 'sound is as it were scouped vp' into the hole of hearing – like an animated funnel, the pinna collects sound and directs it into the body, letting as little of it slip by as possible (p. 582). This is why, according to Crooke, 'such as are halfe deafe ... do set their hands to their eare with the palmes forward to gather in the sound' (p. 576). According to Vicary, the pinna is shaped so 'that the soundes that be very fugitive should lurke and abyde under his shadowe, tyl it were taken of the instrumentes of hearing' (p. 21). Vicary immediately follows this praise of the ear's active reception, however, with an account of its selective function: 'Another cause', he writes, 'is that it should keepe the hole that it standeth over, from things falling in, that might hinder the hearing' (p. 35).
21. Other parts of the ear are described in similarly paradoxical terms. The auditory canal is said to slope upward, becoming increasingly straight and narrow so that sounds are both funnelled in and deflected. Describing the ruts and caverns found inside this passageway, Ambroise Paré notes, 'They have beene framed by the providence of nature into twining passages like a Snailes shell, which as they come neerer to the foramen caecum, or blind hole, are the more straitened, that so they might the better gather the aire into them' (p. 189); he then continues, 'But they were made thus into

crooked winding, least the sounds rushing in too violently should hurt the sense of hearing . . . Other wise also lest that the aire too sodainely entring in should by its qualitye, as cold, cause some harme' (pp. 189–90). His account seems to contradict itself: the canal is both straight and winding, designed to draw sounds in and prevent their 'too sodaine' entrance.
22. This 'openness' is further demonstrated by Stephano's embarrassingly ready revelation to this same servant that 'mine uncle is a man of a thousand pound a year; he hath but one son in the world; I am his next heir, as simple as I stand here, if my cousin die. I have a fair living of mine own too, beside' (1.1.82–6).
23. All citations to *Every Man out of His Humour*, unless otherwise indicated, are taken from Jonson, *Every Man out of His Humour*, ed. Ostovich.
24. McPherson, 'Ben Jonson's Library and Marginalia', p. 67.
25. Alfred Harbage was the first to shift the scholarly focus on these plays from a hunt for satirical references between playwrights to, instead, attention to class rivalry between public and private playhouses; his model has since been questioned and refined by Andrew Gurr, Ann Jennalie Cook and Roslyn Lander Knutson. See Harbage, *Shakespeare and the Rival Traditions*; Gurr, *Playgoing in Shakespeare's London*; Knutson, *Playing Companies and Commerce in Shakespeare's Time*; Cook, *The Privileged Playgoers of Shakespeare's London*. An author-based approach to these plays can be found in Bednarz, *Shakespeare & the Poets' War*.
26. This character is Brabant Signior, the elder brother who 'makes costly suppers to trie wits: / And will not stick to spend some 20. pound / To grope a gull'. See H. Harvey Wood's *The Plays of John Marston*, vol. 3, p. 190.
27. All citations to *Jack Drum* are taken from the third volume of Wood's *The Plays of John Marston*. The text is not lineated, and as David G. O'Neill points out, Woods's Act and Scene numbers are 'more arbitrary than actual' (p. 125, n. 13). I have supplied page numbers for each quotation. See O'Neill, 'The Influence of Music in the Works of John Marston'.
28. For a detailed account of how the romance plot in *Jack Drum* parallels and ridicules the *Arcadia* and *The Trial of Chivalry*, see Andrews, '*Jack Drum's Entertainment* as Burlesque'.
29. 'Composed' here means, according to the *OED*, written – most often in reference to poetry. The musical sense of this term, though anachronistic to the period, may share with the sixteenth-century poetic sense the same connotations of harmony and balance (*OED*, 'composed, v', 5). Jonson frequently uses the term 'composition' to refer to well-constructed poetry in his *Discoveries* – as when, for example, he writes that the good poet will 'behold what word is proper, which hath ornaments, which height, what is beautifully translated, where figures are fit, which gentle, which strong, to shew the composition manly' (p. 748).
30. The two classic studies of the boys' companies are Michael Shapiro's *Children of the Revels* and W. Reavley Gair's *The Children of Paul's*. See also Lucy Munro's *Children of the Queen's Revels* and Menzer, *Inside Shakespeare*.
31. On playbooks versus books, see Brayman Hackel, 'The "Great Variety" of Readers and Early Modern Reading Practices'.

32. The title given here (Go by Hieronimo) is a quote from *The Spanish Tragedy*; no extant printed editions or STC listings use this title. That a remembered line, heard in the playhouse, is here being used to refer to the printed artefact (with a different visible title) seems possible. The play was often referred to by the name of its revenger, Hieronimo, and this quote in particular seems to have been a ready shorthand reference to the play.
33. The word 'conceit', moreover, ties this style of dramatic speech to that which poisons Thorello in the scene discussed above.
34. My terms and quoted definitions here are taken from Peacham, *The Garden of Eloquence*, p. 48.
35. Jonson, *Timber: or, Discoveries*, p. 30.
36. Puttenham, *The Art of English Poesy*, 3.12.196.
37. Jonson, *Timber: or, Discoveries*, pp. 30–1. According to Lorna Hutson, Jonson's criticism is 'indebted to the Latin antithesis between *nervosus* ("sinewy", "phallic") and *mollis* ("soft, womanish"), which is central to Seneca's Epistle 114 and to Quintilian, *Inst*'. *Discoveries*, ed. Lorna Hutson, nn. 515–17.
38. Bacon, *The Advancement of Learning*, IV, 5.
39. Citations to the play are taken from Ben Jonson's *Poetaster*, in *Ben Jonson*, ed. Herford and Simpson, vol. 4.
40. If the lines are in fact taken from an actual play in contemporary performance, this play has since been lost:

    TUCCA Sirrah, you, pronounce. Thou shalt hear him speake, in King DARIUS' doleful strain.
    I PYRGUS *O, doleful days! O direful deadly dump!*
    O wicked world! and worldly wickedness!
    How can I hold my fist from crying thump,
    In rue of this right rascal wretchedness! (3.4.178–83)

    The lines' repetitious alliteration recalls the 'fountains fraught with tears' in Kyd's play; their anaphoric 'O' echoes Kyd's 'Oh eyes, no eyes' and 'Oh world, no world' construction.

41. 　I PYRGUS *Vindicta!*
    　2 PYRGUS *Timoria!*
    　I PYRGUS *Vindicta!*
    　2 PYRGUS *Timoria!*
    　I PYRGUS *Veni!*
    　2 PYRGUS *Veni!* (3.4.230–4)

42. Kidnie attributes the line to Chapman's *Blind Beggar*. See *Poetaster*, in *The Devil is an Ass and Other Plays*. I think it more likely the line was taken from an earlier play, since *Blind Beggar*, too, includes a burlesque of several genres (including revenge tragedy). James Knowles, editor of the Oxford *Eastward Ho!* makes a similar point regarding the line's earlier origin, though he does not speculate as to the genre of play from which it was lifted (p. 340).
43. Something similar seems to be at work in the induction to Marston's *Antonio and Mellida*, when one of the actors mocks a fellow player's pronunciation, 'Rampum scrampum! Mount tufty Tamburlaine! What rattling

thunderclap breaks from his lips?' (Ind. ll. 83–4). While *Tamburlaine* is here the primary referent, another player's 'go by, go by', uttered just a few lines earlier, calls to mind *The Spanish Tragedy* as well.

44. Two records of payment for these additions appear in Henslowe's diary. See Foakes, *Henslowe's Diary*, pp. 182 and 203.
45. Epigram LXXXIX, 'To Edward Alleyn'.
46. Critics have seen this shift in Marston's career as requiring explanation – suggesting that the two forms are still understood as somehow incompatible. Joseph Loewenstein, for example, sees in *Antonio's Revenge* a sort of inescapable, subconscious drive on the author's part towards 'imitative aggression'. See Loewenstein, 'Marston's Gorge and the Question of Formalism', p. 95.
47. See Gurr, Cook and Knutson, cited above; and Dillon, 'Clerkenwell and Smithfield as a Neglected Home of London Theatre'.
48. Lorna Hutson, 'Liking Men', p. 1072. For Hutson, *Every Man In* is the progenitor of a canon of 'urban bachelor fiction' that stretches 'from the Restoration to Noel Coward' (p. 1065).
49. Laughing at the right places, if Jonson's epigrams are to be believed, was a skill cherished by many theatregoers. Epigram XXXVIII, 'To Person Guilty', warns that although the author once 'did advise' Guilty to 'conceal' his faults of understanding, Guilty's compensatory behaviour now gives him away worse than before: 'You laugh when you are touch'd, and long before / Any man else, you clap your hands, and roar, / And cry good! good! This quite perverts my sense, / And lies so far from wit, 'tis impudence.'
50. Gabriele Bernhard Jackson writes of *Every Man in His Humour* that 'the plot of a Jonson comedy is peculiarly hard to recall', to which Hutson adds 'and this one more than most'. See *Ben Jonson: Every Man in His Humour*, ed. Jackson, p. 2 and Hutson, 'Liking Men', p. 1067. Cf. John Dryden's claim that *Epicoene* is 'the pattern of a perfect Play', and Samuel Taylor Coleridge's description of *The Alchemist*'s plot as 'perfect'. Dryden, *An Essay of Dramatick Poesie*, in *The Works of John Dryden*, ed. Samuel Holt Monk, vol. 17, p. 55; and *The Table Talk and Omniana of Samuel Taylor Coleridge*, p. 312.
51. Michael C. Andrews argues that the romance plot comes from Sidney's *Arcadia* and the stage romance *The Trial of Chivalry*. See *'Jack Drum's Entertainment* as Burlesque'.
52. According to John Milsom, manuscript partbooks of Latin-texted motets continued to circulate for use in private 'chamber performances' in England even after the Reformation. See Milsom, 'Sacred Songs in the Chamber'.
53. Morley, *A Plain & Easy Introduction to Practical Music*, p. 141.
54. Quoted in Strunk, *Source Readings in Music History*, p. 189.
55. According to the school's 1560 statutes, students were required to 'spend two hours each week ... in the art of music' under the instruction of the choristers' master. For a detailed study of music education at a different English song school, see Orme, 'The Early Musicians of Exeter Cathedral'. For more on the relationship between song schools and grammar schools, as well as on the history and purposes of playing in these institutions, see Shapiro, *Children of the Revels*; see also Orme, *Education and Society in Medieval and Renaissance England*; and Jewell, *Education in Early Modern England*.

56. *The English Grammar, Made by Ben. Jonson, For the Benefit of all Strangers, Out of His Observation of the English Language, now spoken and in use.* The *Grammar* is reprinted in *Ben Jonson*, ed. Herford, Simpson and Simpson, vol. 8. Quoted at pp. 211 and 213.
57. See also, in a different context, the sixteenth-century Florentine composer Carlo Valgulio's comments in his Latin translation of Plutarch's *De Musica*: 'They [rhythm and harmony] differ, however; rhythm is always a companion to harmony, from which arises melody and song; melody, in addition, is perceived in high and low [pitch]; rhythm, though, in fast and slow motion. When this motion is considered in speech, it is called long and short, but in other things fast and slow. When the feet, raised and lowered alternately with a fit and ordinary step, tap the earth, this motion is called fast or slow. In metric and rhythmic feet, which are an apt composition of syllables although they got their name from feet, they are called short and long. There is, however, both a distinction and a point to it, for acute and grave are qualities, but fast and slow are quantities.' The English translation quoted here is taken from Palisca, *Documentary Studies and Translations: The Florentine Camerata*, p. 36.
58. *OED*, 'division, n'. 7a: 'The execution of a rapid melodic passage, originally conceived as the dividing of each of a succession of long notes into several short ones; such a passage itself, a florid phrase or piece of melody, a run; esp. as a variation on, or accompaniment to, a theme or "plain song"; hence often nearly = DESCANT.'
59. Morley, *A Plain & Easy Introduction to Practical Music*, p. 140 (emphasis added).
60. David G. O'Neill examines music's role in wooing and winning throughout Marston's comedies and tragedies in 'The Influence of Music in the Works of John Marston, II'. See also Kiefer, 'Music and Marston's *The Malcontent*' and Ingram, 'The Use of Music in the Plays of Marston'.
61. Marston frequently associates music with poetry. Consider the Induction to *What You Will*: 'Music and poetry were first approved / By common sense', in *The Works of John Marston*, ed. Bullen, vol. 2, Ind. ll. 61–2.
62. Defined in the *OED* as an 'elaborate orchestral composition in three or more movements'. *OED*, 'symphony, n', 5b.
63. During the sixteenth and seventeenth centuries, importantly, the term could also be applied to well-balanced poetic compositions; Puttenham uses 'symphonies' as a synonym for poetry in his *Arte of English Poesie* (1589). The *OED* defines this sense as 'Harmony of sound, esp. of musical sounds; concord, consonance. Also occas. of speech-sounds, as in verse.'
64. Such an understanding of Jonson's and Marston's plays would complement early modern theatrical practice, since, as Simon Palfrey and Tiffany Stern have shown, professional performers learned their roles or 'parts' out of context, coming together only in performance. According to Palfrey and Stern, cues, which began to appear with greater frequency at the beginning of the sixteenth century, performed the work that had previously been done by the prompter in medieval English and Continental theatre: holding a baton, the prompter 'literally "conducted"' the actors as it was their turn to speak. See *Shakespeare in Parts*, p. 16.

65. Palisca, *Documentary Studies and Translations*, p. 63. I am grateful to musicologist Roger Grant for this reference.
66. Ibid., p. 111. Francisco Bardi, whom I quote here, was host of the Florentine Camerata in which Mei himself was a participant.
67. Ibid., pp. 62–3. Bardi similarly writes that 'while Mr. Bass, formally dressed in semibreves and minims, walks about in the ground-floor rooms of his palace, the soprano walks hurriedly with quick steps on the terrace, adorned with minims and semiminims, and Mr. Tenor and the alto go around in the rooms of the intermediate floors with *still other rates of movement* and dressed otherwise' (pp. 111–12).
68. Onstage, these lines would probably have been accompanied with a visual union as well, as Katherine and Pasquil jointly 'clip with joyful arme each others wast' (p. 236).
69. Consider, for example, when Ned Planet and Brabant decide to entertain themselves by listening to a would-be wit's affected speech in a tavern, which is punctuated by the tobacco smoking for which he is named (Puff): 'Sir I enrowle you in the Legend of my (*Puffe*) intimates, I shall be infinitely proud if you wilt daigne to value me worthy the embracement of your (*Puffe*) better affection' (sig. B4^v).
70. Sidney, 'The Defence of Poesy', in Alexander, *Sidney's 'The Defence of Poesy'*, p. 46.
71. In 1962, Foakes argued that Marston's tone was intentionally over the top – that Marston's plays must be understood as parodic burlesques of adult company performances. See Foakes, 'John Marston's Fantastical Plays' and 'Tragedies at the Children's Theatre after 1600'.
72. In the 1600 quartos, these lines are further distinguished from the rest of the text with italics.
73. The first group consists of Carlo Buffone, the fop Fastidious Briske and the country bumpkin Sogliardo, who longs to be a gentleman. The second includes the greedy farmer Sordido and his son Fungo, who enter the scene later and become (for Carlo, Fastidious and Sogliardo) part of the show. The third group is formed by Mitis and Cordatus, Jonson's chorus, who comment on this scene and others throughout the play.
74. Scholars and modern directors have noted how this play's enormous cast ebbs and flows across the stage. See Barnes, '*Bartholomew Fair*: All the Fun of the Fair'.
75. See Ostovich, '"To Behold the Scene Full"'.
76. Cordatus explains, these 'are mere strangers to the whole scope of our play – only come to walk a turn or two i' this scene of Paul's by chance'; the direction reads, 'They walk together' (3.1.38–40, 42 SD). With them, they bring two serving men and Puntarvolo's dog, and together they form the largest group on stage. Carlo tells the knight that Sogliardo, the would-be gentleman, is at the herald's office, purchasing for himself a coat of arms.
77. These exchanges become even more complicated if we assume that Carlo and Puntarvolo do not yield the centre of the stage to Fastidious and Sogliardo. Audiences would in that case have to focus their ears on different strands of conversation spoken from different parts of the stage.
78. John Earle, *Micro-cosmographie, or, A Piece of the World Discovered*, sig. L7^v.

79. This scene, as it appears in the quartos, has much in common with the crowded 'mise-en-page' and 'typographical games' Holger Schott Syme finds in *The Alchemist* and *Bartholomew Fair*. See Syme, 'Unediting the Margin: Jonson, Marston, and the Theatrical Page'. I disagree with Syme's claim, however, that *Every Man Out* reflects 'an initial attempt' on Jonson's part 'to remove his plays wholly from the theatrical realm' (pp. 144, 170).
80. Gants and Lockwood, 'The Printing and Publishing of Ben Jonson's Works'.
81. Jeremy L. Smith, *Thomas East and Music Publishing in Renaissance England*, p. 86.
82. This sudden explosion of polyphonic music books is explained by a shift in the ownership of the royal patent to print them: from 1561 to 1582, John Byrd and Thomas Tallis held an exclusive monopoly on music printing (with the exclusion of the monophonic psalms), which they chose more or less not to exercise after 1575. In 1585, however, Thomas East took over the deceased Tallis's half of the monopoly and soon reenergised the market. According to Thurston Dart, after 1575 'no new music was published in London at all, with the exception of settings of the Genevan psalm tunes'. See Dart, 'Introduction', in Morley, *A Plain & Easy Introduction to Practical Music*, p. x. See also Jeremy L. Smith's *Thomas East and Music Publishing* for a thorough account of the monopoly's history and its effects on music publishing in England during this period.
83. Dowland refers to his vocal music as 'speaking harmony' in the dedication to his *First Booke of Songes or Ayres*, (sig. a^r).
84. Jean Howard calls this scene 'the first instance of London comedy's preoccupation with St. Paul's Walk as a satiric setting for the display of urban vanity' in *Theater of a City*, p. 22. See also Ostovich's discussion of the scene in her introduction to the play, '"To Behold the Scene Full"', at pp. 59–68.
85. Earle, *Micro-cosmographie* (sig. L7^v–L8^v).
86. On this point, see Howard, *Theater of a City* and Mullaney, *The Place of the Stage*.

Chapter 4

'Caviare to the General'?: Taste, Hearing and Genre in *Hamlet*

In *A Short View of Tragedy*, Thomas Rymer famously glosses a speech from *Othello*, 'So much ado, so much stress, so much passion and repetition about an Handkerchief! Why was not this call'd the *Tragedy of the Handkerchief*? What can be more absurd . . .?'[1] His complaint introduces a nonetheless serious critical claim about Shakespeare's play. This chapter will suggest that *Hamlet* could be accused of a similarly 'absurd' attention to ears. Subjected throughout to poisonings both figurative and literal, the ears of kings, queens, princes, ladies of the court and courtiers prove supremely vulnerable organs in this play, situated at the threshold between the body and its environment. Ears are stabbed with verbal 'daggers', filled with poison, 'abused' by rumour and 'assail[ed]' with stories (3.2.386, 1.5.38, 1.1.30).[2] But *Hamlet* is 'absurd' in a different sense as well. Derived from the French term 'surdus', meaning 'deaf, inaudible, insufferable to the ear', the term 'absurd' invites consideration of theatrical speech and its reception, topics with which *Hamlet* seems to be almost obsessively occupied.[3]

Much has been written about *Hamlet*'s interest in the risks that listening entailed, and more recently critics have begun to turn their attention to the physical, material quality of those risks.[4] This work has importantly enhanced our understanding of Shakespeare's play, but by divorcing itself from the study of dramatic form, it has left unexplored what appears to me to be a crucial aspect of *Hamlet*'s attention to hearing – its intervention in a turn-of-the-century debate over how particular kinds of plays should sound and how they should be heard by their audiences.[5] Key to this metadramatic contest is, on the one hand, an assumption of sound's materiality and, on the other, a set of contradictory models of auditory reception. Early modern anatomists describe sound as an object or force capable of working profound physiological effects on its listeners. Noise slips inside the ear, or 'hole of hearing', and progresses ever more deeply inside the self, passing from the outer ear to the auditory canal and, finally, into the 'afterbrain' and memory.⁶ At each stage, sound presses on the body and reforms the corporeal material with which it comes into contact. The act of hearing is consequently imagined as a somatic transformation over which the listener has only tenuous control. And yet these same anatomical texts also stress the ear's ability to deflect and moderate sounds, implying that listeners can select what they hear and determine how deeply they are affected by it. Such contradictions matter crucially for early modern thinking about language, and by extension theatrical speech, which might be imagined either as sound that penetrates the self regardless of its content or, alternatively, as something that can be sampled and selected according to its sense.⁷ In fact, theatrical speech is always both at once. It is sound, a material object, but it is also a source of meaning that theatregoers are charged with interpreting and negotiating in complex and sometimes competing ways.

This process of negotiation was a central topic in early modern theatre, but as I argued in Chapter 3, it receives special scrutiny in the late-sixteenth- and early-seventeenth-century plays of Ben Jonson, John Marston and other playwrights. At issue for these authors is the way in which sound sometimes threatens to trump sense in the theatre. Their plays repeatedly accuse older dramatic forms, revenge tragedy most of all, of featuring thunderous speeches that subject listeners to dangerous somatic processes, opening up their bodies to the indiscriminate reception of theatrical language. Their own comedies, by contrast, claim to introduce a new sound to London's stages that is more measured and less booming. Most importantly, this new sound is described as affecting listeners differently. Older plays bore into audiences' bodies, but the comedies of Jonson, Marston and others do not; instead, their less bombastic speeches allow audiences to choose what they hear according to the sense of what is said. Less an accurate representation of how plays sounded and were heard than a reflection of a broader competitive strategy, this metadramatic attack nonetheless helped to make theatrical audition a vital topic at the close of the sixteenth century.

All of this matters crucially for *Hamlet*, a play which not only takes hearing as one of its subjects but which does so, importantly, from within the genre of revenge. I argue that Shakespeare's play directly responds to Jonson's complaints about revenge tragedy's rumbling sound and its supposedly inevitable, somatically transformative reception. Instead, *Hamlet* insists that *all* theatrical speeches can be absorbed voluntarily, regardless of their style. It also questions the criteria according to which listeners' choices are to be made. If, as I will show, Jonson describes social status as the main determinant of listeners' choices, *Hamlet* gives the lie to that assumption. Instead, the play emphasises the centrality of other concerns, such as the morality or rationality of a given speech. In doing so, *Hamlet* introduces an alternative model of theatrical audition to the early modern stage while at the same time recuperating this long-popular dramatic form from charges of creaking irrelevance. Simply put, Hamlet's tragedy is one of Jonsonian listening run amok. The mistakes he makes as a listener, coupled with the assumptions that he holds about others' reception, determine the action of Shakespeare's play; together they lead inexorably to the fatal silencing of Hamlet himself and to the installation of Fortinbras on the Danish throne. At the same time, *Hamlet*'s investigation of hearing entails nothing less than the transformation of one of the oldest dramatic forms on the London stage. From a suddenly seemingly outmoded, but still popular, genre, which is preoccupied with the violent effects of audition and the instability of corporeal and political bodies that violence signifies, revenge tragedy is remade into a genre that is attuned to the individual's struggle to protect the self against aural and other onslaughts.

The Tasteful Ear

That *Hamlet* is preoccupied with ears and hearing has become a critical commonplace; so, too, has Hamlet's preoccupation with acting and the theatre.[8] The prince's interactions with the players unite these two themes. When the troupe arrives in Elsinore, the theatre – more specifically, turn-of-the-century English theatre – briefly becomes *Hamlet*'s subject. While the travelling players' performance is both oral and gestural, it is its aural elements that resonate most deeply with Hamlet. He remembers having 'heard' the First Player speak a speech before in the role of Aeneas, and he asks to hear it again; he says he'll hear the rest of that broken-off speech later ('I'll have thee speak out the rest of this soon'); and he announces that he'll have the court 'hear a play' tomorrow (2.2.459–60, l. 472). Alarmed by one boy actor's newly grown beard, Hamlet is at least as worried about his voice: 'Lady and mistress! . . . Pray God your voice, like a piece of uncurrent gold, be not cracked within the ring' (ll. 365–6). According to Hamlet, a cracked voice would ruin the boy's ability to perform women's roles as surely as a beard or an ungainly growth spurt, suggesting the centrality of sound to his understanding of the theatrical project. This interest in how actors sound is displayed once again in Hamlet's advice to the players: 'Speak the speech, I pray you, as I pronounced it to you – trippingly on the tongue' (3.2.1–2). Rather than bellowing their speeches, Hamlet encourages the players to pronounce their lines trippingly, or lightly, for the benefit of 'judicious' hearers like himself (l. 26).

Typically read as a critique of unnaturalistic acting, Hamlet's advice to the players is better understood, I argue, as a metadramatic in-joke.[9] Through these scenes, Shakespeare references a turn-of-the-century fad for skewering a particular theatrical sound, one which was becoming associated with certain kinds of plays – revenge tragedies, heroic romances and other older but still popular forms. The fad is one in which Shakespeare himself participated in *A Midsummer Night's Dream*, mocking Bottom's enthusiasm for a part to 'tear a cat in'.[10] But increasingly, as I argued in Chapter 2, its central participants were John Marston and Ben Jonson. The prince's criticism of players who 'tear a passion to tatters, to very rags, to split the ears of the groundlings' (3.2.9–10) echoes not only Bottom's tear-cat speeches, but also Marston's complaints in *Jack Drum's Entertainment* (perf. 1599, 1600) about 'mouldy fopperies of stale Poetry' that 'torment your listning eares'.[11] Perhaps even more than Marston, Hamlet here seems to ventriloquise Ben Jonson, whose comedies persistently mock older dramatic forms – and particularly revenge tragedies – for how thunderous they sound. Matheo, the pretentious fop of Jonson's *Every Man in His Humour* (first perf. 1598), so admires the 'fine speeches' of Thomas Kyd's *The Spanish Tragedy* that he reads them aloud, gushing over their literary merit: 'Oh eyes, no eyes, but fountains fraught with tears! – There's a conceit! Fountains fraught with tears!'[12] He concludes, 'Is't not simply the best that ever you heard?'[13] And in *Poetaster*, which was first performed either the same year as *Hamlet* or the year after, the gruff soldier Tucca commands his servants to perform a pastiche of his favourite plays, including an unnamed (or unspecific) revenge tragedy and a burlesque of *The Spanish Tragedy*.[14] He insists his servant 'mouth' these lines in the very way Hamlet detests: 'Now thunder, sirrah, you, the rumbling plaier.'[15] Like the players who 'tear a passion to tatters', Tucca's servant bellows his rumbling speech in the manner of *Hamlet*'s 'town-crier' (3.2.3). This theatrical sound synecdochically stands for outdated, unsophisticated drama, the kind of production which, Jonson's play self-servingly suggests, is the distinct opposite of *Poetaster* itself – a cutting-edge play with a similarly cutting-edge sound.

That Hamlet here speaks for Jonson is made clearer in Q1 and the Folio, where the prince's exchange with Rosencrantz and Guildenstern (or 'Gilderstone', in Q1) about the approaching actors is expanded. In Q1, Hamlet asks, 'How comes it that [the players] trauell?' Gilderstone explains, 'the principall publike audience that / Came to them, are turned to priuate playes, / And to the *humour* of children.'¹⁶ The word 'humour' recalls Jonson's *Every Man in His Humour* and *Every Man out of His Humour*, both of which were staged shortly before *Hamlet*, and both of which played a signal role in shaping and introducing Jonson's sound and his idealised, socially significant sense of auditory reception to the early modern stage. The opposition Ben Jonson draws between these two dramatic sounds, both in his humours plays and in his later comedies, is an aesthetic one, but it is understood largely in physiological terms. It is a distinction that only seems to have become clearer, or starker, over the course of his career. If in *Every Man In* and *Every Man Out* there was a possibility, at least, that attentive listeners could be formed within the theatre – that is, that the plays themselves could help train theatregoers to hear more thoughtfully and selectively – then by the time *Epicoene* was first performed in 1609, this possibility seems to have been lost. For Jonson, certain sounds, including rumbling stage speech, inevitably demand unthinking and involuntary reception, while lines that are more trippingly pronounced allow for the possibility of selective engagement.

Like Ben Jonson or John Marston, Hamlet finds certain stage sounds embarrassing, and even painful, to hear: 'O, it offends me to the soul to hear a robustious periwig-pated fellow tear a passion to tatters, to very rags, to split the ears of the groundlings' (3.2.8–10). The physical discomfort produced by these sounds in the moment of their reception is the inevitable by-product of their power – meaning both their volume and their strength. Once again, there is support for such thinking in early modern anatomy texts. While the ear is structurally designed to protect the brain from the most damaging of sounds, which Helkiah Crooke describes as 'vehement and violent noyse such as the shooting of ordenance, thunder & such like', it cannot prevent these noises from entering the body altogether.[17] Thunderous speeches could thus be absorbed through the ear involuntarily and at great risk to the listener. Of course, if this understanding of theatrical audition echoes complaints made by Jonson and Marston, it also complements *Hamlet*'s representations of hearing as a potentially violent, dangerous act. Verbs like 'split' and 'cleave' suggest that sound opens up a wound in the hearer's body, allowing words to pour in unmediated, regardless of their sense. Represented most famously, and most gruesomely, in the description of King Hamlet's murder, this model of audition associates words with poison and suggests that listeners do not always have control over what they hear. The 'juice of cursed hebona in a vial' poured 'in the porches' of the sleeping King's ear resembles the false rumours circulating about the King's death – rumours by which 'the whole ear of Denmark' is 'rankly abus'd' (1.5.62–3, ll. 35, 37). Words threaten to damage their hearers in the play's opening scenes, as the Ghost warns that 'the secrets of [his] prison-house' would 'harrow up thy soul, freeze thy young blood' if Hamlet were to hear them (1.5.14–16). Sound's invasion thus signals the vulnerability of *Hamlet*'s political and corporeal bodies, a conceit familiar from *The Spanish Tragedy*, and one that would become increasingly central to the action of seventeenth-century revenge plays.[18]

Since *Hamlet* is a tragedy of revenge, its emphasis on sound's power to wound makes generic sense. And indeed, Hamlet himself often speaks in the ear-splitting style he derides. After hearing the First Player perform, he bellows, 'bloody, bawdy villain, / Remorseless, treacherous, lecherous, kindless villain' and aches to 'cleave the general ear with horrid speech' (2.2.515–16, l. 498). What are we to make, then, of Hamlet's excoriating attacks on thunderous theatre? These complaints seem not only to echo but also to form part of Shakespeare's response to Jonson's skewering of revenge tragedy. Embedded in this response is the play's critique of Jonson's theories of theatrical audition – how it works, first of all, but also in what ways it is thought to matter. For the prince, as for Jonson, auditory reception is both predetermined by how a play sounds and, paradoxically, shaped by a theatregoer's social status. Certain listeners seem to be better able to resist sound's effects, and to instead make choices according to the sense of what they hear. The problem is that the process of making these choices becomes, both for Hamlet and for Jonson, above all a socially significant one. It reveals where a listener fits within a hierarchy of elite and less privileged hearers or, alternatively, signals affiliations with other kinds of social groups – male or female, guilty or innocent. This model of audition ultimately proves insufficient in *Hamlet* for combating the very real dangers attached to the absorption of certain speeches, or for anticipating how people will be affected by what they hear.

For all of Hamlet's complaints about ear-splitting speeches that 'rankly abuse' the body or 'cleave the ear', this is not how he expects to be affected by theatrical language. Nor, importantly, is the violent, involuntary audition that Hamlet and the Ghost describe the only model of hearing encountered in Shakespeare's play. Noises can damage vulnerable hearers, but they can also be ignored, deflected or selectively sampled by active listeners. This last model of audition, which is just as central to *Hamlet* as the one discussed above, has received far less attention in scholars' analysis of this play.[19] At its core is the possibility of choice, a kind of thinking aural consumption informed by aesthetic, spiritual, social and other concerns. For Hamlet, these aural choices – and, just as importantly, one's demonstrated ability to make them in the first place – become expressive of the possession or lack of social polish, status and refinement. In short, they become expressive of taste. The concept of 'taste' as aesthetic discernment has been assumed to be anachronistic to sixteenth- and seventeenth-century England, a product instead of eighteenth-century thought.[20] Yet we can already see this abstracted sense developing in Hamlet's synaesthetic language: 'We'll have a speech straight', he commands; 'Come, give us a taste of your quality. Come, a passionate speech' (2.2.368–70). 'Taste' here means a small sample, or tidbit, to be examined, weighed and judged.[21] This judging will be performed by the ear, an organ that tastes and swallows words like the mouth tastes and swallows food:

> I heard thee speak me a speech once – but it was never acted, or, if it was, not above once, for the play I remember pleased not the million, 'twas caviare to the general. But it was, as I received it, and others whose judgements in such matters cried in the top of mine, an excellent play, well digested in the scenes, set down with as much modesty as cunning. I remember one said there were no sallets in the lines to make the matter savoury nor no matter in the phrase that might indict the author of affection, but called it an honest method, as wholesome as sweet, and by very much more handsome than fine. (2.2.372–83)

Likened to 'caviare', this 'well-digested' play lacks 'sallets', or spices, that might make it 'savoury'.[22] At the same time, it is both 'wholesome' and 'sweet'. Described in the language of taste, these choices link aural and aesthetic palates in the development of a socially significant critical faculty. Enjoying the caviare-like speech of a particular player, Hamlet seems to appreciate most of all its unsuitability for others' palates and the consequent distinction it affords his own. Those of 'general' tastes include no less a personage than Polonius, the King's counsellor, who finds the whole speech 'too long' and savours only the one line that Hamlet seems to dislike ('"The mobled queen"!'), saying, 'That's good' (ll. 441–2).[23] Polonius's theatrical palate is thus set in opposition to Hamlet's and subordinated to it: 'Prithee say on', the prince commands, 'he's for a jig, or a tale of bawdry, or he sleeps' (ll. 437–8).[24]

Gustatory metaphors for the discerning, synaesthetic reception of sounds also appear in contemporary Puritan sermons, suggesting that this abstracted sense of taste was already forming at the start of the seventeenth century. William Cowper writes in *The Anatomie of a Christian Man* that 'as the mouth tastes the meat, and lets none goe downe to the stomack, vnlesse it be approued; so the eare of the godly tastes words, and lets none goe downe to the soule which is not from God'.[25] Cowper encourages Christians to hear both profitably and discriminatingly, a process that depends on being able to gauge the difference between essential sounds and those which must be winnowed out. This skill was always at risk of being misapplied. William Gouge rails against 'the nice or itching Eare ... that will heare nothing but nouelties, and dainties, that lookes not so much to the goodnesse of the meat, as to the sweet-nesse of the sawce'.[26] Nice or itching ears do not just hear the wrong sorts of sounds – attending to theatrical productions, say, instead of to sermons – they also hear the *right* words the wrong way, sampling the sauce without savouring the meat. Such a listener 'often meets with that hee vnderstandeth not, meate that hee cannot digest, and so seldom or neuer profiteth by the Word of God'.[27] The problem is that writers like Gouge and Cowper simultaneously, if inadvertently, encourage the use of just such a nice or itching ear by training listeners in its cultivation. When Stephen Egerton suggests that individuals read along in their Bibles while the minister recites scripture, 'to see whether they be truly alleaged or no', he fosters the development of a critical ear, one attentive to how well the minister reads or recites the Bible.[28] The application of one sort of critical filter might lead to the use of another: the scripture is accurate, but the sermon is boring; the minister's voice is nasal.

Written roughly twenty years before Egerton's sermon was published and ten years before Cowper's, *Hamlet* nevertheless seems to share these authors' understanding of the ear as, first, the organ of salvation, and second, as a tool for exercising aesthetic discernment. I suggest that it also shares their discomfort with this dual function – as applied not just to religious material, but to a wide variety of sounds, including those of the stage. Scholars attuned to *Hamlet*'s emphasis on ears and hearing have tended to consider the play in a Protestant context, arguing that it participates in a post-Reformation shift from the holy images of Catholicism to the word of God.[29] First performed in an ostensibly Protestant culture that legally required weekly attendance at church services, with their hour-long sermons, *Hamlet*'s emphasis on audition certainly seems religiously resonant. Without arguing for a strictly Protestant, let alone Puritan, reading of *Hamlet*, I nonetheless want to suggest that the play critiques Hamlet's hearing as being superficial in its critical focus and dangerously inattentive to the serious stakes of audition – in *any* setting, and under any circumstances.

Such a reading troubles easy identification of Hamlet's thoughts on hearing with Shakespeare's. Instead, like his polemic against rumbling stage speech, Hamlet's stated preference for tasteful audition seems to echo Ben Jonson, who often used synaesthetic language to describe the discriminating reception of sound and who would emphasise the discerning auditor's social distinction throughout his career. Jonson's persistent use of these classically inflected metaphors suggests their new and specifically contemporary significance, particularly with regard to theatrical reception.[30] The first of Jonson's plays to be performed on the commercial stage, *The Case is Altered*, describes speech in edible terms, likening old maxims to stale bread.[31] When the servant Juniper adopts the habit (or humour) of speaking neologisms and other hard words, the more articulate Valentine's complaint ('O how pittifully are these words forc't. / As though they were pumpt out on's belly') both communicates his own more elevated position in the household, since he is able to hear misusages that Jupiter cannot, and signals to the Blackfriars audience that they, too, should listen for malapropisms in the servant's speech.[32] (The same play also offers an important reminder that ears could literally be made into markers of status, bored to indicate the fact that one occupied a position of service: when the groom Peter Onion puts on a 'Lyons hide', boldly adopting a peremptory manner, he is told, 'your eares haue discouered you ... do not I know you *Peter?*' (1.3.16–17)). *Cynthia's Revels*, which was first performed in 1600, likens one boy actor's wilful delivery of the argument to 'giv[ing] them [the audience] the inventory of their cates aforehand' – or, to reading the audience the menu of the meal they are about to enjoy.[33] The prologue to *Epicoene* (first performed 1609 or 1610) likens the poet's words to 'cates', claiming 'Our wishes, like to those make public feasts, / Are not to please the cook's tastes, but the guests.'[34] And *The Staple of News* (first performed 1625) explains in a separate prologue for the court that the play is meant for 'Schollers, *that can iudge, and faire report / The sense they heare, aboue the vulgar sort / Of Nut-crackers, that onely come for sight.*'[35] Like the scholars who hear 'sense' where the vulgar nut-crackers do not, Hamlet imagines his aural choices and capabilities distinguishing him from those without the taste for caviare. His palate is opposed to those of the non-'schollers', who are unable to appreciate what they hear – or even to hear a play at all. Both the meaning of Hamlet's metaphors and the metaphors themselves could be taken straight from one of Ben Jonson's comedies. But whereas *The Case is Altered*, *Cynthia's Revels*, *Epicoene* and *The Staple of News* all bear out the social logic of this tasteful audition, *Hamlet* does not. By interpolating Jonson's stance on theatrical reception into his own turn-of-the-century revenge play, and by putting that position in the mouth of his eponymous hero, Shakespeare tests the limits of this approach from within the much-maligned revenge tragedy form. Shifting the focus of the debate from theatrical pronunciation (rumbling versus tripping, ranting versus well-seasoned) to its reception, *Hamlet* implies that *why* playgoers hear is every bit as important as what, or even how, they hear. What matters most is the criteria according to which those auditory choices are made.

Hamlet's Hearing

For all of *Hamlet*'s, and Hamlet's, focus on audition, the prince has surprisingly persistent trouble hearing. His mistakes as a listener are not only thematically central but also key to the emplotment of Shakespeare's play: it is because Hamlet has failed to hear the Ghost's command in Act One, 'Taint not thy mind nor let thy soul contrive / Against thy mother aught', that he speaks 'words like daggers' to Gertrude in Act Three, causing Polonius to cry out from behind the arras and precipitating the first in a series of what will then become inevitable acts of violence (1.5.85–6, 3.4.93). Mishearings like these help to determine the play's tragic ending, leading inexorably to the prince's death and the dissolution of Denmark's royal line. Their persistent presence and centrality to the plot undermine the prince's, and hence Jonson's, authority on the subject of sound's reception. Rather than endorsing the ear-splitting sound and indiscriminate reception that both Hamlet and Jonson mock, or the tripping pronunciation and tasteful reception they celebrate, *Hamlet* suggests that both are insufficient for negotiating Denmark's soundscapes. Instead, an altogether new auditory model is needed.

Hamlet's opening act establishes the hearing trouble the prince will have throughout the play. When he first encounters the Ghost, Hamlet begins by attempting to frame his reception in much the way Cowper, Gouge and Egerton encourage, asking it questions to judge whether or not he can hear this speaker safely: 'Be thou a spirit of health or goblin damned, / Bring with thee airs from heaven or blasts from hell' (1.4.40–1). And yet, famously, Hamlet does not wait for the answers to these questions, choosing instead to supply them himself: 'I'll call thee Hamlet, / King, father, royal Dane' (ll. 44–5). This choice exposes the prince to grave spiritual as well as physical risks, potentially placing him in the category of those who allow sounds to 'goe downe to the soule which [are] not from God'. Yet Hamlet does not entirely surrender to this speaker's power. He distances himself from the Ghost once again by using the pronoun 'it' ('It will not speak: then I will follow it' (l. 63)) and sets limits to his obedience by refusing to follow the Ghost beyond a particular point on the ramparts. On the one hand, the Ghost's story affects Hamlet strongly, corporeally wounding him: 'Hold, hold, my heart, / And you, my sinews, grow not instant old / But bear me swiftly up' (1.5.93–5). On the other hand, it does not produce in the prince the transformation that the Ghost seeks – or, indeed, that Hamlet promises to undergo.[36] Focusing his aural attention on the wrong information, he most indelibly 'marks' that on which he is expressly told *not* to dwell: the fact of Gertrude's remarriage. It is an instance of dangerously indiscriminate reception that fundamentally shapes the rest of the play.

This scene introduces hearing as a central subject while at the same time signalling Hamlet's failings as a listener. His initial overeagerness to hear the Ghost's story becomes offset by a protective inattentiveness that prevents him from focusing on and remembering the Ghost's command, a morally ambiguous but generically crucial call for vengeance. If the opening act draws attention to Hamlet's hearing trouble, however, it also highlights a more positive model of auditory reception. Hamlet's mistakes are offset by the comparatively thoughtful, measured audition of Horatio, one of the prince's several foils in the play. Neither indiscriminate nor determined by taste, Horatio's listening presents an alternative to the two dominant auditory modes at play in turn-of-the-century English theatre: it is cautious, thoughtful and always situated to the specific circumstances in which each act of hearing takes place. Like the prince a 'scholar' educated at Wittenberg (Martin Luther's university, and hence coded as a site of Protestant learning), Horatio seems to have learned the lessons taught there better than Hamlet has, attending to speeches – theatrical and otherwise – with a sceptically 'fortified' ear (1.1.41, 31). Because Horatio is something of a bystander, limited in the scope of his action, he cannot make mistakes on as grand or tragic a scale as the prince, and he is thus both protected and limited by his role. As cautious in action as Horatio is, he is similarly cautious in his hearing – a trait that is vital to his comparative identification with the prince. Horatio, for example, 'will not let belief take hold of him' about the Ghost on report alone (l. 23). Only firsthand, empirical evidence, rather than Marcellus and Barnardo's report, will convince Horatio that the dead King Hamlet stalks Elsinore's ramparts. He demands to 'speak to' the Ghost, questioning it and considering its responses before deciding whether to accept the watch's story (ll. 128, 131). His discerning ear samples speeches for more than how they sound, considering their sense, provenance and verifiability before choosing how or even whether to mark them.

As is demonstrated by Horatio's repeated willingness to hear Marcellus and Barnardo, however, he limits only his acceptance of what he hears – not his reception more generally. Simply put, Horatio hears as much as he can, but accepts only certain material. To hear becomes an ongoing process of filtering and sifting stories, rumours, news and other sounds. This is the kind of thoughtful audition Hamlet repeatedly fails to perform, and that the play suggests would best protect him from the aural onslaughts of literally and figuratively poisonous speech that are synonymous with the revenge tragedy genre. Sceptical of the watch's story, Horatio nevertheless asks to 'let us hear Barnardo speak of' the Ghost again, collecting information without necessarily approving or accepting it (l. 33). He listens to, remembers and repeats to Marcellus and Barnardo rumours of an imminent attack on Denmark, but he is also cautious in accepting these rumours as true: 'At least the whisper goes so' (l. 79). Horatio seems capable of determining not just whether or not he should hear, but how deeply. He often accepts speeches only 'in part', judging the worth of individual pieces of discourse while practising a sort of layered, and even inductive, audition. 'I have heard', Horatio explains, that 'The cock . . . is the trumpet to the morn', frightening away spirits with its cry; 'and of the truth herein / This present object made probation' (ll. 148–55). Having heard the cock crow and seen the Ghost depart, Horatio now believes what he has heard about roosters: the specific example has proven the general rule. That the cock sings all night long at Christmas, and no ghosts walk abroad that night (as Marcellus next insists), Horatio remains sceptical: 'So have I heard *and do in part believe it*' (l. 164, emphasis added). He hears Marcellus's theory, considers it and stores it, but with qualifications. Using the particular to prove the general, Horatio is able to absorb more information and to make wiser, sounder judgements as a result.

Such cautious hearing complements traditional readings of Horatio as a Christian Stoic, since his carefully managed audition could be seen as part of a larger project of self-control.[37] But Horatio's hearing is Stoic in a different sense as well. It seems to represent a practical extension of the theories of language described by Diogenes Laertius, Seneca and others that distinguished between the corporeality of speech and the incorporeality of meaning, or sense.[38] The Stoics understood all utterances, including speech, to be corporeal. Comprised of air, itself a material substance, speech was capable (like all other 'bodies') of acting upon matter or of being acted upon. By contrast, meaning, or 'sayables' (*lekta*), subsists but has no bodily form. This distinction enables listeners, at least theoretically, to manage speech's impact on their own bodies, deciding how fully or how deeply it is allowed to matter. Stoic logic demands such sifting. In its breadth, it encompasses all aspects of discourse – phonetics, semantics, stylistics and so on – and provides a linguistic framework for evaluating the truth of what the Stoics termed 'assertibles', a class of sayable.[39] It is the context in which an assertible is spoken that largely determines its truth. (For example, the assertible 'it is day' may be true right now, but it will not be true this evening; it will again be true tomorrow.⁴⁰) Attentive to the circumstances in which speech is delivered as well as to its meaning, Horatio sifts sounds in ways that seem in keeping with this logic.

As with Horatio's stoicism more generally, which Hamlet admires but is unable to put into practice for much of the play, his cautious reception, too, remains elusive for the prince. Hamlet, the play's great theoriser on the subject of audition, hears far less successfully in practice than Horatio – or, in fact, than many of the play's other characters. In addition to mishearing certain sounds, the prince also mistakenly assumes that all individuals will hear predictably and by rule. His underestimation of other listeners' discrimination matters because it shapes his interactions with the men and women of the Danish court and prevents him from interpreting their auditory responses correctly. This second point will have important implications for Hamlet's use of the theatre in his plot against Claudius, and for the 'scourg[ing]' sermon he delivers in the closet scene, both of which I turn to below; but it affects the prince's other exchanges as well. By assuming that audition is categorically predetermined, Hamlet aligns himself with the mainly Puritan authors who produced a sharply gendered schematic in which all women were imagined to hear more indiscriminately than most men. The faultiness of such assumptions forms part of *Hamlet*'s critique of Jonsonian reception. As feminist critics have shown, the goal of controlling the unruly female body became tied in early modern England to managing what it said and heard.⁴¹ Shakespeare undermines such rigidly gendered ways of thinking by giving them voice through Polonius and Laertes, the latter of whose isomorphism of Ophelia's 'credent ear' and 'chaste treasure' renders his harangue against her an incestuous assault, undercutting his moral authority (1.3.29–30). Hamlet also expects groups of listeners to hear by rule, but the key term for him is rank rather than gender. He considers his own tasteful audition, an ability to appreciate that which seems 'caviare to the general', a mark of his birth and education. Similarly, he imagines his supposed imperviousness to sound's violent effects – a quality he boasts of possessing – as tied to social privilege. When Rosencrantz asks Hamlet the 'cause of [his] distemper', he explains he 'lack[s] advancement' and asks Guildenstern to 'play upon this pipe' (3.2.328–9, 331, 342–3): 'It is as easy as lying', he urges, 'give it breath with your mouth, and it will discourse most eloquent music' (ll. 349–51). Guildenstern insists he cannot play, at which point Hamlet explodes:

> Why, look you now how unworthy a thing you make of me: you would play upon me! You would seem to know my stops, you would pluck out the heart of my mystery, you would sound me from my lowest note to my compass.

And there is much music, excellent voice, in this little organ. Yet cannot you make it speak. S'blood! Do you think I am easier to be played on than a pipe? Call me what instrument you will, though you fret me you cannot play upon me. (ll. 355–63)

The analogy creates a sharp distinction between two sets of individuals: those who can be played, or 'sounded', like a pipe, and those who cannot. At issue is one's receptivity to words' material effects. Unlike those who resemble an instrument in their willingness to be sounded by others, Hamlet insists he can hear words without being forced to 'discourse'. The physiological distinction suggests a social one as well.

Hamlet's musical metaphor once again echoes the metadramatic conversations discussed above and further links Hamlet to Ben Jonson. In my third chapter I argued that the fools in *Every Man in His Humour* are likened to instruments upon which others can play: Prospero says of Stephano, a gull, 'Oh, it's a precious good fool . . . I can compare him to nothing more happily than a barber's virginals; for everyone may play upon him.'[42] 'Play[ing] upon' Stephano – that is, saying things to him that compel Stephano to say foolish things in turn – Prospero demonstrates his ability to dominate another man, a meaning that is further stressed through the term 'virginals'. Controlling Stephano's speech, and hence his entire body, through the ear, Prospero establishes a corporeal and sociological distinction between them. Though the instrument has changed – a pipe, rather than a barber's virginal – Hamlet's metaphorical meaning seems similar to Prospero's. What makes Guildenstern's request for information so insulting is that it associates Hamlet with those who have little or no control over their aural reception, and hence over their bodies. Like Polonius or Laertes, or like a wit in one of Jonson's satiric city comedies, Hamlet espouses a model of audition through which individuals are lumped into social categories according to what, and how, they hear: rumbling speeches, in the first instance; openly and submissively in the second.

Relying on this pattern to predict how listeners will absorb aural material, Hamlet also uses it to 'play upon' others himself. 'Do you see yonder cloud that's almost in shape of a camel?' he asks Polonius:

Pol. By th' mass and 'tis like a camel indeed.
Ham. Methinks it is like a weasel.
Pol. It is backed like a weasel.
Ham. Or like a whale?
Pol. Very like a whale. (3.2.367–73)

From camel to weasel to whale, Polonius dutifully sounds out the word Hamlet breathes into his ears. Later, the prince similarly sounds out the courtier Osric, perversely responding to his 'it is very hot' with 'No . . . 'tis very cold.' Osric agrees ('It is indifferent cold, my lord, indeed'), only to be contradicted again ('it is very sultry and hot'). Once more, the courtier adjusts his weather report accordingly: 'Exceedingly, my Lord, it is very sultry' (5.2.80–6). In their desire to please the prince, both Polonius and Osric relinquish control of their sensory perception and of their bodies more generally, allowing themselves to become Hamlet's instruments: though he is the King's counsellor, Polonius is nonetheless subservient to the prince and can therefore be forced, like Osric, to discourse according to his suggestions. The exchanges display Hamlet's power over these men and Guildenstern's comparable powerlessness over the prince. Yet such pliant receptivity is at least in part an occupational hazard; receiving the prince's voice deferentially, Polonius and Osric are pressured to accept what he says as true. Hamlet's mistake is to assume that other listeners will hear him as Polonius and Osric do – deferentially, and without defence – and to attribute this defenceless listening to a defective, unalterable openness. He fails to consider, in other words, the conditions in which these exchanges take place and the social constraints that encourage the men's submissively open reception of his words, assuming instead that how people hear is always inevitably and consistently predetermined by rank or other factors. Hamlet's application of these assumptions to the reception of sermons and theatrical speeches tests their validity while extending *Hamlet*'s interest in audition offstage.

Marking the Play

Given the prince's fixation on the theatre and his assumptions about reception, it is fitting that he chooses a play as both an investigative tool and a weapon to wield against the King. He assumes his stage-managed play will 'prick', 'catch', 'tent' and 'touch' the listening Claudius, setting in motion a physiological process over which he will have no control and, ultimately, effect a reformative cure of the state. The guilty King will be played like a pipe through the players' surgical application of certain sounds:

> I have heard
> That guilty creatures sitting at a play
> Have by the very cunning of the scene
> Been struck so to the soul that presently
> They have proclaimed their malefactions.
> For murder, though it have no tongue, will speak

With most miraculous organ. I'll have these players
Play something like the murder of my father
Before mine uncle. I'll observe his looks,
I'll tent him to the quick. (2.2.523–32)

That a play could inspire the guilty in its audience to confess long-secret crimes was an early modern commonplace, which Hamlet seems to have 'heard' and believed. In his 1612 *An Apology for Actors*, the playwright Thomas Heywood writes that a Norfolk woman who attended a production of the 'History of Fryer *Francis*' by 'the then Earle of *Sussex* players' (which features an adulterous wife who murders her husband) was suddenly compelled to confess a similar crime in the middle of the performance: 'finding her conscience (at this presentment) extremely troubled, [she] suddenly skritched and cryd out Oh my husband, my husband!'[43] Heywood's story offers a model of theatrical listening similar to that which Hamlet describes, and on which his plot seems to depend: like all guilty men or women, Claudius will be made to sound out the desired notes. Though the prince does not speak directly here of listening, his earlier insistence on the aurality of playing suggests that the play's violent effects will be produced primarily through the ear. So, too, does Hamlet's medical language. To 'tent' Claudius 'to the quick' is to perform a surgical procedure: a 'tent' is defined by the *OED* as a 'roll or pledget' that is 'often medicated', and which is 'used to search and cleanse a wound, or to keep open or distend a wound, sore, or *natural orifice*'.[44] Hamlet imagines the play – something the court will 'hear' the following day – invading Claudius's body and propping open the very wound it inflicts. The 'wound' in this case could be the ear itself, an open orifice that Claudius wishes to keep closed.[45] Hearing the players' performance, Hamlet imagines, Claudius will be struck to the soul and tented to the quick: 'The play's the thing / Wherein I'll catch the conscience of the King' (ll. 539–40).

Yet there is something else at work here. Hamlet has chosen to have the players perform a revenge tragedy, *The Murder of Gonzago*, a generic distinction that is crucial for two reasons: first, it suggests that Hamlet has harnessed for his own purposes the theatrical sound that Jonson's comedies mock, one that is imagined as cleaving, pricking, tenting and otherwise wounding its listeners; second, Hamlet's weapon is a play very much like *Hamlet* itself, a highly self-conscious remake of an earlier revenge tragedy (also called *Hamlet*) that had already come to stand synecdochically for this emerging genre.[46] The play-within-the-play therefore tests both Jonson's criticisms of this dramatic form and, at the same time, some of the genre's implicit assumptions. Revenge tragedies depend in part on an understanding of sound as materially dangerous, its reception difficult to control. These plays' final scenes tend to be spectacularly metatheatrical, featuring inset dramatic productions, masques or performances of implicitly theatrical courtly pomp, such as the cannibalistic banquet Titus hosts costumed 'like a cook' in *Titus Andronicus*.[47] Here the revenger's long-concealed hatred is finally released in vehement confessions that his enemies are compelled to hear. Paired with other forms of violence, these wounding words produce catastrophic, near-apocalyptic destruction, and the metatheatricality of these moments invites theatregoers to consider the risks of their own audition.[48] *Hamlet* showcases this trope while departing from it in significant ways. Audiences familiar with *The Spanish Tragedy* and *Titus Andronicus* would probably have expected *Hamlet*'s inset play to work quite differently. Instead of dramatising Denmark's recent past, it should instantaneously transform Denmark's future by ending, as these plays' metatheatrical moments do, in tyrannicide. Rather than sitting in the audience, Hamlet the revenger should be performing; the play-within-the-play typically serves as a screen for violence, as the revenger bursts out of character to stab his listening enemies with accusations of guilt and thrusts of his sword. Even structurally, *Hamlet*'s inset play is not where it is supposed to be: *The Murder of Gonzago* is staged not in *Hamlet*'s final scenes, as such metatheatrical moments usually are in revenge tragedy, but in *Hamlet*'s structural centre – what modern editions label Act Three, Scene Two.[49]

Hamlet assumes his production will work as revenge tragedies are supposed to. It does not. Though Hamlet and his fellow audience members listen to *The Murder of Gonzago* in a variety of ways, no listener 'skritches' out a confession or doubles over in agony. Both Hamlet and Claudius are 'touched' by what they hear, but neither is seriously wounded; and it is Hamlet, not the King, who appears least in control of his response. In fact, Claudius proves a resiliently defensive listener, first seeing and then both seeing *and* hearing the players enact his crime. Performed first as a dumbshow and then restaged with a script, it is only the actors' second, spoken performance that stirs the King.[50] Claudius calls for light ('Give me some light, away' (3.2.261)), stops the show, rises and departs in chaos, demonstrating that he is far from insensible to the script's effects; yet he is nonetheless able to control his body's response, keeping his confession closely kennelled until he is alone.

It is Hamlet, ironically, who seems most 'touched' by what he hears during the performance. This, too, runs counter to his plan. Although Hamlet assumes the King, if guilty, will be compelled to confess, he imagines performing together with Horatio an entirely different auditory practice, one in keeping with the tasteful listening discussed above:

'And after [the play] we will both our judgements join / In censure of his seeming' (ll. 82–3). The two elite Wittenberg scholars will taste Claudius's outburst, consider it and judge it. Instead of coolly analysing Claudius's cry, however, Hamlet exalts at the confession his own imaginative hearing has partly produced. The Folio and First Quarto include an immediate, exuberant rejoinder to the King's outburst: 'What, frighted with false fire?' While Q2 lacks this rejoinder, all three texts feature Hamlet reciting – or perhaps even singing – a jubilant sing-song stanza in triumph to Horatio:

> Why let the stricken deer go weep,
> The hart ungalled play,
> For some must watch while some must sleep.
> Thus runs the world away. (ll. 263–6)

Rather than asking Horatio for his interpretation of the King's response, Hamlet *tells* him what it should be: 'Didst perceive? ... Upon the talk of the poisoning' (ll. 279–81). The prince excitedly hears in Claudius's outburst incontrovertible proof of the Ghost's claims ('O good Horatio, I'll take the Ghost's word for a thousand pound' (ll. 278–9)). He is also tented to the quick – compelled to produce antic, even musical speech in response.

Horatio, on the other hand, continues to hear cautiously. He tempers Hamlet's boast, that the prince is qualified for 'a fellowship in a cry of players', to a mere 'Half a share' (ll. 269–71). This typically Horatian response – that Hamlet deserves a share only *in part* – is not wholly critical, but careful. As with Fortinbras's rumoured attack, superstitions about cocks crowing on Christmas and other speeches, Horatio considers both Claudius's outburst and Hamlet's antic answer to it. His judgement may be further complicated by his having heard other sounds in the hall. Glossing the play's action, Hamlet famously misidentifies the poisoner as 'one Lucianus, nephew to the king' – a slip that identifies Hamlet, Claudius's nephew, as a potential regicide (l. 237). It is therefore unclear whether Hamlet's remark or the 'talk of the poisoning' has motivated the King's strained response.[51] Horatio, who could very well have heard this misidentification, wisely awaits further 'probation' of Claudius's guilt: to Hamlet's 'Didst perceive?' he opaquely responds, 'Very well, my lord'; and to the prince's further prompting, 'Upon the talk of the poisoning', he says, 'I did very well note him' (l. 282). Having attended not only to the play and the King but also to Hamlet's commentary, Horatio remains sceptical, and he is cautious in what he unkennels.

In this way, *The Murder of Gonzago* represents a kind of experiment through which the theatre's aural impact can be evaluated. If Hamlet's misidentification of Lucianus declares, intentionally or otherwise, his plan to kill the King, it also serves a different and equally important function. Collapsing the murder and its revenge into a single act, the word 'nephew' reminds *Hamlet*'s audience that the Danish court is being treated to a revenge tragedy performed by a commercial acting troupe. In other words, they are hearing and seeing a play uncannily similar to *Hamlet* itself. That *Gonzago* is not received as expected critiques not only the prince's ability to listen well and to understand how theatrical audition works, but also the premises that undergird his thinking about sound and its reception. Instead of being predetermined by gender, social status or other factors – including the sound of the actors themselves – theatrical audition is revealed in this scene to be a much more complicated, conscious process. Attentive to both the play and one another's reactions to it, Gertrude, Claudius, Hamlet and Ophelia in particular are able to focus their attention on certain sounds and ignore others, thinking critically about the production's aesthetic and its more substantive qualities. Ophelia begins, for example, by asking Hamlet to interpret both the dumbshow and prologue for her, seeming at first to mark his commentary more than the play itself:

> *Oph.* What means this, my lord?
> *Ham.* Marry, this munching mallico! It means mischief.
> *Oph.* Belike this show imports the argument of the play . . .
> Will [the player-as-prologue] tell us what this show meant?
> *Ham.* Ay, or any show that you will show him. Be not you ashamed to show, he'll not shame to tell you what it means.
> *Oph.* You are naught, you are naught. I'll mark the play. (ll. 129–41)

Willing initially to relinquish her interpretive faculty to Hamlet, Ophelia does not sacrifice it altogether. Instead, she attends to Hamlet's interpretations critically, eventually dismissing them as ridiculous, unhelpful and bawdy. She then returns to 'mark[ing]' the play for herself. Far from displaying the 'too credent ear' that both her brother and father assume she, like all women, must possess, Ophelia proves a skilful theatrical listener: she tunes her ear to the prince, then to the players, then back again, offering critiques of her fellow auditors' criticism and conversation as well as of the actors' lines. Ophelia and Hamlet seem equally capable of sampling the sounds of the stage, critiquing the prologue's brevity as well as its sing-song sound: 'Is this a prologue or the posy of a ring?' ''Tis brief, my lord' (ll. 145–6). The play then becomes fodder for other conversations, including Ophelia and Hamlet's flirtatious banter. Situated within this complicated soundscape, playgoers like Hamlet, Gertrude and Ophelia are faced with the challenge of deciding which piece of dialogue – on or offstage – to 'mark', when to mark it and how to do so.

Used in this passage, the verb 'mark' recalls *Hamlet*'s opening scenes, in which the prince must decide whether to attend to, or 'mark', the Ghost's story. In a play so attentive to sound, this echo cannot be incidental. It signals the shared seriousness of both scenes of audition, and the spiritual and physical risks of listening poorly in the playhouse. Hearing the wrong piece of a play, or only a piece, can skew interpretation and mark listeners in potentially dangerous ways, as Hamlet's listening here attests. 'In second husband let me be accurst', the Player Queen declares, 'None wed the second but who killed the first' (ll. 173–4). Hamlet's interjection, 'That's wormwood', has several meanings for the play's on- and offstage audiences (l. 175). Used medicinally, wormwood was known to have a bitter taste; a medicine that fills up ears to unstop them, *Gonzago*'s 'wormwood' is designed to disabuse the country's 'whole ear' of rumour by first tenting the King's and Queen's.[52] Hamlet's comment reveals how attentive he is to the speech's effects on Gertrude and Claudius. He proves much less attentive, though, to the play itself. He does not 'mark' the speech that follows this one, and cannot therefore be marked by it. Were he to be so, the play could perhaps end quite differently: 'I do believe you think what now you speak', the Player King responds, 'But what we do determine oft we break. / Purpose is but the slave to memory' (ll. 180–2). Referring to the Player Queen's promise not to remarry after her husband's death, these lines' emphasis on broken vows, and on purpose blunted by time, should pierce Hamlet more personally: first, he too has delayed; second, and I think more importantly, these lines offer a crucial reminder to the prince and to *Hamlet*'s audience that remarriage after death is not necessarily monstrous, but natural. Neither meaning penetrates. Hamlet's next interjection ('If she should break it now!' (l. 218)) proves he has continued to concentrate either on the Player Queen's inconstancy or on Gertrude's reaction. He has therefore missed the meaning of the Player King's speech. Wormwood – poisonous or medicinal, destructive or restorative – only works if the ears into which it is poured are attentive to its sense. Otherwise it remains simply 'Poison in jest', carrying 'No offense i'th'world' offstage (ll. 228–9). A play's power to edify, then, is not inevitable, no matter how rumbling it sounds or how trippingly it is pronounced; but this does not render its power insignificant. How and what theatregoers hear becomes in *Hamlet* a question every bit as serious as how and what churchgoers hear, or heads of state, enacting on an individual, personal scale the political instability that sound's violence often signifies in early modern tragedies of revenge.

That Hamlet follows his attempted theatrical 'cure' of the state of Denmark with what is essentially a sermon (the harangue delivered in his mother's closet) further points out the shared stakes of hearing in the church and the playhouse – and, indeed, in any number of other settings. Hamlet casts himself as a 'scourge and minister' sent by heaven to reveal Gertrude's sin, insisting that his speech is meant to edify, not to punish: 'I must be cruel only to be kind' (3.4.173, 176). His words, which Hamlet imagines as stabbing his mother like 'daggers', are intended to pierce her as 'Gods word doth pearse into them [who hear it] and causeth them to tremble at the majesty & power of the same'.[53] '[L]et me wring your heart', Hamlet begins, and concludes by urging her to 'Confess yourself to heaven, / Repent what's past, avoid what is to come' (3.4.33, 147–8).

At first, Hamlet's sermon seems to have the desired effect, reforming Gertrude's heart, mind and spirit through her receptive ear. Calling on Gertrude to look at two pictures, the 'counterfeit presentment of two brothers', Hamlet offers a lengthy description that actually supplants, or perhaps even substitutes for, the images themselves, guiding her perception just as he has that of Osric and Polonius (3.4.51–2).[54] The Queen's sight is then redirected inward, as a self-critical gaze: 'Thou turn'st my very eyes into my soul / And there I see such black and grieved spots / As will leave there their tinct' (3.4.87–9). Gertrude seems to be not just a receptive listener, but an ideally edified Christian one, 'turn[ing her] eyes' inward to examine the sin within.[55] What she 'sees' inside herself – again, under the pressure of Hamlet's description – is the blackened stain, or tinct, of sin. We might therefore expect, as Hamlet certainly does, that Gertrude will do as he urges: confess, repent and avoid. But of course Gertrude does not do any of these things. She never 'confesses' to, or indeed ever gives any sign of having been involved in, the crime of which Hamlet accuses her (King Hamlet's murder); in Q1, in fact, she has a speech in which she explicitly denies involvement. And although she expresses bewildered regret, it is unclear for what, if any, act Gertrude 'repents'. Far from 'avoiding' Claudius after hearing Hamlet's speech, Gertrude instead reaffirms her fidelity to him in the following Act, thrusting herself between the King and the furiously threatening Laertes ('Let him go, Gertrude', Claudius urges, 'Do not fear our person' (4.5.122)).

Earlier critics have explained Gertrude's steadfastness as a sort of daftness: either she has forgotten Hamlet's speech, or she has been dumbly insensible to it. A. C. Bradley writes, for example,

> the Queen was not a badhearted woman, not at all the woman to think little of murder. But she had a soft animal nature, and was very dull and shallow.

She loved to be happy, like a sheep in the sun; and, to do her justice, it pleased her to see others happy, like more sheep in the sun.[56]

The Queen's clearly pained reception of Hamlet's lines, however, demonstrates just how affected she has been by what her son has said. Instead, Hamlet's speech fails to alter Gertrude in the way its speaker hopes because, first, it is pitched more to wound than to reform; and second, because its speaker underestimates Gertrude's considerable listening skills. Like Horatio, Gertrude shows herself to be a far more supple and 'partial' listener than her son.

Although Hamlet famously exhorts himself, before visiting his mother in her closet, to 'be cruel, not unnatural', and to 'speak daggers to her but use none', he has trouble living up to his own promise (3.2.386). Drawing a distinction between actual daggers and words, Hamlet's lines point out the difference between the two.[57] Yet Hamlet's language is far from harmless. It causes Gertrude pain, which we hear in her repeated pleas that he stop speaking ('O Hamlet, speak no more'; 'O speak to me no more!'; 'No more, sweet Hamlet'; 'No more!' (3.4.87, 92, 94, 99)), and in her assertion at its conclusion that Hamlet's speech has 'cleft [her] heart in twain' (l. 154).

The distinction drawn in this scene, and in Hamlet's earlier exhortation to himself, between actual daggers and spoken ones is not between the material and the immaterial, the effective and the ineffectual; rather, it is between two different kinds of material, literal threats that can be 'parried' with varying degrees of success. Surprised by Hamlet's sword, Polonius can do nothing to defend himself against it. Gertrude, however, engages with her son in a sort of aural fencing match, as the two wrest control from one another through creative, defensive listening. The Queen's opening line, 'Hamlet, thou hast thy father much offended', is deflected and redirected back on her by her adeptly listening son: 'Mother, you have my father much offended' (3.4.8–9). Hamlet's echo works like an opposing thrust, and when Gertrude responds dismissively, she is echoed by Hamlet once again: 'Come, come, you answer with an idle tongue'; 'Go, go, you question with a wicked tongue' (ll. 10–11). Rather than continuing to parry Gertrude's questions, which she eventually stops asking, Hamlet next goes on the offensive, forcing Gertrude into a listening position with the command, 'sit you down' (l. 17). As in the opening scene of the play, when Horatio is told to 'Sit down awhile' while Barnardo and Marcellus 'assail [his] ears', sitting here seems to signal Gertrude's submission to her son's aural 'assault' (1.1.29–30).[58] Hamlet then attempts to subject her to violently angry, imperious speech, but the Queen is able to respond to his attack in kind. To Hamlet's 'almost as bad, good mother, / As kill a king and marry with his brother', she echoes, 'As kill a king?' (3.4.26–8). Gertrude's response turns Hamlet's charge back against its speaker – a tactic made all the more effective, given Hamlet's recent misidentification of the poisoner in *The Murder of Gonzago* as the 'nephew to the king' (3.2.237). Having turned the charge against the prince, the Queen then wipes away any record of its ever having been brought against her by repeatedly asking what it is she is supposed to have done: 'What have I done'; 'Ay, me, what act?' (3.4.37, 49). The questions seem to un-say Hamlet's earlier accusation. To use the language of the play, Gertrude refuses to be marked by Hamlet's charge by refusing to 'mark' it.

One of the things at stake in this scene is the question of who will shape the other's interpretation of events, and, by so doing, determine the narrative of King Hamlet's death – as well as of *Hamlet* itself. As *The Murder of Gonzago* has just vividly demonstrated, different audience members can respond to the same scene, even the same lines, differently. In a scene like this one, in which competing versions of past events are presented – and in which the play is literally haunted, through the reappearance of the Ghost, by its own past – the choice of whom to hear and how deeply to be marked by various speakers becomes especially fraught. These are dramatic, aesthetic and ethical dilemmas, as well as physical ones, and they go to the heart of Shakespeare's play.

'Audiences to this Act'

'Shakespeare's *Hamlet*', Margreta de Grazia points out, 'was old on arrival'.[59] Deliberately old-fashioned, *Hamlet* is nevertheless neither outdated nor unoriginal. I have argued that Shakespeare's cutting-edge play in deliberately old-fashioned dress ventriloquises attacks on the revenge tragedy genre made by Ben Jonson and other playwrights, but questions their validity. *Hamlet* is not only about these metatheatrical debates but deeply affected by them. They shape the tragic outcome of Hamlet as a character; the dramatic structure of the play; and, through *Hamlet*, the very form of revenge tragedy itself. By experimenting with generic conventions and theatrical forms, *Hamlet* updates revenge for a changing theatrical marketplace, one that was being reshaped by the interests and expectations of its turn-of-the-century audiences. These interests included an ability to police the body's boundaries – a struggle foregrounded in Jonson's humoral comedies, and one which *Hamlet* ultimately identifies as futile. As a result, *Hamlet* both demonstrates revenge tragedy's continued adaptability to the preoccupations of the moment and questions some of the cultural ideals other plays helped to produce.

In *Hamlet*'s final scenes, the prince's effort to control his own hearing becomes tantamount to the struggle against mortality, a way of resisting the dissolution of the body into an unending cycle of destruction and decay. Having fought to manage his reception of sounds, sometimes successfully and other times not, Hamlet seems at last to have accepted that absolute control of this process is impossible – with regard not only to sounds, but also to the other material elements that sound suggests. No longer boasting, in the end, of his ability to resist being sounded out by others, Hamlet instead becomes willing to relinquish control of his body to the King's command, or perhaps to fate: 'I am constant to my purposes. They follow the King's pleasure. If his fitness speaks, mine is ready. Now or whensoever, provided I be so able as now' (5.2.179–81). This transformation has its genesis, appropriately, in the graveyard scene, as Hamlet moves through the dust of the dead, musing at length over the theme that has disgusted him throughout the play: 'Why may not imagination trace the noble dust of Alexander till 'a find it stopping a bung-hole?' (5.1.193–4). As Horatio warns, ''Twere to consider too curiously to consider so', yet for Hamlet this has long been the only question worth considering (l. 195). It is the twin preoccupation to tasteful audition's social significance. To control what and how one hears is to display the possession of a particular palate, but it is also to display corporeal self-control – to distinguish oneself from a pipe, a barber's virginal or any of the other 'instruments' that can be played and hence controlled by other men. Doing so implies inviolability against even death itself.

Hamlet's struggle against dissolution also revises a familiar revenge tragedy conceit. The destruction of the body is a central feature of this dramatic form, as is the sense that sound is a weapon that rips into the self.[60] Hieronimo concludes his 'play in sundry languages' – *The Spanish Tragedy*'s climactic bloodbath – with a lengthy confession that stuns his audience into silence and, oddly, forgetfulness; his listeners immediately ask to hear this same confession again, as though they have not just heard it spoken ('Why has thou done this undeserving deed?' (4.4.165)).[61] Rather than repeat his rant, Hieronimo bites out his own tongue, reserving for himself the power to both sound out his confession and disarticulate his own body. In Kyd's play, the manipulation of sound's flow is a political act performed through and on the body; Hieronimo's refusal to be *made* to speak constitutes a rebellion against the state and, more specifically, against the systems of power that have denied him justice for his murdered son. Predicated on a king's murder and the subsequent disinheritance of his only child, *Hamlet* is every bit as invested in the authentication and transmission of political power as is *The Spanish Tragedy*. But the struggle to control the body's intake and release of sounds becomes in *Hamlet* a personal one as well. It is not only a matter of disciplining the body for a political act – taking arms against a usurper – but of attaining corporeal self-control.

This thematic difference may account for the best-known formal innovation of Shakespeare's play, its profusion of soliloquies – or, more accurately, its assignment of nearly all its soliloquies to only one character, Hamlet himself.[62] In *Hamlet*, these speeches provide a glimpse inside the solipsistic echo chamber of the tasteful listener, whose ears absorb his own witty speeches more eagerly, and more deeply, than those he selectively samples from others. Rather than understanding Hamlet's soliloquies as thoughts overheard, we might consider them as speeches spoken to an onstage audience of one, delighting in his own discourse.[63] Such persistently self-centred audition could seem the safest alternative in a revenge tragedy like *Hamlet*, with its spoken daggers and poisoned ears, but the prince's recycling of sounds proves equally dangerous. As I argued above, early modern anatomists described the auditory canal as a two-way street that allows sounds to enter and, at the same time, enables the 'expurgation' of 'the superfluities that fall from the heade, by the eare into the mouth, as also to purge and depurate that aire which is implanted in the instrument of hearing'.[64] Excrement secreted from the brain collects in pools about the ears and must from time to time be expelled; so, too, must the inward air (that which is 'implanted in the instrument of hearing') itself. This expurgation occurs through the ears and the mouth, which are connected through a system of canals and other passages. In this way the listener 'is purged and receiueth new Ayre for his perpetuall nourishment'.[65] Like the Galenic humoral economy whose regulation, as Gail Kern Paster and Michael Schoenfeldt have shown, is instrumental to the formation of early modern subjects, the flow of air into, through and out of the body must be kept in balance to ensure good health.[66] Venting passionate, potentially wounding words into only his own ears, Hamlet recycles and reabsorbs his own expurgated matter. On a poetic level, then, the soliloquy enacts the same closed economy glimpsed in Hamlet's musings on mortality: that 'A man may fish with the worm that hath eat of a king and eat of the fish that hath fed of that worm' (4.3.26–7). Like the cycles of corporeal decay with which he is preoccupied throughout the play, this verbal system admits of no release, no exit. In the context of the metatheatrical debates discussed above, *Hamlet*'s soliloquies serve two important functions. First, they demonstrate revenge tragedy's suitability to the investigation of a subject increasingly central to early modern comedy, that of the individual's struggle for corporeal self-control and, ultimately, inviolability. Second, they question the wisdom of the ideal these comedies helped to introduce. The only ears in this play that *do* prove impervious to unwanted sounds are those made fatally 'senseless' to them (5.2.353). All other listeners will continue to be charged with the task of filtering and judging stories – separating rumour from matter 'truly deliver[ed]' – and of fending off the violent physical and political effects of 'warlike noise' (ll. 369, 333). It is only for the dead, for whom the rest is indeed silence, that this process ever becomes complete.

If, then, *Hamlet* incorporates and responds to attacks lobbed against the revenge tragedy genre by Ben Jonson and other playwrights, it also engages in some genre-based criticism of its own. By suggesting that the struggle for corporeal inviolability that their comedies helped to introduce is in fact futile, *Hamlet* refocuses audiences' attention on the ongoing process through which the self is produced. Sampling and judging sounds is a key part of this process, as the listener is charged with winnowing out potential pollutants without sacrificing the benefits of restorative speech. This requires hearing less like the Hamlet of the first two acts of Shakespeare's play and more like the Hamlet encountered in its final scenes, or even like Horatio or Gertrude – meaning, with an open yet still cautious ear, one that absorbs a range of theatrical sounds but that judges all noises, theatrical and otherwise, with a discriminating faculty attuned to their potential power.

Hearing after *Hamlet*

I want to close my discussion of *Hamlet* by briefly considering how it may have influenced the ways in which revenge tragedy and city comedy sounded to early modern audiences in the decades that followed. These are the years in which, in many ways, the two forms that are the subject of this book came into their own. Some of the most commonly anthologised examples of each were written and performed in the opening decades of the seventeenth century: the anonymous, generically self-conscious *The Revenger's Tragedy* (1606); John Webster's *The Duchess of Malfi* (1614); and Thomas Middleton's *Women Beware Women* (1620–4); as well as Ben Jonson's *Epicoene* (1609) and *The Alchemist* (1610); Middleton's *A Chaste Maid in Cheapside* (c. 1613); and Francis Beaumont's *The Knight of the Burning Pestle* (1607), to name just a few. These are vastly different plays, which, for all their currently assured status in the canon of Renaissance drama, experienced varying degrees of popularity and success on the early modern stage, but they each seem to echo *Hamlet*'s intervention in the formal and sonic debates outlined above. Many if not most Jacobean city comedies include aborted revenge plots, as well as mixtures of different styles of speech, which audiences are challenged to absorb and understand. Seventeenth-century revenge tragedies, similarly, stage scenes of horrific violence in which weapons are joined with words in the performance of revenge, but they also implicitly challenge the model of involuntary reception on which such aural violence often depends. In other words, Jacobean revenge tragedies suggest that Shakespeare's project of generic recuperation *worked*. The genre remains vibrant because, after *Hamlet*, revenge plays often incorporate and respond to their own generic critique, as it was put forward by Ben Jonson and others at the turn of the century. This is not to say that this critique – that revenge plays were all sound, and no sense – was *right* – far from it. But it seems to have been effective. And in *Hamlet*, Shakespeare mounts an equally effective defence. Later revenge plays tend to foreground the assumption that it is up to the individual theatregoer to perform different, often readily adaptive, auditory practices in any playhouse, to any play, depending on the sound and sense of what is said onstage. Consider, for example, the 'hideous noise' of a 'consort / Of madmen' that Ferdinand sends to drive his sister to despair in *The Duchess of Malfi*: 'We'll bill and bawl our parts', one of the madmen sings, 'Till yerksome noise have cloyed your ears / And corrosived your hearts' (4.2.1, ll. 2–3, 65–6). That the Duchess is able to withstand this assault is testament to her extraordinary strength and resolve, but her resilience also shows the extent to which revenge's 'breathie swords' can be, and are in fact expected to be, resisted.[67]

A similar transformation can be seen at work in much Jacobean city comedy, which, though it still tends to celebrate selective reception as a valuable, socially significant skill, often subjects theatregoers to a variety of sounds – including more of the brash noises and bombast that Jonson and Marston skewered. Rafe, the servant-turned-player in *The Knight of the Burning Pestle*, demonstrates his acting *bona fides* by 'Speak[ing] a huffing part'; and George and Nell assure the 'gentlemen' in the audience that 'he should have played Jeronimo with a shoemaker for a wager' (Ind., ll. 74–5, 85–6).[68] The play that follows mocks old genres and the sounds and styles of speaking associated with each, all the while assuming on the part of its audiences a thoroughgoing knowledge of them; but *The Knight of the Burning Pestle* also implicitly encourages playgoers to hear this material differently (less enthusiastically, more critically) than do the Grocer and his wife, thereby confirming their status as 'gentlemen'. In many ways, Beaumont's play is unique, but its pastiche of dramatic forms and sounds merely exaggerates the kind of generic melding found in any number of other Jacobean city comedies: for example, *Epicoene*, an astonishingly noisy play, whose plot is shaped by the gallant Dauphine's elaborate revenge against his rich uncle, Morose; *A Chaste Maid in Cheapside*, which concludes with Sir Walter Whorehound's ominous bequest of curses, venereal disease and 'barrenness of joy' to the Allwits ('Oh, my vengeance!') (5.1.110, 69); and *The Alchemist*, which opens with a noisy brawl and features a failed plot by Subtle 'To be revenged upon' his co-conspirator and sometime rival, Face (and which even features a cameo appearance by 'Hieronimo's old cloak, ruff, and hat') (4.3.103, 4.6.71).

My claim here is that *Hamlet* was very likely instrumental in the increased hybridisation of both city comedy and revenge tragedy as dramatic forms, both sonically and structurally. As I will argue in Chapter 5, the hybridisation of revenge tragedy and city comedy could be said to reach its apotheosis in the Cockpit theatre of the 1630s, but this process was already well under way in the opening decades of the seventeenth century. We can see it most clearly, perhaps, in *The Revenger's Tragedy*, which sets itself up as a direct inheritor of Shakespeare's play.[69] (As Scott McMillin succinctly put it, this play, once thought 'to be about the neuroses of its author, is really about *Hamlet*'.[70]) First performed by the King's Men in 1606 or 1607, *The Revenger's Tragedy* all but quotes *Hamlet* directly at various points in the action, and it opens with the revenger, Vindice, holding what was most likely the same skull used as a prop in Shakespeare's gravedigger scene. Although the play is set, like many other revenge tragedies, in a foreign (Italian) court, it is largely preoccupied with the concerns of London comedy: the fate of Vindice's father and the proposed liaison between Lussurioso and Castiza, Vindice's sister, raise questions about social mobility and its limits, as well as about its dependence on economic and sexual exchange. Revenge itself is repeatedly discussed in economic terms (for example: 'Murder' must not go 'unpaid'), and the overall tone of the play is darkly comic (1.1.43).[71] Sometimes labelled a satiric tragedy, a term which helps to point out the play's thoughtful formal mingling, *The Revenger's Tragedy* both follows and ironises revenge tragedy conventions, including that genre's association between aural and physical violence.

As I argued in my introduction, *The Revenger's Tragedy*'s final scene underscores the lethality of Vindice's words as well as his sword. It is the revenger's spoken revelations ("'twas Vindice murdered thee ... / Murdered thy father ... / And I am he') that seem at last to finish off the dying Lussurioso ('So, so, the Duke's departed') (5.3.77–9, 80). And yet, the crucial thing about these words is that they are spoken quietly, 'whisper[ed]' into Lussurioso's ear rather than portentously thundered aloud (l. 77 SD). The fact that actual thunder has sounded earlier in this same scene further emphasises this sonic difference: *The revengers dance; at the end, steal out their swords, and these four kill the four at the table in their chairs. It thunders*' (5.3.41 SD). Vindice urges those who hear this thunder to 'mark' it, as though recognising its generic signification: 'Dost know thy cue, thou big-voiced crier?'; 'When thunder claps, heaven likes the tragedy' (5.3.42–8).

I will return to this scene below, but first I want to consider the series of violent revelations that participate in the murder of Lussurioso's father earlier in the play. As the Duke kisses the poisoned skull of Gloriana, Vindice's murdered betrothed, the revenger-brothers light a torch so that 'his affrighted eyeballs / May start into those hollows' (3.5.147–8). Then they taunt him:

> VINDICE: Duke, dost know
> Yon dreadful visor? View it well; 'tis the skull
> Of Gloriana, whom thou poisonedst last.
> DUKE: Oh, 't'as poisoned me.
> VINDICE: Didst not know that till now?
> DUKE: What are you two?
> VINDICE: Villains all three. The very ragged bone
> Has been sufficiently revenged. (ll. 146–54)

Vindice's incredulous 'Didst not know that till now?' seems almost to point out a flaw in the play: how could the Duke not yet feel that he has been poisoned? It is as if the Duke must not only see the skull, but also be told whose it is, in order for the poison to reach full potency. Like the dumbshow in *Hamlet*, which must be restaged with sound in order for it fully to take effect, the silent spectacle of the skull is somehow insufficient. The brothers then bombard the Duke with revelations designed to 'stick thy soul with ulcers' and 'make / Thy spirit grievous sore': they tell him he is 'a renowned, high, and mighty cuckold' and force him to eavesdrop on his wife's seduction of his bastard son (ll. 174–8). These soul-sticking, ulcerous revelations are gleefully – and, it seems, *loudly* – delivered. At one point, Hippolito jumps up and down, 'stamping on' the Duke, as he shouts 'Treason, treason, treason!'; and in the end, the brothers give 'Thanks to loud music' for concealing their crime (ll. 156 SD, 156, 219). All of these words are absorbed by the Duke without the possibility of vocalising a response: his tongue is 'Nail[ed] down' to the stage as Vindice's 'keep[s] possession / About his heart' (ll. 196–7). Denied the purgative benefits of speech, and even it seems of sound – 'If he but gasp, he dies' – the Duke is essentially forced to feel what is more typically the revenger's agony (l. 197). His final words, 'I cannot brook – ', are stifled mid-sentence, giving voice to the impossibility of withstanding the brothers' relentless aural assault while at the same time demonstrating what has made that assault so painful – his inability to express, in turn, what is being heard, felt and experienced (l. 219).

The revenger-brothers put into deadly practice, in other words, many of the lessons about sound and its reception that I have been arguing early modern revenge tragedies teach. And yet, it takes an excruciatingly long time for the Duke to die. He proves morbidly resilient to the brothers' assault, narrating the process of his own physiological disintegration ('My teeth are eaten out'; 'Oh my tongue!') in ways that Vindice, at least, finds puzzling: 'What, is not thy tongue eaten out yet?' (ll. 159, 162, 193). The brothers' elaborately crafted revenge plot, which dutifully deploys many of that genre's most fearsome weapons – its repetitious oratory, its vehemently spoken 'discoveries' of secret, long-concealed matter – does not exactly fail, but it does not exactly work either. As the Duke continues to speak even after his tongue has been nailed to the stage, the grisly scene becomes savagely funny, its mood slipping between the comic and tragic as the scene both faithfully follows revenge tragedy conventions surrounding violent speech and giddily parodies them. Like *Hamlet*, then, *The Revenger's Tragedy* seems to incorporate its own generic critique – not by putting it into the mouth of a specific character, as Shakespeare's play does, but by amplifying the sonic effects associated with such plays almost to the point of absurdity.

I am using the word 'absurd' here both in the sense of the ridiculous, and in the sense mentioned at the beginning of this chapter: dissonant, unharmonious, even unpleasant to the ear.[72] *The Revenger's Tragedy*'s final scene, in which Vindice whispers his revelations into the ear of the dying Lussurioso, is so chaotically noisy – with thunder clapping, two musical masques of revengers and multiple confessions being 'discovered' onstage to different hearers at different points in the action – as to make it difficult to take seriously and also, perhaps, to hear. When Vindice suddenly, without explanation, volunteers the fact that he and his brother have been responsible for committing all of the crimes that have taken place, he is essentially inviting the audience in on a meta-generic joke: that in early modern revenge plays, 'When murd'rers shut deeds close, this curse does seal 'em: / If none disclose 'em they themselves reveal 'em' (5.3.110–11). The sing-song couplet points out the confession's pat unbelievability, as does Antonio's response to it:

'How subtly was that murder closed!' (5.3.126). The point is not that *The Revenger's Tragedy* mocks revenge plays in the way that Jonson's *Poetaster* or his humours plays do; rather, it assumes its audiences can simultaneously experience and reflect upon such sonic bombardment. It anticipates on the part of theatregoers the kind of adaptive, even tasteful reception that Jonson, however unfairly, associates more with city comedy than with revenge. And it is in this, as much as in any of its other all but citational references to *Hamlet*, that *The Revenger's Tragedy* is so deeply indebted to Shakespeare's play. Like *The Knight of the Burning Pestle*, it is perhaps an extreme example of a much more widespread phenomenon in Jacobean theatre: the melding, in both sound and structure, of the two forms that, just a decade or so prior, had seemed to exist in direct, starkly competitive opposition with one another.

Notes

An earlier version of this chapter was published as an essay in *Shakespeare Quarterly*. I am grateful to Jean E. Howard and Alan Stewart, as well as to David Schalkwyk and to the journal's anonymous readers, for their comments and suggestions.

1. Rymer, *A Short View of Tragedy*, sig. K6^r.
2. Here and throughout, unless otherwise noted, I refer to Ann Thompson and Neil Taylor's 2006 modernised edition of the 1604 Second Quarto, *Hamlet*, Arden 3. Rather than work with a conflated edition, which we know was never staged and in fact did not exist in the seventeenth century, I have chosen the text scholars tend to agree most closely represents Shakespeare's first written version of the play.
3. 'absurd, *adj.* and *n.*' OED.
4. For the symbolic, figurative risks of listening in *Hamlet*, see Gross, 'The Rumor of *Hamlet*', in *Shakespeare's Noise*, pp. 10–32; Cummings, 'Hearing in *Hamlet*: Poisoned Ears and the Psychopathology of Flawed Audition'; Berry, 'Hamlet's Ear'; and Thompson and Thompson, *Shakespeare, Meaning and Metaphor*, pp. 102–4. For attention to the material, physical risks inherent in hearing, see Gina Bloom, 'Fortress of the Ear', in *Voice in Motion*, pp. 111–59; Tanya Pollard, 'Vulnerable Ears', in *Drugs and Theater in Early Modern England*, pp. 123–43; Wes Folkerth, *The Sound of Shakespeare*; and Bruce R. Smith, *The Acoustic World of Early Modern England*. Pollard deals directly with *Hamlet*; Bloom, Folkerth and Smith concentrate on other literary texts, but return to *Hamlet* almost unavoidably.
5. For an exploration of the ways in which this debate, and the contradictory models of audition on which it depends, shaped *The Tempest*, see Deutermann, '"Repeat to me the words of the Echo"'.

6. Crooke, *Microcosmographia* (1615), pp. 573–612; the 'hole of hearing' is introduced at p. 576; the 'afterbrain' is discussed at p. 475. See also my discussion in Chapter 2, pp. 28–30.
7. I use the term 'sense' here as it is deployed by philosophers of language, who distinguish between the sense, or meaning, of a given phrase and its reference, as well as the phonemes out of which it is composed. See Geach and Black, *Translations from the Philosophical Writings of Gottlob Frege*. I am especially interested in points of intersection between modern philosophical and early modern anatomical and rhetorical claims about the material efficacy of language and the centrality of the listener to the production of linguistic meaning. See J. L. Austin's discussion of perlocutionary, locutionary and illocutionary acts, as well as his definition of 'uptake', in *How to Do Things with Words*, pp. 94–120, 139; and Ludwig Wittgenstein's discussion of public language as a kind of game, or rule-governed activity, in *Philosophical Investigations*. For a recent application of this work to Shakespeare, see Schalkwyk, *Speech and Performance in Shakespeare's Sonnets and Plays*.
8. On the first point, see Bloom, Folkerth, Gross and Pollard, cited above. Shankar Raman links the play's aural focus to a shift in the period's 'sensory and affective discourses', which he sees as brought on by the loss of the Aristotelian concept of *kinesis*, or movement, to theories of cognition. See 'Hamlet in Motion', esp. pp. 119–20. On the second point, see Danner, 'Speaking Daggers'; Weimann, 'Mimesis in *Hamlet*', 'Society and the Individual in Shakespeare's Conception of Character' and *Author's Pen and Actor's Voice*, pp. 18–28 and 151–79.
9. See Joseph, *Elizabethan Acting* and Shakespeare, *Hamlet*, ed. Jenkins, pp. 498–9n.
10. Shakespeare, *A Midsummer Night's Dream*, ed. Brooks, 1.2.25.
11. Citations to *Jack Drum* are taken from *The Plays of John Marston*, ed. Wood, 3: 179. The text is not lineated; the lines quoted here appear in the Induction.
12. Citations to Jonson's original, unrevised play are taken from *Every Man in His Humour: A Parallel-Text Edition of the 1601 Quarto and the 1616 Folio*, ed. Lever, 1.3.129–31.
13. Jonson, *Every Man In*, 1.3.134–5.
14. Citations to *Poetaster* are taken from *Ben Jonson*, ed. Herford and Simpson, vol. 4.
15. Jonson, *Poetaster*, 3.4.236.
16. See Shakespeare, *The Tragicall Historie of Hamlet Prince of Denmarke*, sig. E3ʳ, emphasis added. James Bednarz argues (in *Shakespeare & the Poets' War*, p. 227) that audiences would have recognised the reference to Jonson. In *Shakespeare Only*, Jeffrey Knapp also sees Hamlet as echoing Ben Jonson, linking this exchange to the production of competing modes of authorship.
17. Crooke, *Microcosmographia* (1615), p. 588.
18. See Hillman, *Shakespeare's Entrails*.
19. Bloom is an important exception to this rule, though her attention to 'resistant hearing' is tied to the romances rather than to *Hamlet*, pp. 111–59.
20. George Dickie calls the eighteenth century 'the century of taste' and claims

it was during this period that authors shifted their focus from 'objective notions of beauty' to subjective ones. See *The Century of Taste*, p. 3.
21. The OED defines 'taste' in this sense as 'A trying, testing; a trial, test, examination.' See 'taste, *n.*1', 2a.
22. Thompson and Taylor gloss 'sallets' as 'salads', noting that the term is 'usually glossed as "spicy bits"'; they suggest instead the term could be used to refer to 'just a variety of ingredients', p. 266n. Either way, Shakespeare's use of the term suggests flavouring, or spice, in a 'well-seasoned' piece of dialogue.
23. The distinction in reception is clearer in Q1 and the First Folio than in Q2. Q2 has Hamlet echo, 'The mobled queen' while Polonius chimes in, 'That's good.' The Folio replaces 'mobled' with 'inobled' and punctuates Hamlet's echo with a question mark ('The innobled Queene?') which, in early modern printing practice, could signal either a question or an exclamation. Q1 and the Folio also extend Polonius's response into the more fatuous, 'That's good, Mobled Queene is good' (2.2.440–1n). This extended response seems more ridiculous and suggests that Hamlet's echo, unlike Polonius's, is less than enthusiastic.
24. Compare Polonius's earlier critique of the 'vile phrase' in Hamlet's letter ('most beautified Ophelia') (2.2.108–9). Here, too, differences in taste may be established, although it seems more likely that Polonius is reacting to the insult embedded in Hamlet's phrasing.
25. Cowper, *Anatomie of a Christian Man*, pp. 202–3.
26. The quote appears in the letter to the reader introducing Stephen Egerton's *The Boring of the Eare*, sig. A5^r.
27. Egerton, *Boring of the Eare*, sig. A5^r.
28. Egerton, *Boring of the Eare*, p. 38. Egerton's listener is encouraged to judge whether the scriptures she hears match those she sees, gauging the accuracy of their delivery. See OED, 'allege, *v.* 2', 2.
29. Grace Tiffany argues that *Hamlet*, an example of 'aural theater', rejects spectacle in favour of a 'morally superior, spoken performativity' in line with Protestant thinking. See '*Hamlet* and Protestant Aural Theater', esp. pp. 308 and 313. For a description of the Protestant 'cult of the ear', see Crockett, '"Holy Cozenage" and the Renaissance Cult of the Ear', in *The Play of Paradox*, pp. 50–70.
30. R. V. Holdsworth links such gustatory similes to Martial, *Epigrams*, IX.lxxxi, and notes Jonson's fondness for them. See Jonson, *Epicoene, or the Silent Woman*, ed. Holdsworth, p. 7n. Subsequent citations are to this edition.
31. Jonson, *The Case is Altered*, in *Ben Jonson*, ed. Herford, Simpson and Simpson, 3: 1.2.44–5. Subsequent citations are to this edition.
32. Jonson, *Case is Altered*, 1.4.18–19.
33. Jonson, *Cynthia's Revels*, in *Ben Jonson*, ed. Herford, Simpson and Simpson, 4: Induction, ll. 185–8.
34. Jonson, *Epicoene*, Prologue, ll. 9–10.
35. Jonson, *The Staple of News*, in *Ben Jonson*, ed. Herford, Simpson and Simpson, 6: Prologue ll. 6–8, emphasis original.
36. Promising to record only the Ghost's command for revenge in 'the book and volume of my brain', Hamlet instead jots down the commonplace, 'one

may smile and smile and be a villain' (1.5.103, 108). The observation is set down in his 'tables', suggesting impermanence (l. 107). See Stallybrass et al., 'Hamlet's Tables and the Technologies of Writing in Renaissance England'.
37. See Braden, *Renaissance Tragedy and the Senecan Tradition* and Miola, *Shakespeare and Classical Tragedy*.
38. See Long and Sedley, *The Hellenistic Philosophers, Vol. 1*, pp. 158–437, esp. pp. 183–235.
39. Barnes and Bobzien, 'Logic: "The Stoics"'.
40. The example is taken from Diogenes Laertius, *The Lives of the Philosophers* 7: 65, quoted in Long and Sedley, *Hellenistic Philosophers*, p. 203.
41. See Green, '"Ears Prejudicate" in *Mariam* and *Duchess of Malfi*'; Graham, 'Virgin Ears'; and Stallybrass, 'Patriarchal Territories'.
42. Jonson, *Every Man In*, 2.3.175–7.
43. Heywood, *An Apology for Actors*, sig. G^v.
44. 'tent, *n*. 3', 2, emphasis added.
45. That this 'pricking' is accomplished through the ear is later suggested by Claudius himself; responding to an aphoristic speech of Polonius's, the King murmurs in an aside, 'How smart a lash that speech doth give my conscience!' (3.1.49).
46. Though shaped by classical models, revenge tragedies like *The Spanish Tragedy* were largely an early modern invention – hence my characterisation of it as 'emerging'. See Chapter 2. Most likely written by Thomas Kyd, this earlier *Hamlet*, or Ur-Hamlet, was lampooned by Nashe in his 1589 preface to Greene's *Menaphon*; Thomas Lodge quoted it in his 1596 *Wit's Miser*. See de Grazia, *Hamlet without Hamlet*, pp. 7–9, 173.
47. Shakespeare, *Titus Andronicus*, ed. Bate, 5.3.25 SD. The stage direction appears in both the First Folio and the 1594 Quarto.
48. See my second chapter for a fuller discussion of these claims.
49. This might be yet another way in which John Marston's *Antonio's Revenge*, performed contemporaneously with *Hamlet* though probably shortly after Shakespeare's play first hit the stage, echoes *Hamlet*. For a discussion of *Antonio's Revenge* and what he reads as its derivative, less effective use of *Hamlet*'s more spectacular moments, see Jenkins, pp. 7–13.
50. This has become one of *Hamlet*'s most famous critical cruxes: why doesn't Claudius's conscience catch at the dumbshow, or why must the play's action be performed twice? The question has been answered, at least partly, by critics attentive to the play's interest in theatre's aurality. See Pollard, 'Vulnerable Ears', esp. pp. 136–43.
51. Scholars have explained the misidentification of Lucianus as both a dramatic trick of Shakespeare's and a subconscious slip of Hamlet's; either way, it conflates the original crime with its revenge. See Alexander, *Poison, Play, and Duel* and Jenkins, pp. 145, 156, 508. I am interested in the generic implications of this conflation.
52. 'wormwood, *n*.', 1a. The 1597 *Herball, or Generall Historie of Plantes* instructs its readers, '[F]or worms in a man's ears ... take the juice of wormwood and put it in the ear of the patient.' Quoted in Hockey, 'Wormwood, Wormwood!'.

53. Gifford, *A Sermon on the Parable of the Sower*, sig. B4^v.
54. Presumably Hamlet gestures either to two large images hanging onstage behind mother and son or, as theatre historians have argued is more likely, to two miniatures. It is also possible that there are no pictures onstage at all, and that instead Hamlet is drawing the likenesses for Gertrude (and the audience) through his own description. Such an interpretation was followed by the nineteenth-century actors Henry Irving and Tomasso Salvini. Harold Jenkins dismisses this interpretation, but I think it worth considering and, without any stage directions to prove otherwise, certainly possible.
55. This is a Protestant rhetorical commonplace. In his 'The Church-Porch', George Herbert instructs churchgoers to 'seal up both thine eyes, / And send them to thine heart . . . Those doors being shut, all by the ear comes in.' *The Complete English poems*, ll. 415–18.
56. See Bradley, *Shakespearean Tragedy*, p. 135.
57. In 'Speaking Daggers', Bruce Danner reads this as a shift from literal violence to figurative, and specifically theatrical, violence. Anatomical theories current in the period, however, encourage a more literal reading of the violence embedded in spoken daggers, a claim I make more fully in my second chapter.
58. Horatio accedes to this request, 'Well, sit we down / And let us hear Barnardo speak of this' (1.1.33–4). Sitting, listening and storytelling in fact continue to be linked throughout the opening scene: 'Good now', Marcellus says, 'sit down, and tell me he that knows / Why this same strict and most observant watch / So nightly toils the subject of the land' (1.1.69–71).
59. de Grazia, p. 8.
60. This is not to say that dismemberment features only in revenge tragedy, but that it appears consistently as a trope in these plays. For more on dismemberment in early modern drama, see Owens, *Stages of Dismemberment*.
61. Citations to *The Spanish Tragedy* are taken from Calvo and Tronch's edition.
62. In terms of the number of lines spoken in soliloquy, *The Spanish Tragedy* far outranks *Hamlet*. By my count, there are 354 lines spoken out of the earshot of others in *The Spanish Tragedy*; Q2 *Hamlet* features 216 lines, not including the thirty of the 'To be or not to be' speech, which is delivered before Ophelia and the eavesdropping Claudius and Polonius. (*Titus Andronicus*, by comparison, contains only seventy lines of soliloquised speech.) *The Spanish Tragedy*'s soliloquies are distributed among Hieronimo, Isabella, Lorenzo, Pedringano; all but two of *Hamlet*'s soliloquies (not including the First Player's speech, which is of course delivered to a listening onstage audience, or Ophelia's, which is spoken before the eavesdropping Claudius and Polonius) are spoken by Hamlet himself. The two that are not spoken by Hamlet both belong to Claudius (3.3.36–72, and again at 97–8; and 4.3.56–66).
63. Cf. Harold Bloom's claim (in *Ruin the Sacred Truths*, pp. 111 and 54) that Shakespeare 'represent[s] . . . inner change by showing characters pondering their own utterances' 'and being altered through that consideration'.
64. Crooke, sig. Ddd6^r.
65. Crooke, sig. Fff^v.
66. Paster, *The Body Embarrassed*; and Schoenfeldt, *Bodies and Selves in Early Modern England*.

67. Peele, *David and Bethsabe*, in *The Dramatic Works of George Peele*, ed. Benbow, at l. 1830.
68. *The Knight of the Burning Pestle*, ed. Hattaway.
69. We might also look to Chettle's *The Tragedy of Hoffman; or, Revenge for a Father*, which I follow Thomas Rutter's lead in dating to 1603 (though first published in 1631) – a play which includes a number of similarities to *Hamlet* (in terms of both plot and characterisation), and which includes numerous verbal echoes. Like *The Revenger's Tragedy*, Chettle's play seems to have been written partly in response to *Hamlet*'s thoughtful engagement with the revenge tragedy genre, and Jonson's skewering of it. The play's indebtedness not only to *Hamlet*, but also to *The Spanish Tragedy* (which was being revised for performance with new additions by the Admiral's Men in 1602) is well charted by Rutter in 'Marlowe, Hoffman, and the Admiral's Men'.
70. McMillin, 'Acting and Violence: *The Revenger's Tragedy* and its Departures from *Hamlet*', p. 275. McMillin is building on Felperin, *Shakespearean Representation*, pp. 159–70.
71. Citations to *The Revenger's Tragedy* are taken from *Thomas Middleton: The Collected Works*, ed. Taylor and Lavagnino.
72. See also 'absurdity', n. 1: '*Music*. Lack of harmony, dissonance; an instance of this', OED.

Chapter 5

Listening for Form at the Cockpit Theatre

Introduction

In 1630, a battle erupted in print between James Shirley, the principal dramatist associated with Drury Lane's Cockpit theatre, and William Davenant, whose *The Just Italian* was staged at Blackfriars the year before. Davenant's play had been a flop, and in the commendatory verses that accompanied it into print his supporters blamed its failure on audiences' preference for 'bad' plays on offer elsewhere – for choosing 'the untun'd pipe' of Pan over Apollo's lyre.[1] The Cockpit came in for their sharpest criticism. Its actors were accused of braying like an 'untun'd Kennell', and its 'adulterate stage' was pointed to as a place where 'Now noyse prevayles'.[2] The language Davenant's supporters used could be borrowed directly from Ben Jonson's turn-of-the-century comedies, and Shirley and his supporters responded in kind. In the commendatory verses for his *The Grateful Servant* (1630), it is Shirley's language, not Davenant's, that is likened to Apollo's ('So smooth, and so sweet, that Apollo might rehearse / To his own lute'), and it is his rivals who are accused of writing unintelligible noise: their lines 'like Nile-cataracts do fall / With a huge noise, and yet not heard at all'.[3]

This back-and-forth between Davenant, Shirley and their respective supporters has been credited with starting a 'second poets' war', one which pitted the amateur gentleman dramatists of Blackfriars against the professional playwrights associated with the Cockpit.[4] Since several of these men wrote on occasion for both theatres, and since the line between professional and gentleman-amateur was at best a blurry one, such distinctions seem more manufactured than genuine. The battle, however, shows the extent to which the theatre of the 1630s was talked about as an aural phenomenon, even as it also became more visually spectacular. It also suggests that the dramatists associated with these two playhouses understood them as existing in competition with one another. Distinguishing each theatre's repertoire from the other's seems therefore to have been considered a competitive necessity, and one of the ways in which Shirley sought to do so was by celebrating the dramatic variety on offer at the Cockpit, as opposed to at Blackfriars. This means making a virtue out of what Davenant's crowd considered a fault – the blending together of vastly different plays and the sounds and styles of acting that went along with them. In the Prologue to *The Example* (first perf. 1634), Shirley complimented his audience for its assumed appreciation of variety – for enjoying more than 'one stage', and for not being 'over partial' to any one group of actors (and, by extension, to any one style of 'voice and gesture').[5] He suggested that good judgement depended on the cultivation of a less partial palate than that celebrated decades before by Ben Jonson, or more recently by Davenant and his followers, and on the ability to appreciate multiple aesthetic and aural dimensions.

This chapter argues for an understanding of the Cockpit's 1630s repertoire as participating in the self-conscious cultivation of a playhouse brand, one that celebrated formal variety and hybridity as well as theatregoers' ability to appreciate it aurally. The Cockpit's audience is imagined as hearing in much the same way Shakespeare's *Hamlet* encouraged playgoers to do decades earlier – widely, but also always thoughtfully, taking in a variety of sounds and styles. Such an approach may have been especially well suited to the Cockpit's 'adulterate stage', where revivals of tear-throat plays like Christopher Marlowe's *The Jew of Malta* were performed alongside fashionable new comedies of manners by Shirley and others, and where audiences would have encountered, at various points, actors from the Red Bull as well as from Queen Henrietta's Men and Beeston's Boys. But Shirley's celebration of variety could also apply to many of the roughly thirty-seven new plays that, to the best of our knowledge, were performed at the Cockpit during this decade.[6] Many of these were what we might call 'adulterate' forms: tragicomedies, which make up a large portion of the Cockpit's repertoire, but also other, less immediately recognisable mixtures, such as Thomas Heywood's commercial masque, *Love's Mistress*.

This adulterate-ness, or hybridity, had vital implications for the form and reception of the two genres discussed throughout this book. The new revenge tragedies and city comedies written for the Cockpit engage in sophisticated formal play, often incorporating elements from one another wholesale: they mix the domestic with the foreign; stock characters from Jonsonian city comedy with revenge tragedy's ghosts, accusatorily fresh-bleeding wounds and metatheatrical set pieces. Such widespread formal mingling would have invited playgoers to reflect upon the tropes and conventions that continued to give the genres of city comedy and revenge tragedy their shape, including the sounds and styles of listening with which each had become associated. For the most part, sound continues to be a tool for social distinction in the Cockpit's comedies, its tasteful consumption serving as a sign of a character's eligibility for membership within Town culture; while in its tragedies, sound tends to function as a powerful, even apocalyptic, weapon in the revenger's arsenal.[7] But these distinctions would come to be less sharp than they had been decades earlier, part of an ongoing process that (as I argued in Chapter 4) we can already see at work in Shakespeare's *Hamlet*.

As formal distinctions became more muddled, what emerged instead at the Cockpit was a set of conventions that could be traced across, as opposed to only within, dramatic genres. Several of these grew directly out of the theatre's sustained attention to its own aural reception, which I have been charting throughout this book. These devices were not new in and of themselves. They include eavesdropping, in which characters listen in on a speaker who is unaware he or she is being overheard, and the 'roaring', or 'railing', speech of boisterous gallants – a kind of social noise pollution that other characters must filter or avoid. These familiar (in the case of eavesdropping, even hackneyed) dramatic features take on different meaning when read across the Cockpit's repertoire. First, their use in these plays often signals moments of formal intrusion – that is, moments when the tragic becomes comic, or the comic threatens to become tragic – that depend on aural cues. Railing is a comic misfiring of revenge tragedy's violent speech, but one that carries the potential to hit its mark nonetheless. Eavesdropping, which makes listening dramatically visible, enables onstage listeners to provide comic choric commentary (as well as for their toes to be seen jutting out beneath a curtain), but it also threatens to derail marriage plots and set revenges in motion. Both railing and eavesdropping serve as auditory flashpoints, then, for formal mingling. Their presence signals to playgoers that a generic, and hence often a sonic, shift is coming or is taking place. Second, the persistent, almost hyperbolic, use of railing (and, even more so, of eavesdropping) becomes something of a running joke in which the Cockpit's audience is invited to participate. This sense of conspiratorial inclusion – of being 'in the know' – could be used to direct audiences' sympathies and responses (as I will argue John Ford does to great effect in *'Tis Pity She's a Whore*), or to showcase an author's ingenuity. Ultimately this persistent self-reflection helped to cultivate a sense of the theatre as an institution, complete with its own richly accumulated history and established set of performance and reception practices, in the final years before London's playhouses were shuttered.

This chapter begins with a brief survey of how railing and eavesdropping function within the 1630s repertoire of the Cockpit. It then focuses in on two plays that I argue exemplify how the forms and models of listening discussed throughout this book evolved in the final decade of the commercial theatre's existence: James Shirley's comedy of manners *The Ball* (first perf. 1632), and John Ford's urban tragedy, *'Tis Pity She's a Whore* (first perf. 1629–1633). Both plays are generic hybrids, and both feature episodes of roaring and eavesdropping that invite reflection on audience reception, albeit in markedly different ways. Each also demands of its audiences (and, in turn, helps to train them in the practice of) a kind of flexibility of reception. It has been one of the central claims of this book that aural cues were crucial agents for shaping the recognition and reception of different dramatic genres. The Cockpit's adulterate plays primed theatregoers to shift rapidly between modes of hearing, and ways of conceptualising that hearing, within a single production or even a single scene – revitalising what I argued in Chapter 3 was a signature feature of the earliest London comedies. The pages that follow explore this process and ask questions about its effects on the men and women who, according to Davenant's supporters, did 'in crowded heapes throng' to the Cockpit theatre in the mid-seventeenth century.[8]

Railing and Eavesdropping

In his dedicatory poem for John Ford's *Perkin Warbeck* (1634), George Donne assures the dramatist that his play will outlast works by the 'sicke Poet' who 'finde[s] men / To roare, *HE is THE WIT'S; His NOYSE doth sway*' (sig. A3ʳ).[9] These roaring supporters threaten to drown out not only others' better judgement, but also Ford's play itself by sheer force of volume. As in the commendatory verses discussed above, which marked the 1630 rivalry between Davenant and Shirley, here an opposition is being drawn between unintelligible 'noise' on the one hand and poetry on the other. The problem is that the shouting roarers threaten to make hearing, let alone appreciating, Ford's poetry all but impossible.

Donne's poem offers a literary-critical version of a familiar dramatic conceit. For decades, London city comedies had featured bands of roaring gallants (and, less often, 'city-roaring girls') who roam about the city 'braving' authority with their bold and boastful speeches.[10] The Cockpit's comedies, especially, build on this tradition, but roarers populate many of its tragicomedies as well. In Shirley's *The Lady of*

Pleasure (first perf. 1635), Frederick (a university student who longs to be a gentleman wit) announces, 'We'll have music; I love noise! We will outroar the Thames and shake the bridge, boy!'[11] In calling for music and noise, Frederick apes the gallants found in countless city comedies, including Thomas Nabbes's *The Bride* (first perf. 1638), which features 'Three or four Blades' described as 'Wilde roaring fellowes' in the dramatis personae.[12] In the Cockpit's tragicomedies, roaring tends to take the form of martial bluster: instead of being spoken by gallants, it is often delivered by soldiers and generals. But this style of speech is similarly represented as drowning out otherwise more intelligible and tasteful, even musical, language – particularly that of romance. Ford's comedy *The Lady's Trial* knits together the two kinds of roarer in the character of Guzman, a 'braggadocio Spaniard' who cannot help speaking of battle even as he practises how to woo a woman:

> Not to affright your tender soul with horror,
> We may descend to tales of peace and love,
> Soft whispers fitting ladies' closets; for
> Thunder and cannon, roaring smoke and fire,
> As if hell's maw had vomited confusion,
> The clash of steel, the neighs of barbed steeds,
> Wounds spouting blood, towns capering in the air . . .
> Become great Guzman's oratory best.[13]

No matter how hard he tries to speak in 'soft whispers', Guzman cannot help but roar, his 'oratory' filling with increasingly violent images of battle until in the end he is all but quoting *Tamburlaine*. It is as though the thunderous sound effects of the early commercial theatre have been displaced onto the bodies of these pretentious social upstarts or, in the tragicomedies (and in *The Lady's Trial*), onto the bodies of the martial men responsible for drumming up the noise of battle.

As different as these two types of 'roaring' or railing often are, they both share the potential to rattle London's very foundations – to 'shake the bridge', as Frederick puts it in *The Lady of Pleasure*. And in this sense, it has much in common with the often devastating speech of early modern revengers. The blades who roar their way through Nabbes's city comedy *The Bride*, for example, threaten to rape the bride of the title. Their roaring serves as both a prelude to and a prefiguring of that sexual assault ('Her chaste eares / Never received such sounds', Theophilus insists (2.6, p. 36)). The same holds true for tragicomic roarers, those often martial men who seem to be incapable of modulating their violent, warlike language. In Henry Glapthorne's *Argalus and Parthenia* (first perf. 1632–8), the comically unsuitable 'blunt phrase of war' spoken by Demagoras (who 'must speake / In the Heroick Dialect' even when he tries to woo) in fact prefigures the physical threat he will later embody – when, after having been rejected by Parthenia, he seeks 'revenge / Upon [her] beauty' by sacking her uncle's castle.[14] Whether spoken by the blades and gallants of city comedy or the martial men of tragicomedies, roaring is almost always ridiculous, but it is also often dangerous. It is a sonic sign of disorder as well as a means of producing such disorder.

Eavesdropping is even more omnipresent than railing on the Cockpit's stage. By my count, of the thirty-seven new plays performed there from 1629–39, at least twenty-one feature some form of eavesdropping, in which a character deliberately overhears speeches or snatches of conversation without the speaker's (or speakers') knowledge.[15] Of course, eavesdropping is a feature common to lots of plays, staged in most (if not all) early modern theatres. What makes the Cockpit's use of this device so striking is the frequency with which it appears – both within individual plays and across the repertoire as a whole – and its often exaggerated quality. Scenes of eavesdropping tend to be repeated or doubled in these plays, and to be highlighted through metatheatrical pointing. Again, this is not in itself an innovation – think of *Love's Labour's Lost* or *Troilus and Cressida*, to name just two examples – but the frequent, even obsessive, returning to this device by the Cockpit's dramatists is. When, in Robert Davenport's *King John and Matilda*, Young Bruce discovers the still-warm body of the murdered Matilda, he assumes her killer is still close by and decides to mislead the 'Eves dropper[]':[16] 'Thou honest soul, / That (by the heat of thy happy han[d]y-work,) / Canst not I am sure but be in hearing ... be not asham'd to let / Thy unknown friend possess thee' (sig. I^r). Incredibly, his plan works: 'S'foot, this is one of our side', remarks the eavesdropping killer (sig. H4^v). A similarly metatheatrically flagged example of eavesdropping occurs in Henry Glapthorne's city comedy *Wit in a Constable*: the titular constable seems to eavesdrop on all of London, and his benevolent surveillance is essential to the play's romantic plots ('I have o're-heard them all', Busie tells the audience at the end of Act Three, 'and it conduces / Much to my purpose').[17]

Some of the Cockpit's most elaborate scenes of eavesdropping were written by its principal dramatist, James Shirley. Towards the end of his *The Traitor*, the seditious plotter Depazzi asks his co-conspirator, Lorenzo, 'Is no body within hearing? all clear behind the arras?'[18] Multiple things are happening here at once. First, and most obviously, the line is a reference to *Hamlet* (in fact, it is the second such reference in this tragedy, building on Depazzi's earlier 'I smell a rat behind the hangings' (3.1)). Second, Depazzi's question winkingly references *The Traitor*'s frequent, almost hyperbolic, eavesdropping. In several scenes, someone *is* in fact listening behind the arras, or just beyond the door, and in one memorable scene a would-be eavesdropper is surprised to discover another listener already hidden behind the hangings. Finally, the episode functions intertheatrically, linking Depazzi to Polonius and to the countless other characters who have stood on stage listening behind a curtain.

A similarly baroque episode of eavesdropping occurs in Shirley's comedy *The Opportunity* between a quartet of lovers. As the lovesick Duke of Ferrara stands in the shadows outside the Duchess of Urbino's palace, his rival, Borgia (actually the young Aurelio in disguise), enters complaining that he is torn between two women: the Duchess and her attendant, Cornelia. Suddenly Cornelia 'appears at an upper window' and, hearing Borgia/Aurelio, decides to speak to him in the person of the Duchess in order to discourage his pursuit of her mistress.[19] The Duke, hearing Cornelia (and, like Aurelio, mistakenly believing her to be the Duchess), is relieved, and exits, at which the point the *real* Duchess suddenly enters and shoos Cornelia from the window. ('I heard your voice more loud than usual', she says. 'Whom spake you to?') The Duchess then picks up where Cornelia left off with Borgia/Aurelio, but she does so while claiming to be Cornelia, and to have been *pretending* to be the Duchess all along. The dizzying artifice of this charade is metatheatrically signalled by the Duchess-as-Cornelia's ironic compliment to the still-deceived Aurelio at the scene's conclusion: 'You well distinguish voices', she says; 'yes, [the Duchess] is gone' (2.3, p. 401). Here, as in *The Traitor*, multilayered eavesdropping points out the theatricality of the device while at the same time gesturing intertheatrically to other, earlier dramatic moments: Romeo and Juliet's exchange at her window, for one, but also *'Tis Pity She's a Whore*, which I discuss below.[20]

The Cockpit's obsessive staging and restaging of eavesdropping could be understood as reflecting an actual part of the lived, urban experience of early modern London. As historians of sixteenth- and seventeenth-century England have shown, eavesdropping was an inevitable consequence of urban overcrowding. It served as a tool for community policing, as neighbours listened in on one another and acted as witnesses in legal disputes, but it was also a pastime, or a source of entertainment.[21] Etymologically, eavesdroppers were both auditory and spatial intruders who were essentially 'built in' to early modern English architecture: to eavesdrop was to 'stand within the "eavesdrop" of a house in order to listen to secrets', or to stand within 'the space of ground which is liable to receive the rain-water thrown off by the eaves of a building'.[22] Crammed within one another's eavesdrip, and often subdivided to hold multiple families, London's houses would have made eavesdropping all but unavoidable, both inside and out. This would have been less true of the relatively less densely crowded West End, where the Cockpit was located.[23] But many of the new kinds of spaces and architectural features most associated with this part of the city, and with the cultivation of Town culture, would have introduced particular challenges for speakers and listeners alike, which may have drawn new attention to audition. Balconies, for example, which figure centrally in many of the Cockpit's eavesdropping scenes, were (as Adam Zucker has shown) an entirely new feature in 1630s West End London that placed individuals in distinctly liminal space between inside and out, public and private.[24] And the royal parks introduced in West End London (e.g., Hyde Park, St James's Park) allowed fashionable Londoners to engage in highly conspicuous, publicly visible retreats into 'private' walks for more intimate conversation. These public-private spaces, which broadcast one's desire for privacy as well as the ability to access it, would inevitably have invited the very auditory scrutiny that their use would seem intended to avoid.[25] The Cockpit's persistent use of eavesdropping may reflect this paradox.

And yet: the highly artificial, intensely self-referential quality of eavesdropping in a play like *The Traitor* makes it difficult to understand such scenes as mimetically referencing a broadly experienced urban phenomenon. Surely they do this, but they also do something else. Above all, these scenes place audience members in the position of being 'in' on something, and what they are being let 'in' on is the history of the theatre itself – a history that, as I have been arguing throughout this book, has always been embedded in thinking about sound. *The Traitor*'s richly intertheatrical eavesdropping not only makes listening something that audiences can *see* – reminding theatregoers that they, like Depazzi, are hearers – it also highlights the decades-long accumulation of raw material, rules and conventions on which a dramatist like Shirley could draw, and in fact *had* to draw, by the 1630s. Put another way: Depazzi's question ('Is no body within hearing? all clear behind the arras?') presumes on the part of its audience a deep knowledge of London's commercial theatre history, and in doing so it both celebrates the existence of that history and compliments playgoers for their understanding and appreciation of it. Railing serves a similar purpose. It skewers a certain style of speaking (the fashion for 'roaring' that these plays suggest was always more gauche than gallant) while simultaneously referencing a whole roll call of railers: if Depazzi calls to mind Polonius, then Frederick in Nabbes's *The Bride* recalls Bobadilla from Ben Jonson's *Every Man in His Humour* and Chough and Trimtram from Middleton and Rowley's *A Fair Quarrel*, as well as *The Roaring Girl*'s Moll Cutpurse, to name just a few. While the uses to which these dramatic devices are put vary greatly from play to play, their reiteration calls attention to them *as* devices, and, moreover, as devices that foreground audition. Like a play-within-a-play, railing and eavesdropping invite metatheatrical reflection on dramatic production and sensory reception, and on the formal codes through which the two are linked. In performance, railing is recognisable as such not only through how it sounds (its style, as well as its blustery content), but also through how it is heard by its onstage listeners. Eavesdropping, similarly, is a highly stylised dramatic representation of the act of hearing. Both devices function citationally across London's commercial theatre history while serving as reminders of the role audition has played in shaping that history. The next two sections examine the uses to which railing and eavesdropping are put in a pair of Cockpit plays and ask what the effect of such relentless, metatheatrical self-scrutiny may have been.

'Take our Scourges Patiently'

In both its representation of sound and its expectations of how audiences are to hear, James Shirley's *The Ball* is a clear inheritor of the model of tasteful hearing introduced by Ben Jonson at the close of the sixteenth century. Like Jonson's *Epicoene*, it is a comedy of manners set in London's West End, where a crucial skill required of the men and women of leisure who move through its socially significant spaces is being able to filter out the unwanted sounds of the city. Much like Shakespeare's *Twelfth Night* and *The Merry Wives of Windsor*, however, *The Ball* is also what we might call a revenge-comedy. It includes multiple revenge plots, and although these are all defused by the time we reach the play's conclusion, their presence threatens at times to derail the comic action.[26] The first, and most ominous, of these subplots is introduced in Act Two, when the wealthy widow Lucina decides to humiliate her unsuitable suitors; and it is set in motion by an elaborately stage-managed episode of eavesdropping. After inviting each of her suitors to visit her at home, Lucina puts on a kind of improvised play for the benefit of her maid: 'Now, Scutilla, we are ripe, and ready / To entertain my gamesters', she begins, before ushering Scutilla behind the hangings: 'Away, Scutilla, and / Laugh not [too] loud between our acts' (2.3, p. 27). As each gallant is brought in, Lucina humours him, praising the dancing skills of the foppish Sir Ambrose Lamount, for example, and telling the aristocratically pretentious Bostock that she could love him if only he 'were / Not half so noble, nay, indeed, no gentleman' (2.3, p. 32). The performances are a hit – Scutilla tells Lucina she 'is almost dead with stifling my laughter' (2.3, p. 31) – but what Lucina does not know is that Scutilla has already invited one of these suitors, Colonel Winfield, to listen in on Lucina's performance. ('[B]e but pleas'd to obscure / Yourself behind these hangings a few minutes', she directs him before the others arrive (2.3, p. 26).) Since his eavesdropping enables the Colonel to outwit both his romantic rivals and, eventually, Lucina (whom he will later persuade to marry him by putting to good use what he has overheard), we might understand this scene as lumping the widow together with her victims, and of placing the Colonel in a position of power over all of them. But such a reading is complicated by the fact that he has been placed in this aurally advantageous position by Lucina's maid. In fact, sets of speakers and eavesdroppers are nested within one another like matryoshka dolls, and while the innermost speakers (Lucina's socially pretentious suitors) are subjected to the greatest humiliation, the outward listeners do not escape ridicule entirely. Even the Colonel is exposed to the women's laughter, since he, too, must take his turn being humiliated by Lucina for the listening Scutilla's benefit. 'Come', Lucina concludes afterwards: 'we'll laugh, and lie down in the next room, Scutilla' (2.3, 35, 36). The Colonel may be in on their joke, but he is also at least partly its object.

Even more than this scene of eavesdropping points out power differentials between characters, then, it seems to draw attention to the act of listening itself – and, more specifically, to the act of hearing a play. This is after all what Lucina has imagined she has been preparing for Scutilla all along: a play in several 'acts', designed for her 'entertain[ment]'. Scutilla and the Colonel's eavesdropping therefore functions similarly to the multilayered eavesdropping encountered in *The Traitor* and countless other Cockpit plays. It reflects the audience's own sensory reception as though through a funhouse mirror, with exaggeration and doubling, and it does so just before a sudden shift in dramatic mood. As a result, the audience is encouraged to think about its own auditory experience at the precise moment when the formal identity of Shirley's play is about to become briefly unmoored. As the Colonel leaves Lucina's chamber, he mutters, 'Why did not I strike her?' and declares his rather dark intent to 'do something' (2.3, p. 36). At this point in the play, we can have no idea what this 'something' is. But by pairing the Colonel's vague threat with his professed regret over not having retaliated physically (with a 'strike'), Shirley opens up the possibility, at least, that the Colonel's response will be violent.

This potential for violence seems to be on the verge of being realised later in the play, when the Colonel successfully persuades his fellow suitors to 'join wi' [him] in revenge' against Lucina (3.2, p. 42). And it is on the form their revenge will take that I want to focus. Together, the men decide to return to Lucina's chamber and 'rail upon her' – 'confound[ing]' and 'tortur[ing]' her with their 'bitter' insults (3.2, pp. 42 and 43). The plan, which is clearly coded as ridiculous from the moment it is proposed, nonetheless depends on the same logic undergirding the most gruesome revenge plots of the period. It is not just what the men say, but the physical fact of the sounds they make – spoken in the small, enclosed space of Lucina's chamber – that matters. Bostock, who appoints himself the suitors' spokesperson, allows that the Colonel may 'relieve me: / When I take breath, then you may help, or you, / Or any, to confound her' (3.2, p. 43). The idea that Bostock's cursing will wear him out, so that he must 'take breath', highlights the physicality of railing – meaning both the materiality of his words, which are comprised of breath and air, and also the physical work their production entails. His emphasis on the breathlessness brought on through physical exertion, and of his need for the others to 'relieve' him, recasts their verbal assault as a kind of rape. This is further suggested by Shirley's use of the word 'discharge', which likens railing both to the firing of a weapon and to ejaculation, explicitly casting the attack in sexual terms: 'if we all discharge at once upon her, / We shall but make confusion', warns Sir Ambrose Lamount, 'let us choose one / To curse her for us all' (3.2, p. 42).

The gallants' attack on Lucina introduces violent language that is jarringly uncivil and delivered at what the play's language and punctuation suggest may have been a higher volume.[27] Their bitter invective therefore represents a stark departure in both sound and style from much of what has preceded it:

> I spit
> Defiance: stand further off, and be attentive,
> Weep, or do worse; repentance wet thy linen,
> And leave no vein for the doctor!
> . . . let thy tongue be silent,
> And take our scourges patiently; thou hast,
> In thine own self, all the ingredients
> Of wickedness in thy sex; able to furnish
> Hell, if't were insufficiently provided,
> With falsehood, and she-fiends of thy own making! (3.4, pp. 49–50)

The politely civil language that characterises Bostock's earlier exchange with Lucina has been replaced with violent and grotesque images of bleeding, or possibly urinating, bodies, as well as with fiercely misogynistic tropes (such as that linking women's bodies with hell). As he delivers his 'scourge' – itself a term associated with the tear-throat speech of Tamburlaine – Bostock imagines its potency as practically knocking Lucina off her feet ('stand further off'). Yet his 'discharge' proves harmless. As Lucina and her maid parry Bostock's verbal thrusts, it is this speaker's relative impotence and masculine insufficiency that are exposed, not the harmlessness of speech in general.[28] Colonel Winfield's threats prove much more potent. As Bostock pauses to 'breathe awhile', the Colonel shocks his companions by stepping forward, striking him, and then reprimanding them all for having spoken to Lucina so roughly: 'dare but lift thy voice / To fright this lady, or but ask thy pardon, / My sword shall rip thy body for thy heart, / And nail it on her threshold' (3.4, p. 51). For the audience, this is the moment when the violence first threatened by the Colonel's desire to 'strike' Lucina, and further hinted at in his plan to seek revenge against her, is erased (or, rather, comically displaced). As the gallants quickly realise, 'his plot, to have us rail' was intended all along as a way to win Lucina's favour by allowing the Colonel to take her part against them (3.4, p. 51). But the Colonel's language – like his strike itself – is almost too rough. Even the charmed Lucina is, at first, alarmed: 'This is no place for blood, nor shall my cause / Engage to such a danger' (3.4, p. 52). Colonel Winfield's lines have the power almost to retroactively reinvigorate Bostock's limp assault: his choice of phrase ('lift thy voice') equates that earlier language with a raised hand. The gallants' railing may be ineffectual, a comic misfiring of potentially violent speech, but the Colonel's has the capacity to hit its mark.

Eavesdropping and vengeance are paired throughout *The Ball*. In fact, nearly every time a character deliberately listens in on another's conversation, the act of overhearing helps to instigate a (quickly defused) revenge plot. When the ladies Honoria and Rosamond, rivals for Lord Rainbow's affection, realise he has overheard them arguing, they decide to pursue his friend Barker out of spite ('I may be even / With this May lord'; 'I will love some other in revenge' (3.3, p. 47)). And when the pretended traveller Jack Freshwater learns he has been overheard betraying his ignorance of foreign places, he vows to 'venture one drowning to be reveng'd' on his debtors (5.1, p. 91). As it does in the pair of scenes discussed above, eavesdropping seems, at these other moments, to precipitate and announce revenge's formal intrusion into Shirley's comedy. As a theatrical device, it therefore might have helped to signal impending changes in mood, tone and – in the gallants' revenge plot – even theatrical sound. The scene set in Lucina's chamber, which modulates between the comic and the potentially tragic, also combines two very different ways of thinking about speech: it is a 'scourge', an assault, but it is also something of 'no danger' (3.4, p. 50). Like Lucina and Scutilla, who are exposed to this variously affective speech within the intimate, enclosed space of a private chamber, the Cockpit's theatregoers, too, are being made to hear such language in an enclosed West End space. The decades-long theatrical history on which *The Ball* so explicitly draws, moreover, would have trained theatregoers to consider the risks such audition might carry – that railing speech, even or perhaps especially in a space like this, could harm its hearers. Eavesdropping draws attention to this possibility by pointing out the shared experience (and exposure) of on- and offstage audiences, just as the consequences of that exposure seem to be most in question. For playgoers as steeped in theatre history as a play like *The Traitor* (also by Shirley) suggests the Cockpit's audiences were likely to be, such shifts would have demanded auditory flexibility, but they may also have invited admiration.

Overhearing, Overdone: John Ford's *'Tis Pity She's a Whore*

Enter Giovanni, with a heart upon his dagger.
John Ford, *'Tis Pity She's a Whore* (London, 1633)[29]

When, at the conclusion of *'Tis Pity She's a Whore*, Giovanni enters the banquet hall with Annabella's heart impaled upon his dagger, Soranzo's guests are bewildered: 'What means this?'; 'What strange riddle's this?' (5.6.13, 28). Annabella's heart, long an object of frustrated scrutiny for the men in this play, becomes in the end a 'grisly tautology', as Michael Neill puts it – a lump of flesh 'brutally stripped of all vestiges of metaphor' and emptied out of meaning.[30] The bewilderment felt by Giovanni's onstage audience has long been mirrored in the critical reception of Ford's play, which, though it has inspired a rich body of work, has often left readers unsure what to make of its final, bloody tableau. From earlier scholars, who dismissed the scene as an embarrassing example of the decadence and sensationalism of Caroline drama, to more recent ones, who have emphasised the heart's opacity as a symbol or signifier, a sense emerges that this scene (and consequently this play) are difficult, if not impossible, to talk about.[31]

Rather than being a sign of dramatic (or, for that matter, of critical) failure, I want to suggest that the bewilderment that greets this image – both onstage and off – may itself be the point. It is in fact the necessary by-product of *'Tis Pity*'s intensely self-referential formal and sonic play, the seemingly inevitable endpoint of the decades-long process of generic self-scrutiny that I have been charting throughout this book – a process through which revenge tragedy and city comedy as forms came to be associated with specific auditory modes. *'Tis Pity She's a Whore* is famously hybrid, a city comedy that ends with a bloodbath instead of a wedding. Set in a distinctly urban space, and shaped by the traditionally city-comic question of who will marry the wealthy merchant's daughter, *'Tis Pity* is also very much a revenge tragedy, and it shares with such plays an emphasis on the violence that sound (particularly vehement speech) can perform on the bodies that hear it.[32] Giovanni's final, grisly revelation – that he has murdered his sister, Annabella, who had also become his lover – mortally wounds their father ('Cursed man! Have I lived to – *Dies*' (5.6.59, 59 SD)), and the play is suffused with metaphors linking words with weapons.[33] As I argued in Chapter 2, such metaphors were literalised by early modern anatomical theory, which imagined sound as piercing and puncturing the body or poisoning and corroding it from within. But in *'Tis Pity*, such thinking must compete throughout with a sense of sound's more selective reception. Giovanni is, above all, a man who hears only what he *wants* to hear. His partial hearing of the philosophical and religious lectures he has attended in Bologna, as well as of the Friar's advice, is ultimately what plots his destruction. It is his highly selective reception and subsequent misapplication of this knowledge (as 'school points' and 'nice philosophy') that enables Giovanni to dismiss incest as no more than 'a peevish sound' (1.1.2, 24).

As in so many Cockpit plays, in *'Tis Pity* eavesdropping plays a crucial role in shaping its decidedly hybrid plot. But Ford's use of eavesdropping differs markedly from Shirley's, for example, in both its staging and its function. The Cockpit's balcony is often used to separate speakers from their (unknown) hearers, a choice of staging that helps to make listening dramatically visible and one that imbues specific characters with moral and critical authority. As they stand on the balcony above the stage, commenting on the suitors they have just heard squabbling on the street below, Annabella and her nurse, Puttana, form a kind of chorus. 'How like you this, child?' Puttana asks (1.2.67). It is as though the two women have just been treated to a performance on which they are now able to comment critically and, it turns out, astutely:

> PUT. Here's threatening, challenging, quarreling and fighting on every side, and all is for your sake . . . Take the worst with the best. There's Grimaldi, the soldier, a very well-timbered fellow . . . But faith, charge, I do not like him, an't be for nothing but for being a soldier: one amongst twenty of your skirmishing captains but have some privy maim or other that mars their standing upright. (1.2.67–86)

Grimaldi may or may not be diseased, but he is certainly not represented as a viable romantic option; and Soranzo, who fares far better in Puttana's estimation, is nonetheless as flawed and sexually compromised as she recognises him to be. Although initially Annabella resists participating ('Fie, how thou prat'st' (l. 90)), by the time Bergetto appears, she has joined Puttana's chorus: 'This idiot haunts me too' (1.2.130). Their commentary is by now fully in step with the critical perspectives assumed by Ford's play, which in turn prepares theatregoers to share in Annabella's deeply problematic, but apparently correct, assessment of her brother's superiority at the end of this scene: 'But see, Puttana, see, what blessed shape / Of some celestial creature now appears?' (1.2.140–1). It goes to the heart of Ford's tragedy, in fact, that she is right.

In this scene, eavesdroppers become proximate audience members who serve as critics or interpreters of the play's events. They are, quite literally, *over*-hearers, whose reception and responses the play seems to privilege. This is particularly true for Annabella, who appears on the balcony most often, but it is also the case for Giovanni, who later stands on the same balcony listening to, and commenting on, Soranzo's attempt to woo Annabella:[34]

> SORANZO: Did you but see my heart, then you would swear –
> ANNABELLA: That you were dead.
> GIOVANNI [aside]: That's true, or somewhat near it. (3.2.23–5)

Spoken as an aside, Giovanni's 'That's true' hovers somewhere between the world of the play and the world outside it. His interjection invites *'Tis Pity*'s audience in on his own, private joke, essentially dovetailing their reactions. If extant seventeenth-century drawings accurately depict the design of the Cockpit theatre, then over-hearers on the balcony would practically have been incorporated into the audience above the stage.[35] And while *'Tis Pity* permits no easy links between the upper stage and heaven, or between below-stage and hell, the spatial logic of over-hearing nonetheless recalls the theatrical tradition in which such associations were forged. Compare Annabella and Puttana's eavesdropping with the Friar's in Act Five: as Annabella appears (once again) on the balcony, 'confess[ing]' that she is 'lost', the Friar enters below, listening unobserved, and announces that 'heaven hath heard you / And ... ordained that I / Should be minister for your behoof' (5.1.11, 11, 30, 37–9). The Friar's position below Annabella undercuts the sense, however, that her words have been heard by 'heaven' above – as does his rather ineffectual turn, thus far, as 'minister' of her protection. Rather than assuring the audience of Annabella's spiritual absolution, the exchange seems to underscore the hopelessness of her current plight. Trapped 'like a turtle, mewed up in a cage' where she 'converse[s] with air and walls, / And descant[s] on [her] vile unhappiness', Annabella has long been forced to be her own confessor (5.1.14–16). Speaking now into the open air, her thoughts fly up to heaven, but her words, it seems, remain below.

These two scenes of eavesdropping – the first, in which Annabella and Puttana over-hear her suitors; the second, in which the Friar listens in on Annabella's confession from below – bookend the play's action. Together, they help to make visible *'Tis Pity*'s preoccupation with the ways in which sounds circulate – a process that seems both to symbolise and, crucially, to help *produce* the moral and physical decay at Parma's centre. As Ford's use of the balcony suggests, in this play sounds move within a seemingly closed, and therefore stiflingly unhealthy, system. Confessions are repeatedly 'unripped' from speakers' bodies and poured into confessors' ears in an endlessly staged cycle of purgation and reabsorption. Such 'foul and guilty' secrets, once spoken aloud, can harm the hearer's body as well as his soul. When Giovanni confesses to the Friar that he and Annabella have consummated their affection, the Friar responds, 'I'm sorry I have heard it. Would mine ears / Had been one minute deaf before the hour / That thou cam'st to see me' (2.5.3–5). Beginning with a command to stop talking ('Peace!'), and ending with a longing for deafness, the Friar's lines suggest discomfort, even danger, in hearing this 'tale whose every word / Threatens eternal slaughter to the soul' (2.5.1–2). It is surely the meaning of these 'word[s]' that matters most, but to protect himself from the risk of having heard them, the Friar would willingly sacrifice his ability to hear any sounds at all.

When he later hears Annabella's confession in his cell, the Friar seems to take an even greater risk – not because the content of Annabella's confession is more threatening, but because the space in which she vents it is so intimately close, permitting no dissipation of her potent vocal matter.[36] The Friar and Annabella are revealed 'in his study, sitting in a chair; ANNABELLA kneeling and whispering to him; a table before them and wax-lights' (3.6.37, 3.6.1 SD). The semi-darkness of this scene communicates intimacy but also constriction – an effect that, as Sonia Massai points out, would have been exacerbated by the relatively small size of the Cockpit itself (which may have been even smaller than Blackfriars).[37] The cramped setting helps to make the lovers' incestuous nearness, and the extent to which Annabella is now 'trapped' in a desperate situation, materially visible, but I argue that the audience is made to feel the unhealthiness of their closeness through sound. In the dark, claustrophobically enclosed space of the Friar's study – where, initially, Annabella is seen and possibly heard whispering – secrets are not just spoken, but 'unripped' from the body in speeches that reverberate against the walls of the Friar's study and, ultimately, of the enclosed, private playhouse in which that study is being represented (3.6.2).[38]

These potent speeches accumulate with suffocating pressure until there is nowhere for them to go but into the bodies of the men and women who populate the Cockpit's stage and its benches.

This dramatic fact is emphasised by the play's language, which becomes increasingly thick with metaphors of smothering, decay and rot.[39] Late in the play, Soranzo accuses the pregnant Annabella of having in 'thy lewd womb even buried me alive!' (4.3.115), and demands to know why she has 'picked [him] out to be cloak to your close tricks' (4.3.11).[40] Such language serves symbolically to point out the corruption that plagues all of Parma, but it also serves as a reminder that absorbing sounds without giving them vent can be dangerously corrosive. In *'Tis Pity*, as in other tragedies of revenge, keeping secret is synonymous with keeping quiet – a process that threatens to produce physiological damage, but one that is also necessary for fuelling the would-be revenger's fury. When Vasquez urges Soranzo to 'smother [his] revenge' and 'leave the scenting out your wrongs to me', he is advising him to keep his anger secret by not expressing it aloud (4.3.99–101). Like Hieronimo's efforts to 'dissembl[e] quiet in unquietness' in *The Spanish Tragedy*, Soranzo's 'smother[ed] revenge' may be strategically necessary, but it produces tremendous physical strain, even madness: 'The less I speak, the more I burn', he assures Vasquez, 'And blood shall quench that flame' (5.4.22–3).[41]

This sense that sound is being smothered, kept inside the bodies of the men and women who move through Parma, only builds throughout the play, as the secrets mount and the plotted revenges multiply.[42] But *'Tis Pity*'s sonic and spatial logic seems to undercut the possibility that a healthful purgation would even be possible anyway – not just for the play's many revengers, but for virtually all of Parma's citizens, and even, I will argue, for Ford's audience. Whether, in Parma's too-intimate spaces, secrets are kept quiet or 'disclosed', these spaces pollute the bodies that move through them, and ultimately the Cockpit is just another of them. The structure, staging and language of Ford's play all but demand that theatregoers acknowledge the potential risks entailed in their own claustrophobic reception – that they feel the 'gallimaufry that's stuffed' in their own too-pregnant ears (4.3.13). Ford seems to have used the ways in which the Cockpit's size and structure would have conditioned playgoers' reception, in other words, to reproduce for them on an intimately physical, uncomfortably individual, level something like the experience of his doomed lovers, as well as something like that of the play's many revengers.

Part of the 'gallimaufry' being 'stuffed' into Ford's audience's ears (as my own infelicitous paraphrase of Olivia's 'pregnant and vouchsafed ear' might remind us) is an abundance, or even an over-abundance, of references to other English Renaissance plays. This is one of the most remarked upon aspects of *'Tis Pity* – whether it is being pointed to as a sign of the play's derivativeness or of Ford's ingenuity.[43] Like *'Tis Pity*'s seemingly smothering accumulation of sounds, its progressive piling on of intertheatrical references becomes leaden, heavy. Its intertheatricality thus functions both as yet another dramatic representation of the incestuous relationship at this play's centre and, at the same time, of the dramatic-historical fact that I want to conclude this chapter by arguing Annabella and Giovanni's relationship is being used, in part, to explore. As the theatre draws on its own history, again and again, in order to produce something 'new' – or rather to *re*-produce examples of what were, by then, long-established and almost obsessively self-reflexive dramatic forms – it runs the risk of entailing its own disintegration. Put differently: under the pressure of so much metatheatrical attention and self-scrutiny, revenge tragedy and city comedy as forms threaten to come apart at the seams.

Some of Ford's borrowings function citationally, as though explicitly inviting the audience to consider the dramatic lineage of which this play is an inheritor. For example, the letter, 'double-lined with tears and blood' (5.1.34), which Annabella drops from her balcony to the listening Friar, serves almost as a quotation or dramatic paraphrase of Bel-Imperia's 'bloody writ' (another 'letter' dropped from above, which the passing Hieronimo picks up in Act Three of *The Spanish Tragedy*. Similarly, Vasquez's enthusiastic response to Soranzo's description of his burning blood – 'Now you begin to turn Italian!' – confirms his master's transformation into a bloody-minded revenger while at the same time signalling his membership in a long line of Italian revengers on the early modern stage (5.4.22–31). By the time we reach the end of *'Tis Pity*, its metatheatrical references have become so dense, it is as though they have invaded the world of the play. Annabella almost seems to recognise herself as a character in a revenge tragedy when she warns her brother that 'these gay attires were not put on / But to some end' (5.5.20–1). Dressed, like the doomed Desdemona, in her wedding clothes as she lies 'on a bed' with her brother, Annabella knows how to read the dramatic codes that give this scene its meaning: 'Be not deceived, my brother: / This banquet is an harbinger of death / To you and me' (5.5.1 SD, 5.5.26–8). It is not just that Soranzo's banquet follows hard upon another, earlier feast that also ended in bloodshed. It is also that banquets, like Italian revengers and letters written in blood, had by the time *'Tis Pity* was first performed become features firmly associated with revenge tragedy as a genre. The Friar expresses a similar formal awareness earlier, when he warns Giovanni not to attend the banquet: 'You will not go, I trust . . . This feast, I'll gage my life, / Is but a plot to train you to your ruin. / Be ruled: you sha' not go' (5.3.56–9). Their knowing references to bloody banquets reach beyond and outside the world of the play into the space of the Cockpit itself – where, either shortly before or after *'Tis Pity* was first performed, a revenge tragedy with the telling title of *The Bloody Banquet* was staged.

We are made to feel the full weight of these intertheatrical references in *'Tis Pity*'s final scene – when, after having killed Annabella, Giovanni enters the banquet hall with her heart 'reeking blood' upon his dagger (5.6.9). Suddenly, the action of Ford's play seems to stop, as all eyes become riveted on what has been called 'the most shocking, eloquent and unforgettable' of Ford's 'stage pictures' – a bloody tableau that functions like the gests of Brecht's epic theatre to distil in a single moment the meaning of the entire play.[44] What this picture so vividly discovers is the essentially metatheatrical, and therefore even more frustratingly meaningless, quality of Giovanni's revenge. It threatens to turn the play into a parody at precisely the moment when its action becomes most disturbingly, deadly serious, a perverse transposition. 'Shrink not, courageous hand; stand up, my heart', Giovanni urges himself, 'And boldly act my last and greater part' (5.5.106–7). The 'greater part' that he must 'boldly act' is that of the conventional stage revenger, a role that has been thrust upon him, but one that he nonetheless now assumes in all its phantasmagorical glory:

> that times to come may know
> How as my fate I honoured my revenge,
> List, father: to your ears I will yield up
> How much I have deserved to be your son. (5.6.34–7)

To Giovanni's father, this stentorian speech is the railing of a 'rage'-filled 'madman' or 'frantic madman', but to a theatregoing audience well steeped in dramatic conventions and practices, it is the unmistakable sound of the revenger: booming, portentous and oratorically outdated (5.6.50, 33, 41). With its 'List, father', the lines might even hold a reverse echo of the Ghost's command that Hamlet 'list, list, oh list' to his tale of 'most unnatural murder' (1.5.22, 25). It is, in short, a markedly old-fashioned sounding kind of bluster – of the revenger's, rather than of the gallant's, railing – and it seems to shift this decidedly hybrid play into an entirely different register. No longer are we in the Parma of Ford's urban tragedy, but in the Italy of Middleton's and Webster's Jacobean revenge plays, a formal and geographical space in which long-withheld confessions are unleashed to produce apocalyptic violence.

As the bewildered response of Giovanni's onstage audience suggests, however, this analysis does not quite ring true. Like countless revengers before him, Giovanni at last delivers a lengthy confession detailing how, and why, he committed the murder suddenly 'discovered' onstage; but like Hieronimo's confessional oration at the end of *The Spanish Tragedy*, Giovanni's fails at first to resonate. It is dismissed by its hearers as false ('Oh, his rage belies him! (l. 50)), and so he must repeatedly assert its veracity ("'Tis the oracle of truth, / I vow 'tis so' (5.6.51–2)). The problem is that, initially, Giovanni seems to believe that the heart speaks for itself, and so his railing, though full of sound and fury, signifies nothing and wounds no one. By the time Giovanni realises his mistake – that, despite the spectacularly visual revelation of the heart, an explanation is also necessary – it is almost too late. The verbal discovery of Giovanni's secret matter (his incestuous affair, Annabella's pregnancy) has been all but drowned out by the vividly visual materiality of Annabella's heart.

Rather than challenging the logic, or even the anatomical assumptions, that underlie the gruesome violence of revenge tragedy's verbal discoveries, I suggest that *'Tis Pity*'s final scene showcases Giovanni's misunderstanding of how verbal violence works, both physiologically and dramatically. For all its spectacular grisliness, Annabella's heart is not a weapon, but an organ in which sound's damage is most painfully, viscerally felt. Ford's almost exactly contemporary *The Broken Heart* concludes when the newly crowned Calantha dies of an eerily audible heart-break ('Crack, crack' (5.3.77)).[45] For Calantha, the cause of her own death is aural: she has been forced to hear a series of escalatingly awful revelations ('one news straight came huddling on another, / Of death, and death, and death. Still I danced forward; / But it struck home, and here, and in an instant' (5.3.68–71)).[46] The discovery of this 'news', which we see and hear being 'whispered' 'In Calantha's ear' in the preceding scene, is made lethal when Calantha cannot give it vent: 'They are the silent griefs', she concludes, 'which cut the heart-strings' (5.3.75). While Calantha's stoicism may signal her fitness as a ruler, physically it is unsound. She cannot hear so much and say so little. Bottling up speech entails stifling the body's circulation of air, the matter out of which the voice is formed, and doing so while absorbing others' breath (a form of waste) imperils the body's 'ayrie substaunce'. It is in the heart, the figurative seat of feeling and the locus for the production of vital spirits, that this imbalance would be felt most keenly.[47] Breathed into the body through the lungs, air was thought to mix almost alchemically with blood in the heart, which was then 'strayned . . . betwene the Ventricles' via a pair of portals. Incredibly, these portals in the heart were called 'eares', a coincidence of terminology that suggests the organs were linked conceptually as well as physiologically in the circulation of air, breath and sound. The 'heart hath little eares or auricles', explains the anatomist John Banister, that are 'two Appendaunces, growyng to the seate of the hart'.[48] And according to the English translator of Ambroise Paré's works, these auricles are uncannily similar to the proper ears in their purpose and function: they 'break the violence of the matters entring the heart with great force when it is dilated' and act as 'stayes or props to the Arteria venosa and great Arterye'.[49]

When, at the end of *'Tis Pity*, Giovanni enters the hall with Annabella's heart on his dagger 'proud in the spoil / Of love and vengeance', it is as if he has turned everything – Annabella's body, this play, the logic of revenge tragedy itself – inside-out (5.6.10–11). For all his thoughtful, apparently studied, appropriation of the revenger's role, he gets it wrong, and in this sense he has a surprising amount in common with Bostock of James Shirley's *The Ball*. His railing misfires in ways that threaten to destabilise the seemingly settled question of just what kind of play this is.[50] The point is not that *'Tis Pity She's a Whore* should be reclassified as a comedy, or even that Giovanni's error is best understood satirically; rather, it is that Ford's play is persistently hybrid to the very end.[51] When the Cardinal delivers his maddeningly pat rhyming couplet to conclude the play ('Of one so young, so rich in nature's store, / Who could not say, "'Tis pity she's a whore?"'), he condenses into two lines of iambic pentameter both the 'lightness of title' and 'gravity of subject' Ford mentions in his dedication (5.6.162–3). The tinny-sounding couplet perfectly encapsulates this play's uneasy union of comic and tragic elements: of sounds that pierce and kill with words that misfire; of bodies that pulse with smothered sounds, with hearts that are dumbly, yet almost shriekingly, silent. Unlike *The Revenger's Tragedy*, which concludes with a kind of generic in-joke (that revengers, no matter how savvy, will be made to 'confess' their crimes in ways that guarantee their own destruction), there is nothing funny about *'Tis Pity*'s hyper-generic awareness. It is horrifically relentless, the revenge itself ham-fistedly literal. This seems, in fact, to be what Giovanni's onstage listeners cannot accept: the blunt literalness of his acts. 'Have you all no faith / To credit yet my triumphs? Here I swear . . . / These hands have from her bosom ripped this heart' (5.6.54–8).

It is a quality Ford's critics have long had trouble accepting as well. For earlier scholars, the spectacular sensationalism of *'Tis Pity*'s ending points up the play's belatedness, the sense that it comes at the tail-end of a once-vibrant theatrical tradition. According to T. B. Tomlinson, for example, 'the need to cultivate sadism and unnatural sex relationships of the kind Ford displays herald the exhaustion of the literary convention, the increasing temptation to re-invigorate it by concentrating more and more on the abnormal, the merely stimulating'.[52] Yet the 'too-muchness' of this ending, like that of the thick patchwork of intertheatrical references woven throughout the play, could ultimately be the point. Collectively, these references threaten to bury Ford's play under the weight of the theatre's own accumulated history and, in the process, to stifle theatregoers with an almost incestuous dramatic self-referentiality. This is the challenge that faces all playwrights, and all theatregoers, operating within the vividly self-aware, and by now well-established, cultural institution of London's commercial theatres in the final decade of their operation: how is the theatre to make use of its own history without being buried alive within it? Such questions would have been even more pressing for those authors who, like Ford and Shirley, were writing from within the genres of revenge tragedy and city comedy – which, as I have been arguing throughout this book, developed out of a dialectical relationship spanning several decades of theatrical performance. By the time *'Tis Pity* was first performed, these genres had become almost hysterically self-aware, an effect that is felt throughout the Cockpit's repertoire, with its persistent mingling of elements from these two genres, again and again, in a single play. And it is not just felt within, but is in many ways the subject of, Ford's urban tragedy – a city comedy–revenge tragedy blend that is relentlessly, even obsessively, preoccupied with its own formal history.

'Calm Ears'

As different as they are in mood, content and form, then, *'Tis Pity She's a Whore* and *The Ball* have a surprising amount in common, both with each other and with the rest of the Cockpit's 1630s repertoire. It is tempting to see these similarities as developing out of a shared sense of what the Cockpit's audiences might want, or expect, to see and hear at this particular playhouse. Dramatists' pointed, almost winking use of eavesdropping and railing, and of the kind of formal mingling these dramatic features so often signalled, could have helped forge a reputation for the Cockpit as a site for sophisticated formal and auditory play, as well as for deeply self-referential theatrical productions. If the Blackfriars' gentlemen-amateurs were branding their playhouse as a destination for the socially and culturally elite, then the Cockpit's dramatists may have been building a name for its rival as a site for the theatrically knowledgeable.[53]

Consider, for example, Shackerley Marmion's *The Antiquary*, a city comedy that includes an elaborate inset performance sending up some of revenge tragedy's most recognisable features.[54] Like *The Ball* and *'Tis Pity She's a Whore*, *The Antiquary* is a formal hybrid that celebrates its audience's assumed knowledge of theatrical conventions and their aural cues. As a crowd of characters listen in, the seemingly guilt-ridden revenger, Bravo, addresses his murdered victim's ghost:

> Look where the ghost appears, his wounds fresh bleeding,
> He frowns, and threatens me, could the substance
> Do nothing, and will shadow's revenge?
> . . .
> What's he that seeks to hide himself? come forth thou mortall,
> Thou art a traytor or a murderer:
> Oh is it you? (sigs K^v–K2^v)

Bravo's speech recalls the glut of ghosts stalking the early modern stage and the revenge tragedies in which so many of them appear. His final line ('Oh is it you?') could be a direct reference to the same unknown play skewered in Ben Jonson's *Poetaster* ('Who cries out murder? Lady, is it you?'), while his speech's hyperbolic metatheatricality recalls that of specific plays, like *The Spanish Tragedy*, and parodies the use of such language more generally.[55] The whole speech, however, is a fake – an elaborate performance organised by Bravo (who turns out to be Aurelio's father in disguise) and his future daughter-in-law, Lucretia, in order to scare the elderly lecher, Moccinigo, straight. As Moccinigo listens in, suddenly he cries out, 'How can you have the heart to look upon him? pray let me go, I feel a loosnesse in my belly' (sig. K2^r). Seeing and hearing Bravo's performance affects Moccinigo more than the other listeners because he is guilty of having attempted to plot Aurelio's death, but Moccinigo's involuntary physical response is represented as being of a piece with his desire for revenge in the first place. Both are a form of incontinence, or an inability to control oneself, that is embarrassing, uncivil and linked to old age.[56] Marmion's comedy seems, then, to be parodying revenge tragedy and the desires and passions that fuel its central action. It is the old men in this play who long for vengeance, and it is the younger characters (Lucretia, Aurelio) who plot how to cure them of their incontinence. That they do so through the careful application of a mini-revenge play, however, which does what *all* revenge tragedies suggest they are capable of doing (working an involuntary, in this instance restorative, physical transformation upon them), complicates this seemingly simple parodic structure. The scene both mocks and depends upon the revenge tragedy model of violent audition, assuming on the part of playgoers an impressive generic competency.

My point is that by the mid-1630s, when *The Antiquary* was first performed, Bravo's old-fashioned sounding speech and Moccinigo's incontinent reception of it could not *help* but function synecdochally. *The Antiquary*, like *The Ball* and *'Tis Pity*, echo earlier revenge tragedies and city comedies, both individually and collectively, in ways that the Cockpit's listeners are expected to hear, recognise and appreciate. It is not that this expectation is new, but that it has intensified over time – as have the number and the intricacy of the references themselves – accumulating into what can seem, to us at least, to be exquisitely, baroquely self-reflective productions.

This relentless self-referentiality could be seen as the inevitable outcome of the 'exhaustion ... of literary convention', as Tomlinson put it – a sign that the theatre of the 1630s had run out of ideas.[57] Or it could be understood, as I have been arguing it should be, as part of a much larger and longer theatrical tradition – one that dates back even to the very first decades of the commercial drama's existence – of examining its own aural impact. As Agnes Mure Mackenzie put it in 1927: 'To turn from Middleton at his best, Tourneur and Webster, to Beaumont and Fletcher, Massinger and Ford, is like coming out of a thunderstorm into – a theatre.'[58] But this is precisely the point. To attend *The Ball*, *'Tis Pity* or any number of other Cockpit plays, is to engage in vigorous and thoughtful experiments with what were by then well-established rules of playing. The Cockpit's comedies, tragedies and tragicomedies are always, at least in part, about the theatre itself – about its history, its conventions and above all its sounds – as well as about the ways in which audiences were expected and being trained to hear them. They are, in short, about the theatre's development into an integrated institution – a collectively produced commercial entertainment with an established set of practices, codes and traditions – and about the role which audition has played in shaping its history.[59]

The Prologue to Shirley's 1634 *The Example* speaks to an audience that is understood to be a productive member of that institution – knowledgeable about its practices and capable of determining the shape of its aesthetic output. Such thinking inspires what initially sounds like an anxious plea: 'we have nam'd our play / THE EXAMPLE', Shirley's Prologue begins, 'and for aught we know it may be made one':

> since the praise
> Of wit and judgment is not, now a days,
> Owing to them that write; but he that can
> Talk loud, and high, is held the witty man,
> And censures finely, rules the box, and strikes
> With his court nod consent to what he likes. (Prologue, ll. 7–12)

Shirley's complaint about 'loud' playgoers who 'censure finely' echoes George Donne's, which I quoted above (that 'roare[rs]' are shouting down good poets: '*HE is THE WIT'S; His NOYSE doth sway*'). It also, of course, sounds an awful lot like Ben Jonson: for example, his complaint in the Induction to *Bartholomew Fair* about playgoers who sit 'on the bench' and 'indict and arraign plays daily'.[60] For Shirley, the answer to this problem of 'loud' 'censure' is not to banish would-be critics, but to welcome them, provided that they keep an open ear. It is not just, as I argued at the beginning of this chapter, that audiences are encouraged to appreciate more than 'one stage' (and consequently more than one style of 'voice and gesture'). They are also urged to hear thoughtfully and attentively, and above all to hear 'calm[ly]'. Having dismissed those 'delinquents' whom the Prologue imagines do not belong in this particular playhouse to begin with, it continues,

> to the rest we say,
> Hear patiently ere you condemn the play.
> 'Tis not the author's confidence, to dare
> Your judgments, but your calm ears to prepare,
> That, if for mercy, you can find no room,
> He prays that mildly, you pronounce his doom.

There is no hope, in this space, that playgoers will *not* judge; and indeed, judging seems to be part of the pleasure of playgoing, as well as part of the playgoer's expected and anticipated role at the Cockpit. All that can be asked is that theatregoers prepare their critical faculty by first preparing their ears. And this is what the poet, via the actors, requests the audience to do. Rather than drawing up a contract and demanding a certain kind of behaviour or response, the Prologue asks that theatregoers participate in the play's production, and that they do so more 'mildly' than they may otherwise be inclined. In other words, the Prologue assumes a posture of deep respect towards its audience, complimenting them in order to achieve a particular end (a favourable response, rather than the 'loud talk' and 'censure' the poet fears), but also to prepare them for the auditory *work* that follows. Part of this work, to return to Mackenzie's complaint, is to hear the 'thunderstorms' that precede, and echo within, the plays of this theatre.

Afterword: Behind the Hangings

I want to conclude my discussion of the Cockpit's 1630s repertoire by thinking briefly about its afterlife in mid-seventeenth-century England.

A strange story recounted in William Sanderson's *Aulicus Coquinariae* (London, 1650) offers the tantalising possibility that the conventions outlined above continued to shape thinking about sound and its reception outside the playhouse as well as within it, even after the theatres had been shut down at the start of the Civil War.[61] It might therefore offer another way into considering the relationship between the formal, sonic contests that I have been tracing throughout this book and the culture of which early modern London's commercial theatre was a part.

Sanderson's pamphlet describes a supposedly real-life performance of highly artificial overhearing that could be borrowed directly from the stage. Sometime during 1617–19, Anne Lake, Lady Ros and her mother accused the Countess of Exeter of having tried to poison her. According to Sanderson, King James investigated the 'quarrel' (which had been 'blazon'd at Court, to the *King's eare*') with great patience, '*examin[ing]* each party' 'as privately as could be, singly' and then consenting to read 'a whole sheet of paper' presented to him by the Lakes, which they claimed contained the Countess's confession (sig. H3ᵛ). After demanding of the Lakes the '*place, time, and occasion*' of its being written, the King was told that the Countess had made her confession at Wimbledon, and that she wrote it out while situated 'at the *Window*, in the upper end of the great *Chamber* . . . in presence of the *Mother* and the *Daughter*, the Lord *Rosse*, and one *Diego* a *Spaniard* his confiding *Servant*'. The Lakes insisted on the letter's veracity even after it was proved a forgery, and at the King's suggestion, they promised to produce another witness:

> they assure[d] *him*, That one *Sarah Swarton*, their *Chamberesse* stood behind the hanging, at the entrance of the *Room*, and heard the *Countesse* reade over, what she had *writ*. (sig. H4ᵛ)

The account reads like the summary of a stage play, with an eavesdropping servant lurking behind the hangings of a private residence's great room as the telltale, confessional letter is read aloud. Doubtless informed by the legal imperative to witness, an anticipation of the need to provide proof, the description also calls to mind the countless 'discoveries' of violent deeds supplied by murderers' spontaneous, seemingly wholly unprompted, confessions (although, in this instance, the 'confession' is false). There is even a 'confiding' Spanish servant. But then the account gets even stranger:

> To make further *tryal*, the *King* in a hunting journy, at *New Park* neer Wimbleton, gallops thither, viewes the *Room*; observing the great distance of the *Window*, from the lower end of the Roome, and placing himself, behind

the *hanging*, and so other *Lords* in turn; they could not *hear* one *speak aloud*,[62] from the *window*. Then the *House-Keeper* was call'd, who protested those hangings had constantly furnisht that *room*, for 20. Years; which the *King* observed, to be two foot *short* of the ground, and might discover the *woman*, if hidden behind them. I may present also, the King saying, *oaths cannot confound my sight*. (sigs H4^v–H5^r)

Here, sound and sight become tools for measuring space and, by extension, for testing the veracity of the Lakes' claim. If the King, who has stowed himself behind the hangings, cannot hear what is being said by the window, then the 'place' offered by the Lakes (to the King's demanded '*place, time, and occasion*') cannot be accurate, and the whole story crumbles. But this highly stylised performance of eavesdropping is also just that – a performance – staged for the benefit of an audience of lords. It is as much entertainment as evidence-gathering, as the King re-enacts (and then invites the lords to re-enact his *own* performance, in turn) of the maid Sarah Swarton's overhearing. As in *The Traitor* and *The Ball*, eavesdropping becomes a layered, almost nested, activity, performed by teams of speakers and listeners over and against one another. There is a kind of hyper-theatricality to this performance, an exaggeration brought on through elaborate repetition. And, finally, in the King's gesture towards the two-foot gap between the hangings and the floor, there is also a touch of farce. The scene, in short, veers between the tragic and the comic, the deadly serious and the seriously funny, as an actual woman's innocence or guilt is tested, but at the same time a servant's feet (and a King's) are seen to be poking out from beneath a comically short set of hangings.

The point is not that William Sanderson borrowed details of his description of James's listening from a particular play, or even from a group or category of plays; rather, it is that regardless of whether or not Sanderson had ever been to a playhouse, the elements of performance discussed in this chapter (which are themselves highly elaborate reflections on much earlier, by now well-established dramatic features) seem to have affected how individuals thought about the world around them. Sanderson's account makes sense without a single theatrical referent, but it makes much more sense, and is therefore made much more convincing, by having access to a whole storehouse of such references. The anecdote, which admittedly is too idiosyncratic to be used as the basis for making grand historical claims – and which is itself, most likely, a fabrication – nonetheless shows us some of the ways in which the theatre, to again paraphrase Douglas and Isherwood, could be good for thinking in early modern England. How else, after *Hamlet*, let alone after the host of hybrid Jacobean revenge plays it inspired, was one to imagine eavesdropping as a means of attaining evidence? Sanderson's hangings, like Shirley's in *The Traitor*, are so crowded with the theatre's history that, in a sense, it does not matter whether Sanderson himself was even aware of it. From our entirely different perspective, it is impossible not to hear these echoes.

Notes

1. William Hopkins, 'To my Friend M. D'Avenant, on his legitimate Poeme', *The Just Italian* (London, 1630), sig. A3^r.
2. The phrases are all taken from Thomas Carew's 'To my worthy friend, M. D'Avenant, Upon his Excellent Play, The Just Italian', *The Just Italian*, cited above. All but the phrase 'Now noise prevails' (which appears at sig. A3^v) are found at sig. A4^r.
3. John Fox, 'To my learned friend James Shirley upon his Grateful Servant', *The Grateful Servant* (London, 1630), sig. A1^r; Thomas Randolph, untitled poem, *The Grateful Servant*, sig. A3^r.
4. Andrew Gurr outlines and criticises this characterisation of the dispute in *The Shakespearian Playing Companies*, p. 151.
5. Shirley, *Dramatic Works and Poems*, vol. 3, ed. Gifford and Dyce.
6. A survey of the roughly thirty-seven new plays performed at the Cockpit between 1629 and 1639 reveals a wide range of dramatic genres and poetic styles. Of these, two have been classified by contemporary scholars as histories: John Ford's *Perkin Warbeck* and Robert Davenport's *King John and Matilda* (although the latter identifies itself as a 'tragedy' on its title page as well as in its dedication and running title). One, Thomas Heywood's *Love's Mistress*, has been called both a classical legend and a masque, and another two are pastoral tragicomedies (Rutter's *Shephered's Holiday* and Glapthorne's *Argalus and Parthenia*). The remaining thirty-two plays can be divided into tragedies, tragicomedies and comedies, and while it is difficult to draw distinct lines between these categories, it is safe to say that the majority of these fall into either the comic or tragicomic (as opposed to the tragic) camp. On tragicomedy as a form and the difficulty, even reluctance, of early modern playwrights to provide a definition for it, see Gordon McMullan and Jonathan Hope's introduction to *The Politics of Tragicomedy*. My chronology, here and throughout this chapter, is based on S. Schoenbaum's revision to Alfred Harbage's *Annals of English drama, 975–1700*; and on Andrew Gurr's 'A Select List of Plays and Their Playhouses', *The Shakespearean Stage*, pp. 232–3.
7. Martin Butler defines Town culture as belonging to 'that fashionable society which, though partly overlapping with the court, was also distinct from it and had a separateness and identity of its own' (p. 109); its members were 'the precursors of the Restoration *beau monde*, a class coming to London principally as a place of leisure' in the 1630s (p. 102). See Butler, *Theatre and Crisis*.
8. Carew, 'To my Friend M. D'Avenant', sig. A4^r.
9. It is tempting, though almost definitely wrong, to imagine the unusual typesetting of this line as suggesting an uptick in volume, or even a shout.

10. For the most part, this is a male character type. Moll (Frith) Cutpurse of Middleton and Dekker's *The Roaring Girl* is the famous exception. I am grateful to Gavin Hollis for shaping my discussion of railing in Caroline drama through his comments on an earlier draft of this chapter.
11. Shirley, *Dramatic Works and Poems*, vol. 4, 4.2, pp. 158–9. The edition is not lineated.
12. Nabbes, *The Bride*, in *The Works of Thomas Nabbes*, ed. Bullen, vol. 2, p. 5. Subsequent citations to the play are taken from this edition, which is not lineated.
13. Ford, *The Lady's Trial*, ed. Hopkins, 2.1.62–70.
14. Glapthorne, *Argalus and Parthenia*, sigs B3^v and D4^v.
15. These include, in roughly chronological order of performance, *King John and Matilda* (1628–34), *The Grateful Servant* (1629), *Love's Cruelty* (1631), *The Traitor* (1631), *Love's Sacrifice* (1632?), *Hyde Park* (1632), *'Tis Pity She's a Whore* (1629?–33), *The Ball* (1632), *Perkin Warbeck* (1629–34), *Covent Garden* (1633), *The Bird in a Cage* (1633), *The Example* (1634), *The Opportunity* (1634), *The Prisoners* (1632–6), *The Antiquary* (1634–6), *The Coronation* (1635), *The Lady of Pleasure* (1635), *The Lady's Trial* (1638), *Wit in a Constable* (1636–8), *The Bride* (1638) and *The Bloody Banquet* (1639). A compelling case for a much earlier date for *The Bloody Banquet* is made by Gary Taylor and Julia Gasper in Taylor and Lavagnino eds, *Thomas Middleton and Early Modern Textual Culture*, pp. 364–8.
16. Davenport, *King John and Matilda*, sig. H4^v. Subsequent citations are to this edition.
17. Glapthorne, *Wit in a Constable*, sig. G3^v.
18. Shirley, *Dramatic Works and Poems*, vol. 2, 4.1, p. 155. The edition is not lineated. Subsequent citations to *The Traitor* will be taken from this edition, with Act, Scene and page numbers provided in the main text.
19. See *The Opportunity*, in Shirley, *Dramatic Works and Poems*, vol. 3, 2.3, p. 400.
20. Ford's play is also referenced through the supposedly incestuous romance of Cornelia and her 'brother', Borgia, who turns out not to be Borgia, but Aurelio in disguise.
21. On the first and second point, see Orlin, *Locating Privacy in Tudor London*, esp. pp. 173–92; and Gowing, *Domestic Dangers*, pp. 98–9. On eavesdropping as pastime, see Griffiths, 'Meanings of Nightwalking in Early Modern England'. John Rastell's legal dictionary, *Les Termes de la Ley*, defines 'Euesdroppers' as 'such as stand vnder walles or windowes by night or day to heare newes and to carrie them to others to make strife and debate amongst their Neighboures, those are euill Members in the Commonwealth and therefore by the Statute of Westminster I. cap. 33 are to bee punished. And this misdemeanor is presentable and punishable in the Courte Leete, Kitch.fol.ii', p. 191.
22. 'eavesdrop', v.; 'eavesdrip', 'eavesdrop', n. *OED*
23. Although, as R. Malcolm Smuts points out, the West End was not as homogeneously privileged as is often assumed. See 'The Court and Its Neighborhood'.
24. Zucker, 'Covent Garden', in *The Places of Wit in Early Modern English Comedy*, pp. 102–43.

25. On the association of these (and other) outdoor spaces with a desire for privacy, see Crane, 'Illicit Privacy and Outdoor Spaces in Early Modern England'.
26. Its revenge plots include: the rejected suitors of the wealthy widow, Lucina, seek revenge against her when they learn of their humiliation; the ladies Rosamond and Honoria, who are initially 'in contention' with one another for Lord Rainbow's affections, vow revenge when they learn he has mocked them to the cynic Barker (1.2, p. 16); and, finally, Jack Freshwater, the 'pretend traveler' whose debtors refuse to repay him on his 'return', decides to go abroad out of vengeance: 'I'll venture one drowning to be reveng'd' just moments before the play ends (5.1, p. 91). These and all subsequent citations to *The Ball* are taken from Shirley, *Dramatic Works and Poems*, vol. 3.
27. This is not the only incidence of railing in Shirley's play. Each time railing occurs, it introduces a rupture in civility that is figured both sonically and physically. Cf. Barker's threat to 'kick ... to death' the French dancing master, Monsieur Le Frisk, who has mocked him for the difficulty he has in learning French steps. Le Frisk responds to Barker's insult ('jackalent') in kind: 'Jack-a-lent! ... if I had my weapon you durst not affront me.' A delighted Lord Rainbow, listening in on their exchange, announces, 'Rail upon him, monsieur, I'll secure thee; ha, ha, ha!' (3.2, p. 39). Barker's inability to modulate his tone and control his tongue (as well as the French dancing master's inability to keep from 'railing' in return) similarly identify the men as failing to embody the new masculine ideals emerging within this culture of manners.
28. The effect is further highlighted in Scutilla's scoffingly dismissive response: 'There is no danger, madam; let us hear 'em; / If they scold, we two shall be hard enough for 'em, / An they were twenty' (3.4, p. 50).
29. All subsequent citations to *'Tis Pity* are taken from Sonia Massai's edition, *'Tis Pity She's a Whore*, The Arden Early Modern Drama series.
30. Neill, '"What strange riddle's this?"'. Of course, the heart is never 'just' flesh, particularly since it is Annabella's heart we are told we are seeing. According to William Slights, the heart 'preserves a magical aura that keeps it from being simply a bloody piece of meat or an affectively neutral specimen from the anatomist's laboratory' even in this final scene, with its grisly literalisation of 'affective metaphors' (p. 35). Lisa Hopkins finds the metaphorical meanings of the heart to be more resilient in this scene than does Neill, arguing that here (and in other of his late plays), Ford is willing to 'let [the heart's] most obvious and traditional meaning stand ... unchallenged' (p. 154). I agree that the heart is never just a lump of flesh, but the horror of this scene lies in its perverse insistence that it may in fact be just that. See Slights, *The Heart in the Age of Shakespeare* and Hopkins, *John Ford's Political Theatre*.
31. See, for instance, Catherine Silverstone's claim that while Annabella's 'heart is obsessively referred to and both metaphorically and literally anatomized', her heart nonetheless 'refuses to give up its secrets' (p. 84). Silverstone, 'Fatal Attraction'.
32. Like the Jacobean revenge tragedies with which it has so much in common, Ford's play includes episodes of exquisitely dark humour, but it goes beyond

them in its wholesale incorporation of formal features firmly associated with the city comedy genre. For example, the foolish heir, Bergetto, who loves puppet shows and marmalade, would be perfectly at home in one of Ben Jonson's turn-of-the-century London comedies; yet he is killed midway through the play in a way that crucially redirects Ford's plot. A stock city comedy figure, Bergetto is not incidental, but vital to *'Tis Pity*'s tragic action. Verna Foster labels the play a 'city tragedy', calling it 'a perfect tragic analogue to the greatest Jacobean city comedies'. See Foster, *"Tis Pity She's a Whore* as City Tragedy', p. 182. At the same time, *'Tis Pity* is also very much a tragedy of revenge. Multiple characters seek revenge, and for the most part these revenges are delayed until the play's final moments. Their performance is elaborate and apocalyptic, resulting in the destruction not of an entire royal family (as in *The Spanish Tragedy*'s 'whole succeeding hope [of] Spain'), but of all secular civic authority: Parma's merchant class, figured in the wealthy citizen Florio's family, is wiped out, and so too is the nobleman Soranzo, leaving only the morally dubious Cardinal to deliver this play's deeply unsatisfying moral.

33. For example: 'These words wound deeper than your sword could do', Annabella confesses to a furious Soranzo in Act Four (4.3.131).
34. On Annabella's association with this space, see Hopkins, *"Tis Pity She's a Whore* and the Space of the Stage'.
35. Two drawings, possibly by Inigo Jones in 1617 or by his assistant, John Webb, at a much later date, have long been assumed to give us a sense of what the Cockpit looked like. While it is unclear, as Frances Teague points out, whether these images 'depict buildings to be built or renovated, plans that may or may not have been realized' or 'indeed, if they even represent the building in question', the drawings do give some indication as to how a cockpit might be converted into an indoor playhouse. And since this is precisely what the Cockpit was – a converted game house – their value in helping to imagine the Cockpit's architecture seems indisputable, at least in the years before it was burned down during the apprentices' riot of 1617 (and, I would argue, even after the Cockpit was rebuilt and reopened three months later). Even without definite knowledge of the Cockpit's structure and design, however, it seems safe to assume that the balcony was an intermediate space. See Teague, 'The Phoenix and the Cockpit-in-Court Playhouses', p. 243.
36. On the materiality of the voice, see Gina Bloom, *Voice in Motion*. On the materiality of spoken confessions, see my 'Hearing Iago's Withheld Confession'.
37. Massai, 'Introduction', in *'Tis Pity*, pp. 44–6.
38. While *'Tis Pity*'s audience is not exposed to either of the lovers' confessions, they do hear the Friar's responses, which recapitulate their speeches in vividly titillating terms: he speaks of 'lawless sheets' and 'secret incests', and warns Annabella that Giovanni will groan in hell for 'each kiss' given 'when she did yield to lust' (3.6.25, 26, 27, 30).
39. Other critics have noted the ways in which the spatial logic of *'Tis Pity*, particularly when performed in the physical space of an indoor, private theatre, invokes the claustrophobia of incest. See Foster, *"Tis Pity She's a Whore* as City Tragedy', p. 184, and Massai, 'Introduction', p. 45. Hopkins discusses

the relationship between the spatial logic of Ford's play and its impulse to expose private interiors in *"Tis Pity She's a Whore* and the Space of the Stage'. Zenon Luis-Martinez makes a similar point in passing in *In Words and Deeds*, p. 196 (also qtd. in Hopkins, p. 162).
40. When Annabella 'unripp[s]' her 'soul so foul and guilty' through confessional speech, the Friar declares her 'Almost condemned alive' (3.6.8). For the Friar, it is as if Annabella has been buried while still breathing, smothered under the weight of her (until now) unspoken sin. (That the child of this act grows within her, and must now be concealed under the cover of marriage to another man, doubles and even trebles this sense of a living burial.)
41. And again: 'I carry hell about me', he later insists, 'all my blood / Is fired in swift revenge' (4.3.153–4).
42. And Parma is rotten with secrets *and* revengers. When Vasquez assures Hippolita that he will remain 'secret to [her] counsels' and assist her in seeking revenge against Soranzo, he promises 'never [to] disclose it till it be effected' (2.2.134, 163–4). Keeping her plot 'secret' means storing this knowledge silently within himself and not 'disclosing' it through speech. The *OED* divides the definitions for 'disclose' into 'physical' and 'nonphysical' senses, but when disclosures are being made verbally, the two senses inform one another: disclosing a secret, especially one as 'foul and guilty' as revenge or incest, entails the venting of corrosive matter (secrets) materially – that is, through speech, which is itself comprised of breath and sound (3.6.2).
43. A useful summary of the play's indebtedness to earlier drama is provided by Hopkins, who points out that the play 'is shaped and conditioned by a number of previous plays' (p. 2). For Hopkins, these include Shakespeare's *Romeo and Juliet* and Middleton's *Women Beware Women*, as well as (more provocatively) *A Midsummer Night's Dream*. See Hopkins, 'Introduction', in *'Tis Pity She's a Whore: A Critical Guide*, pp. 1–13.
44. See Neill, '"What strange riddle's this?"', and Hattaway, 'Scene Building'.
45. First published in 1633, the play was performed by the King's Men at Blackfriars sometime between 1625 and 1633. All subsequent citations to *The Broken Heart* are taken from T. J. B. Spenser's edition.
46. The revelations are that the King, her father, is dead; that her husband's sister has been 'starved'; and finally that her husband has been 'murdered, murdered cruelly' (5.2.13, 16).
47. How, exactly, this process worked was in the sixteenth and seventeenth centuries a source of some contention. John Banister writes, summarising Galen, 'as touchyng the instruments that restore the ayrie substaunce, whiche continually waste, and refresh the innated heate ... that, of the ayre drawen in by the lunges, part is receiued by the surcles and braunches of the veniall Arterie, and there hence, beyng prepared by the elaboration of the lunges, is by the same vessel caryed into the left ventricle of the hart, where, metyng with the bloud lately strayned through the hedge betwene the ii. Ventricles, it doth together by the workyng of the hart, ordaine that famous composition, the vitall spirite'. Banister, *The Historie of Man*, sig. CCi^r.
48. He adds, 'They are called by the name of eares, not for their use, nor any

action, but for similitude sake, which they obtaine, in situation, like unto the proper eares'. Banister, *The Historie of Man*, sig. Ddi^r.
49. Paré, *The Workes of that famous Chirurgion Ambrose Parey*, p. 145.
50. This seems to be part of what troubled early-twentieth-century critics of Ford, like T. B. Tomlinson, who complained that in *'Tis Pity*, Ford is essentially having too much fun (he accuses Ford, as well as John Fletcher, of a 'frank enjoyment of sin'). See Tomlinson, *A Study of Elizabethan and Jacobean Tragedy*, p. 265.
51. In fact, despite the horror and poignancy of Ford's final scene, it also incorporates features familiar from other genres: a comic revelation (Richardetto, long thought dead, turns out to be alive and well) is paired with the promise of another, oddly festive gathering still to come. 'We shall have time / To talk at large of all' the Cardinal assures the dead Soranzo's guests. Complicating things yet further is the fact that this comic revelation may itself kick off a new revenge cycle ('Sir, was it you –' Donado asks Richardetto, seeming to realise he may have had a hand in his son's murder).
52. Without sharing Tomlinson's moralising impulse, I nonetheless want to take seriously his claims about 'the exhaustion of . . . literary convention', which he shares with Bradbrook and Oliver, quoted above. See Tomlinson, *A Study of Elizabethan and Jacobean Tragedy*, p. 85.
53. Although a number of playwrights wrote for both houses (as well as for other theatres), the contest initiated in 1630 via the printed editions of Davenant's *The Just Italian* and Shirley's *The Grateful Servant*, which I discussed above, suggests that certain authors, at least, saw Blackfriars and the Cockpit as existing in competition with one another.
54. *The Antiquary* (London, 1641). This is the only one of the dramatist's three extant plays to have been staged at the Cockpit. *Holland's Leaguer* and *A Fine Companion* were both performed at Salisbury Court.
55. Bravo imagines the 'horrid tragedy' of Aurelio's murder being 'acted over every night in hell' to great 'applause' in an 'infernall Theater', where 'squalid Actors' perform with 'tragick pomp' (sig. K2v).
56. Lorenzo, who like Moccinigo is described in the cast list as 'an old Gentleman', announces in Act One, 'Revenge! of all the passions of my blood, / 'Tis the most sweet; I should grow fat to think on't' (sig. B4v).
57. Tomlinson, *A Study*, p. 85.
58. See Mackenzie, *The Playgoer's Handbook*, p. 129.
59. See Zucker and Farmer, 'Introduction', in *Localizing Caroline Drama*, pp. 1–16, at p.1.
60. Jonson, *Bartholomew Fair*, New Mermaids, ed. Hibbard, Induction, l. 95.
61. [Sanderson], *Aulicus Coquinariae*. I am grateful to Hillary Nunn for sharing with me her paper on this pamphlet at the Shakespeare Association of America conference in Toronto in 2013.
62. The original accound reads '*speaka loud*'.

Chapter 6

Epilogue

In 1668, after attending his seventh performance of *The Tempest, or the Enchanted Island*, Pepys writes that he slipped backstage to ask the actor Henry Harris 'to repeat to me the words of the Echo, while I writ them down'. Though he had tried to record the part as it was being performed, 'having done it without looking upon my paper', he explains, 'I [found] I could not read the blacklead', or pencil. 'But now, I have got the words clear.'[1] Sitting in the newly darkened Restoration playhouse, attempting to jot down the words to a song he had heard at least six times before, Pepys cuts a figure that is at once both familiar and, in many ways, entirely new. His dramatic consumption both reflects and is part of the cultivation of his social ambition, marking affiliations with men and women of influence while simultaneously signalling Pepys's suitability for such circles. As such, it is anything but unthinking or accidental. But as Pepys's diary entries also repeatedly show, he could be just as interested in what was happening offstage as he was in what was happening on it. In fact, Pepys's first account of Dryden and Davenant's play is strikingly different from the one quoted above:

> [November 7, 1667] Up, and at the office hard all the morning; and at noon resolve with Sir W. Penn to go see *The Tempest*, an old play of Shakespeares, acted here the first day. And so my wife and girl and W. Hewer by themselfs, and Sir W. Penn and I afterward by ourselfs, and forced to sit in the side Balcone over against the Musique-room at the Dukes-House, close by my Lady Dorsett and a great many great ones: the house mighty full, the King and Court there, and the most innocent play that ever I saw, and a curious piece of Musique in an Echo of half-sentences, the Echo repeating the former half while the man goes on to the latter, which is mighty pretty. The play no great wit; but yet good, above ordinary plays. Thence home with W. Penn, and there all mightily pleased with the play; and so to supper and to bed, after having done at the office.[2]

Unlike the avidly attentive playgoer imagined above, this one is only partly interested in the play itself. Instead, he seems much more intent on his nearness to the 'great many great ones' in attendance. Largely ignoring the business of the stage in favour of other sights and sounds, concentrating his aural attention only on parts of the production, Pepys would seem in this entry to be a playwright's worst nightmare. But even here, his theatrical audition remains active, conscious and selective. The Echo's part – the same song Pepys would later try to jot down during the performance, and then ask the actor Henry Harris to repeat to him backstage – seems already to have been of particular interest to him. It is a piece of the play that he has chosen to hear differently – fixedly, intently, doggedly.

Given Pepys's financial and emotional investment in his skill as both a singer and instrumentalist, his focus on this musical number makes sense. A kind of hearer's duet, this 'curious piece of musique', as Pepys termed it, begins with Ariel echoing Ferdinand's weary 'here I am', temporarily distracting him from the grief he feels over the supposed death of his father.[3] As Ferdinand 'sing[s]' his 'sorrows to the murmurs of this Brook', the unseen spirit answers him (3.4.25–6). The Echo therefore represents a moment of staged (pretend) composition *extempore*, in which a pair of artistically adept listeners produce music in response to one another's notes. It is a beautifully productive kind of listening, which not only creates a new piece of music (the duet itself), but also transforms Ferdinand's despair into hope:

> *Ferd. What cares or pleasures can be in this Isle?*
> *Within this desart place*
> *There lives no humane race;*
> *Fate cannot frown here, nor kind fortune smile*
> *Ariel. Kind Fortune smiles, and she*
> *Has yet in store for thee*
> *Some strange felicity.*
> *Follow me, follow me,*
> *And thou shalt see.* (ll. 36–44)

Their exchange persuades Ferdinand to 'take thy word for once' and follow the unseen singer, his experience of this desolate ('desart') place transformed from one in which fortune cannot smile to one in which 'Kind Fortune' has his felicity in store.

Over the course of the seventeenth century, from Shakespeare's romance through Dryden and Davenant's revision to the opera by Thomas Shadwell, *The Tempest* would become increasingly spectacular and more musical.[4] These successive changes would seem to complement Pepys's, and quite likely other Restoration theatregoers', tastes, as well as the auditory choices Pepys's diary suggests those tastes both reflected and informed. Pepys's 1668 entry, in which he describes himself scribbling blindly, his eyes fixed not on the paper but somewhere else, reveals a theatregoer who is especially 'tuned in' to musical innovations of the sort Shadwell would even more extensively introduce. The later, operatic revision of Shakespeare's play would have given Pepys and other auditors even more opportunities to listen to, remember and perform such pieces, suggesting a collaborative theatrical process in which actors, playgoers and playwrights are all engaged.

What is most striking, however, about Pepys's diary entries is the frankness with which he admits that such attentive, aesthetically productive listening takes *work*. In an entry dated 3 February 1668, he writes, 'this day, I took pleasure to learn the tune of the Seamens dance – which I have much desired to be perfect in, and have made myself so' (p. 48).[5] His desire to be 'perfect in' the Seamen's dance, another song from *The Tempest, or the Enchanted Island*, is only realised by 'ma[king] himself so' over time, through repeated trips to the playhouse and through whatever focused effort he spent learning it 'this day'. This may itself be a source of 'pleasure', but it is still work. The same holds true for Pepys's effort to 'get the words [to the Echo] clear'. Like the scribbling commonplacer Littleword in Thomas Nabbes's *Covent Garden*, who copies down elegant phrases he hears because 'Hee is taking a humour for a Play', Pepys sometimes needs to write in order to hear as he wishes – lastingly, productively.[6] As with Littleword's scribbling, Pepys's frantically moving pencil both displays and corrects for a kind of aural deficiency, but it does not seem to suggest in the same way a lack of wit or invention, as it does in Nabbes's play. Rather, for Pepys, who does not efface all of this effort from his diary but instead records it almost as a point of pride, it helps to demonstrate just how fully engaged a listener he can be. Recording the Echo's part is presumably part of what enables Pepys to make better use of it later on, reproducing the song at will for his own and others' consumption.

Although he exists outside this book's temporal frame, Samuel Pepys seems almost to be its inevitable endpoint. An avid theatregoer who frequently wrote in his diary about hearing and seeing plays, Pepys offers tantalising evidence of how the modes of listening outlined above may have been adapted for the Restoration theatre, and perhaps beyond. I turn to Pepys at the end of this book not to make claims about Restoration theatrical practice and auditory reception, however, but to help situate the early modern moment within a much longer theatre history. Listening has continued to matter, both as a dramatic subject and as an experience that is simultaneously felt and socially legible, long since the theatres were shut down in 1642. One need only think of the opening lines of *The Importance of Being Earnest*, when Algernon's manservant, Lane, tells him he did not hear the music he was playing because 'I didn't think it polite to listen, sir.'[7] Their exchange highlights the difference between hearing (as a not necessarily voluntary act) and listening (as an act with intention) at the very start of Wilde's play – a comedy that is formed, after all, almost entirely out of *bon mots* to be heard, appreciated and enjoyed by attentively listening playgoers. But the absurdity of Lane's response, which often elicits this play's first laugh in performance, also underlines the artificiality of such distinctions and the class differences they are intended to reify. How could two men standing in the shared space of a London flat *not* hear the same music, whether they are trying to listen to it or not? Particularly when all of us in the audience are hearing it, too?

The Importance of Being Earnest is, in many ways, a direct descendent of Jonson's *Epicoene* and the Restoration comedies of manners that first West End play helped inspire – all of which are indebted in turn to late-sixteenth-century city comedy. Part of this formal inheritance is on display in Wilde's celebration of the tasteful consumption of goods and of sounds, and in his representation of both as essential to the establishment of intimacy between men. But while listening has continued to matter, both in the theatre and outside of it, through the Restoration and beyond, the association of particular dramatic sounds with emerging formal categories and the modes of reception advanced by each are emphatically early modern. Paying attention to theatrical sound and its reception in this period can therefore help us to understand how the codes and conventions through which the period's drama became legible took shape in performance.

It can also help, I think, to challenge some of the assumptions that we hold about how these plays were understood in connection with one another. One of my goals throughout this book has been to rethink the patterns of relationships through which early modern commercial theatre was experienced, felt and understood by its audiences, and to ask how the experiencing, feeling and understanding of its sounds may in turn have shaped the formal and aesthetic history of early modern drama. But one of the ancillary pleasures of writing this determinedly historicist project has been in considering how many of the questions that it raises are, perhaps surprisingly, still with us. In cities like New York, where I currently live and write, learning how to process sounds selectively remains a pressingly practical concern. And as anyone who has taken public transport, or waited in a train station, bus station or airport during the ascendancy of the iPhone knows, who and what we choose to hear – or, perhaps even more importantly, who and what we choose *not* to hear – are socially, politically and ethically meaningful and determinant acts. By listening to music, an audio book or a podcast, individuals become linked into a network of listeners who are making similar choices; while in public spaces, these same individuals are also sharply distinguishing or even isolating themselves from the people sitting near them, from the men and women asking for change, from the sound of other people's music, voices and breath. These acts of auditory isolation undercut some of the potential for contact that spaces like the bus or subway, as nodes of unexpected social interaction, have for so long made possible in urban settings. Hearing continues to matter to lived, embodied social experience in the twenty-first century in ways that we are only beginning to understand, and that even a strictly historicist project can help, I think, to illuminate. In the early modern theatre, such questions, very differently articulated and experienced, were aesthetically, formally productive. They played a crucial role in shaping the period's drama, as well as in the development of the theatre itself as a cultural institution. I have tried to show throughout this book that such questions, then as much as now, matter for understanding the ways in which men and women experienced the world around them – outside the theatre as well as within it.

Notes

1. Pepys would see the play a total of eight times. Unless otherwise indicated, all references to Pepys's diary are from *The Diary of Samuel Pepys: A New and Complete Transcription*, ed. Latham and Matthews, here vol. 9, p. 195. I discuss the relationship between Shakespeare's play and its revision, and the role of both in the sound and reception of revenge, in 'Repeat to me the Words of the Echo'.
2. Pepys, *The Diary*, vol. 8, pp. 521–2. It is not 'an old play of Shakespeares', in fact, but the Dryden and Davenant revision that Pepys saw and heard performed.
3. 3.4.6. References to *The Tempest, or the Enchanted Island* are to that in Novak and Guffey, *The Works of John Dryden*.
4. Whether Thomas Shadwell wrote the operatic *Tempest* is a matter of debate. The attribution originates in John Downes's 1708 *Roscius Anglicanus*, which claims the play was 'made into an opera by Mr. Shadwell' (p. 64).
5. The song referred to is one sung by Stephano, Trincalo and Mustachio (the Boatswain in Shakespeare's text).
6. Nabbes, *Covent Garden*, in *The Works of Thomas Nabbes*, ed. Bullen, 4.5.
7. Wilde, *The Importance of Being Earnest*, ed. Jackson (1.1.2).

Bibliography

Agnew, Jean-Christophe. *Worlds Apart: The Market and the Theater in Anglo-American Thought, 1550–1750*. Cambridge: Cambridge University Press, 1986.
Alexander, Nigel. *Poison, Play, and Duel: A Study in Hamlet*. Lincoln, NE: University of Nebraska Press, 1971.
Altman, Joel B. *The Tudor Play of Mind: Rhetorical Inquiry and the Development of Elizabethan Drama*. Berkeley: University of California Press, 1978.
Andrews, Michael C. '*Jack Drum's Entertainment* as Burlesque', *Renaissance Quarterly* 24 (1971): 226–31.
Anon. *The True Tragedie of Richard III*. London, 1594.
Anon. *Herball, or Generall Historie of Plantes*. London, 1597.
Anon. *The Famous Victories of Henry V*. London, 1598.
Aristotle. *Aristotle's Poetics: Translated with Commentaries and Glossary*, ed. and trans. Hippocrates G. Apostle, Elizabeth A. Dobbs and Morris A. Parslow. Grinnell: Peripatetic Press, 1990.
Austern, Linda. *Music in English Children's Drama of the Later Renaissance*. Philadelphia: Gordon and Breach, 1992.
Austin, J. L. *How to Do Things with Words*, ed. J. O. Urmson and Marina Sbisà. Cambridge, MA: Harvard University Press, 1975.
Bacon, Francis. *The Advancement of Learning*, ed. William Aldis Wright. Oxford: Clarendon Press, 1876.
Baker, J. H. *An Introduction to English Legal History*. London: Reed Elsevier, 2002.
Banister, John. *The Historie of Man, sucked from the sappe of the most approued Anathomistes, in this present age, comprised in most compendious fourme, and now published in English, for the vtilitie of all godly Chirurgians, within this Realme*. London, 1578.
Barish, Jonas. *Ben Jonson and the Language of Prose Comedy*. Cambridge, MA: Harvard University Press, 1960.
Barnes, Jonathan and Suzanne Bobzien. 'Logic: "The Stoics"', in *The Cambridge History of Hellenistic Philosophy*, ed. Keimpe Algra, Jonathan Barnes, Jaap Mansfeld and Malcolm Schofield. Cambridge: Cambridge University Press, 1999, pp. 92–176.
Barnes, Peter. '*Bartholomew Fair*: All the Fun of the Fair', in *Jonsonians: Living Traditions*, ed. Brian Woolland. Aldershot: Ashgate, 2003, pp. 43–50.

Beaumont, Francis. *The Knight of the Burning Pestle*, ed. Michael Hattaway. London: New Mermaids Series, A&C Black, 2002.
Beaver, Dan. 'The Great Deer Massacre: Animals, Honor, and Communication in Early Modern England', *Journal of British Studies* 38 (1999): 187–216.
Beaver, Dan. *Hunting and the Politics of Violence before the English Civil War.* Cambridge: Cambridge University Press, 2008.
Bednarz, James P. *Shakespeare and the Poets' War.* New York: Columbia University Press, 2001.
Berek, Peter. '*Tamburlaine*'s Weak Sons: Imitation as Interpretation Before 1593', *Renaissance Drama* 13 (1982): 55–82.
Berger, Harry. *Imaginary Audition: Shakespeare on Stage and Page.* Los Angeles: University of California Press, 1989.
Berry, Philippa. 'Hamlet's Ear', *Shakespeare Survey* 50 (1997): 57–64.
Billing, Christian. 'Modelling the Anatomy Theatre and the Indoor Hall Theatre: Dissection on the Stages of Early Modern London', *Early Modern Literary Studies* 13 (2004), 1–17.
Bloom, Gina. *Voice in Motion: Staging Gender, Shaping Sound in Early Modern England.* Philadelphia: University of Pennsylvania Press, 2007.
Bloom, Harold. *Ruin the Sacred Truths: Poetry and Belief from the Bible to the Present* Cambridge, MA: Harvard University Press, 1991.
Bly, Mary. *Queer Virgins and Virgin Queans on the Early Modern Stage.* Oxford: Oxford University Press, 2000.
Bourdieu, Pierre. *Distinction: A Social Critique of the Judgement of Taste*, trans. Richard Nice. Cambridge, MA: Harvard University Press, 1984.
Bourus, Terri. *Young Shakespeare's Young Hamlet: Print, Piracy, and Performance.* New York: Palgrave Macmillan, 2014.
Bowers, Fredson. *Elizabethan Revenge Tragedy.* Princeton: Princeton University Press, 1940.
Bradbrook, M. C. *Themes and Conventions of Elizabethan Tragedy.* Cambridge: Cambridge University Press, 1935.
Braden, Gordon. *Renaissance Tragedy and the Senecan Tradition: Anger's Privilege.* New Haven, CT: Yale University Press, 1985.
Bradley, A. C. *Shakespearean Tragedy: Lectures on Hamlet, Othello, King Lear, Macbeth.* London: Macmillan and Company, 1904.
Braudel, Ferdinand. *The Wheels of Commerce*, vol. 2, *Civilization and Capitalism, 15th–18th Century.* Los Angeles: University of California Press, 1982.
Brayman Hackel, Heidi. 'The "Great Variety" of Readers and Early Modern Reading Practices', in *A Companion to Shakespeare*, ed. David Scott Kastan. Oxford: Blackwell, 1999, pp. 139–57.
Bremmer, Jan and Herman Roodenberg. *A Cultural History of Gesture.* Ithaca, NY: Cornell University Press, 1992.
Brenner, Robert. *Merchants and Revolution: Commercial Change, Political Conflict, and London's Overseas Traders, 1550–1653.* New York: Verso, 2003.
Butler, Martin. *Theatre and Crisis, 1632–1642.* Cambridge: Cambridge University Press, 1984.
Cannon, Charles D. *A Warning for Fair Women*, ed. Charles D. Cannon. The Hague: Mouton, 1975.

Cartelli, Thomas. *Marlowe, Shakespeare, and the Economy of Theatrical Experience*. Philadelphia: University of Pennsylvania Press, 1991.

Cartwright, Kent. *Theatre and Humanism: English Drama in the Sixteenth Century*. Cambridge: Cambridge University Press, 1999.

Cave, Richard Allen. 'Ben Jonson's *Every Man in His Humour*: A Case Study', in *The Cambridge History of British Theatre*, vol. 1. Cambridge: Cambridge University Press, 2004, pp. 282–97.

Chapman, George. *An Humorous Day's Mirth*. London: Printed for the Malone Society by J. Johnson at the Oxford University Press, 1938.

Chettle, Henry. *The Tragedy of Hoffman*. London: Oxford University Press, 1951.

[Chettle, Henry and Robert Greene]. *Greene's Groatsworth of Wit, Bought with a Million of Repentance (1592), Attributed to Henry Chettle and Robert Greene*, ed. D. Allen Carroll. Binghamton, NY: Medieval & Renaissance Textual Studies, 1994.

Churchill, George B. *Richard the Third up to Shakespeare*. Berlin: Mayer & Müller, 1900.

Coleridge, Samuel Taylor. *The Table Talk and Omniana of Samuel Taylor Coleridge*. London: Oxford University Press, 1917.

Cook, Ann Jennalie. *The Privileged Playgoers of Shakespeare's London, 1576–1642*. Princeton: Princeton University Press, 1981.

Cowper, William. *Anatomie of a Christian Man*. London, 1611.

Craik, Katharine and Tanya Pollard, eds. *Shakespearean Sensations: Experiencing Literature in Early Modern England*. Cambridge: Cambridge University Press, 2013.

Crane, Mary Thomas. 'Illicit Privacy and Outdoor Spaces in Early Modern England', *Journal for Early Modern Cultural Studies* 9 (2009): 4–22.

Crawford, Julie. *Marvelous Protestantism: Monstrous Births in Post-Reformation England*. Baltimore: Johns Hopkins University Press, 2005.

Crockett, Bryan. *The Play of Paradox: Stage and Sermon in Renaissance England*. Philadelphia: University of Pennsylvania Press, 1995.

Cronk, Nicholas. 'Aristotle, Horace, and Longinus: The Conception of Reader Response', in *The Cambridge History of Literary Criticism*, vol. 3, *The Renaissance*. Cambridge: Cambridge University Press, 1999, pp. 199–204.

Crooke, Helkiah. *Microcosmographia: A Description of the Body of Man. Together with the Controversies Thereto Belonging*. London, 1615.

Crooke, Helkiah. *Microcosmographia, A Description of the Body of Man*. London, 1616.

Cummings, Peter. 'Hearing in *Hamlet*: Poisoned Ears and the Psychopathology of Flawed Audition', *Shakespeare Yearbook* 1 (1990): 81–92.

Danner, Bruce. 'Speaking Daggers', *Shakespeare Quarterly* 54 (2003): 29–61.

Davenant, William. *The Just Italian*. London, 1630.

Davenport, Robert. *King John and Matilda*. London, 1655.

Dekker, Thomas. *The Seven Deadly Sins of London*, in *The Non-Dramatic Works of Thomas Dekker*, vol. 2, ed. Alexander B. Grosart. New York: Russell & Russell, 1963, pp. 1–82.

Dent, R. W. *Shakespeare's Proverbial Language: An Index*. Berkeley: University of California Press, 1981.

Dessen, Alan C. 'Robert Greene and the Theatrical Vocabulary of the Early 1590s', in *Writing Robert Greene: Essays on England's First Notorious*

Professional Writer, ed. Kirk Melnikoff and Edward Gieskes. Burlington, VT: Ashgate, 2008, pp. 25–37.
Deutermann, Allison Kay. '"Repeat to me the words of the Echo": Listening to *The Tempest*', in *Knowing Shakespeare: Senses, Embodiment and Cognition*, ed. Lowell Gallagher and Shankar Raman. New York: Palgrave Macmillan, 2010, pp. 172–91.
Deutermann, Allison Kay. 'Hearing Iago's Withheld Confession', in *Shakespearean Sensations: Experiencing Literature in Early Modern England*, ed. Katharine Craik and Tanya Pollard. Cambridge: Cambridge University Press, 2013, pp. 47–63.
Dickie, George. *The Century of Taste: The Philosophical Odyssey of Taste in the Eighteenth Century*. New York: Oxford University Press, 1996.
DiGangi, Mario. *The Homoerotics of Early Modern Drama*. Cambridge: Cambridge University Press, 1997.
Dillon, Janette. 'Clerkenwell and Smithfield as a Neglected Home of London Theatre', *The Huntington Library Quarterly* 71 (2008): 115–35.
Douglas, Mary and Baron Isherwood. *The World of Goods: Towards an Anthropology of Consumption*. New York: Routledge, 1996.
Dowland, John. *First Booke of Songes or Ayres*. London, 1597.
Downes, John. *Roscius Anglicanus*, ed. Montague Summers. New York: Ayer Publishing, 1968.
Dugan, Holly. *The Ephemeral History of Perfume: Scent and Sense in Early Modern England*. Baltimore: Johns Hopkins University Press, 2011.
Dunn, Leslie C. and Nancy A. Jones, eds. *Embodied Voices: Representing Female Vocality in Western Culture*. Cambridge: Cambridge University Press, 1994.
Dryden, John. *The Works of John Dryden*, 20 vols, ed. Edward Niles Hooker, H. T. Swedenberg, et al. Berkeley: University of California Press, 1956–2000.
Earle, John. *Micro-cosmographie, or, A Piece of the World Discovered, in Essays and Characters*. London, 1633.
Egerton, Stephen. *The Boring of the Eare*. London, 1623.
Erne, Lukas. *Shakespeare as Literary Dramatist*. Cambridge: Cambridge University Press, 2003.
Fawcett, Mary Laughlin. 'Arms/Words/Tears: Language and the Body in *Titus Andronicus*', *ELH* 50 (1983): 261–77.
Felperin, Howard. *Shakespearean Representation: Mimesis and Modernity in Elizabethan Tragedy*. Princeton: Princeton University Press, 1977.
Ferrell, Lori Anne. 'How-To Books, Protestant Kinetics, and the Art of Theology', *Huntington Library Quarterly* 71 (2008): 591–606.
Foakes, R. A. 'John Marston's Fantastical Plays: *Antonio and Mellida* and *Antonio's Revenge*', *Philological Quarterly* 41 (1962): 229–39.
Foakes, R. A. 'Tragedy at the Children's Theatres after 1600: A Challenge to the Adult Stage', in *The Elizabethan Theatre*, ii, ed. D. Galloway. Toronto: Macmillan, 1970, pp. 39–59.
Foakes, R. A., ed. *Henslowe's Diary*. Cambridge: Cambridge University Press, 2002.
Folkerth, Wes. *The Sound of Shakespeare*. New York: Routledge, 2002.
Ford, John. *The Broken Heart*, ed. T. J. B. Spencer. Manchester: Manchester University Press, 1980.

Ford, John. *The Lady's Trial*, ed. Lisa Hopkins. Manchester: Manchester University Press, 2011.
Ford, John. *'Tis Pity She's a Whore*, ed. Sonia Massai. The Arden Early Modern Drama Series. London: A & C Black, 2011.
Foster, Verna. '*'Tis Pity She's a Whore* as City Tragedy', in *John Ford: Critical Re-Visions*, ed. Michael Neill. Cambridge: Cambridge University Press, 1988, pp. 181–200.
Fox, Adam. *Oral and Literate Culture in England, 1500–1700*. New York: Oxford University Press, 2000.
Frede, Michael. 'Categories in Aristotle', in *Essays in Ancient Philosophy*. Minneapolis: University of Minnesota Press, 1987, pp. 29–48.
Gair, W. Reavley. *The Children of Paul's: The Story of a Theatre Company, 1553–1608*. New York: Cambridge University Press, 1982.
Gallagher, Lowell and Shankar Raman, eds. *Knowing Shakespeare: Sense, Embodiment and Cognition*. New York: Palgrave Macmillan, 2010.
Gants, David L. and Tom Lockwood. 'The Printing and Publishing of Ben Jonson's Works', in *The Cambridge Edition of the Works of Ben Jonson Online*. Cambridge University Press, 2014. Online. http://universitypublishingonline.org/cambridge/benjonson/k/essays/printing_publishing_essay/3/ (accessed 17 January 2016).
Geach, Peter and Max Black, eds. *Translations from the Philosophical Writings of Gottlob Frege*. Oxford: Blackwell, 1980.
Gifford, George. *A Sermon on the Parable of the Sower, taken out of the 13. of Mathew*. London, 1582.
Gilbert, Alan H., *Literary Criticism: Plato to Dryden*. New York: American Book Company, 1940.
Glapthorne, Henry. *Argalus and Parthenia*. London, 1639.
Glapthorne, Henry. *Wit in a Constable*. London, 1640.
Gosson, Stephen. *The Schoole of Abuse*. London, 1579.
Gowing, Laura. *Domestic Dangers: Women, Words, and Sex in Early Modern London*. New York: Oxford University Press, 1996.
Graham, Jean E. 'Virgin Ears: Silence, Deafness, and Chastity in Milton's *Maske*', *Milton Studies* 36 (1998): 1–17.
de Grazia, Margreta. *Hamlet without Hamlet*. Cambridge: Cambridge University Press, 2007.
Green, Reina. '"Ears Prejudicate" in *Mariam* and *Duchess of Malfi*', *Studies in English Literature, 1500–1900* 43 (2003): 459–74.
Greene, Robert. *Perimedes the Blacksmith*. London, 1588.
Greene, Robert. *Menaphon*. London, 1589.
Greene, Robert. *The Dramatic Works of Robert Greene*, 2 vols., ed. Alexander Dyce. London: William Pickering, 1831.
Griffiths, Paul. 'Meanings of Nightwalking in Early Modern England', *The Seventeenth Century* 13 (1998): 212–38.
Gross, Kenneth. *Shakespeare's Noise*. Chicago: University of Chicago Press, 2001.
Gurr, Andrew. *The Shakespearean Stage, 1574–1642*, 2nd edn. Cambridge: Cambridge University Press, 1980.
Gurr, Andrew. *The Shakespearian Playing Companies*. New York: Oxford University Press, 1996.

Gurr, Andrew. *Playgoing in Shakespeare's London*, 3rd edn. Cambridge: Cambridge University Press, 2004.
Gurr, Andrew. *The Shakespeare Company, 1594–1642*. Cambridge: Cambridge University Press, 2004.
Harbage, Alfred. *Shakespeare and the Rival Traditions*. New York: Macmillan, 1952.
Harbage, Alfred. *Annals of English drama, 975–1700: An Analytical Record of All Plays, Extant or Lost, Chronologically Arranged and Indexed by Authors, Titles, Dramatic Companies & c*. London: Methuen, 1964.
Harvey, Elizabeth D., ed. *Sensible Flesh: On Touch in Early Modern Culture*. Philadelphia: University of Pennsylvania Press, 2003.
Hattaway, Michael. 'Scene Building', in *Elizabethan Popular Theatre: Plays in Performance*. London: Routledge and Kegan Paul, 1982, pp. 56–60.
Herbert, George. *The Complete English Poems*, ed. John Tobin. London: Penguin Books, 1991.
Heywood, Thomas. *An Apology for Actors*. London, 1612.
Hillman, David. *Shakespeare's Entrails: Belief, Scepticism and the Interior of the Body*. New York: Palgrave MacMillan, 2007.
Hirschkind, Charles. *The Ethical Soundscape: Cassette Sermons and Islamic Counterpublics*. New York: Columbia University Press, 2006.
Hobgood, Allison. *Passionate Playgoing in Early Modern England*. Cambridge: Cambridge University Press, 2014.
Hockey, Dorothy C. '"Wormwood, Wormwood!"', *English Language Notes* 2 (1965): 174–7.
Hopkins, Lisa. *John Ford's Political Theatre*. Manchester: Manchester University Press, 1994.
Hopkins, Lisa. *''Tis Pity She's a Whore* and the Space of the Stage', in *'Tis Pity She's a Whore: A Critical Guide*, ed. Lisa Hopkins. London: Continuum, 2010, pp. 152–67.
Horowitz, Seth S. *The Universal Sense: How Hearing Shapes the Mind*. New York: Bloomsbury, 2012.
Howard, Jean. *Theater of a City: The Places of London Comedy, 1598–1642*. Philadelphia: University of Pennsylvania Press, 2007.
Hunt, Arnold. *The Art of Hearing: English Preachers and their Audiences, 1590–1640*. Cambridge: Cambridge University Press, 2010.
Hurley, Erin and Sara Warner. 'Affect/Performance/Politics', *Journal of Dramatic Theory and Criticism* 26 (2012): 99–107.
Hutson, Lorna. 'Liking Men: Ben Jonson's Closet Opened', *ELH* 71 (2004): 1065–96.
Ingram, R. W. 'The Use of Music in the Plays of Marston', *Music and Letters* 37 (1956): 154–64.
James, Heather. 'Dido's Ear: Tragedy and the Politics of Response', *Shakespeare Quarterly* 52 (2001): 360–82.
Jewell, Helen M. *Education in Early Modern England*. New York: St Martin's Press, 1998.
Johnson, James H. *Listening in Paris: A Cultural History*. Berkeley: University of California Press, 1995.

Jonson, Ben. *The Comical Satyre of Every Man Out of his Humor*. London: Printed [by P. Short] for William Holme, 1600.
Jonson, Ben. *Every Man in His Humour*. London: [by S. Stafford] for Walter Burre, 1601.
Jonson, Ben. *Ben Jonson*, ed. C. H. Herford, Percy Simpson and Evelyn Simpson, 11 vols. Oxford: Clarendon Press, 1925–52.
Jonson, Ben. *Discoveries, 1641. Conversations with William Drummond of Hawthornden, 1619*. Edinburgh: Edinburgh University Press, 1966.
Jonson, Ben. *Ben Jonson: Every Man in His Humour*, ed. Gabriele Bernhard Jackson. New Haven, CT: Yale University Press, 1969.
Jonson, Ben. *Every Man in His Humour: A Parallel-Text Edition of the 1601 Quarto and the 1616 Folio*, ed. J. W. Lever. Lincoln, NE: University of Nebraska Press, 1971.
Jonson, Ben. *Epicoene, or, The Silent Woman*, ed. R. V. Holdsworth. London: A&C Black, 2002.
Jonson, Ben. *Ben Jonson: The Devil is an Ass and Other Plays*, ed. Margaret Jane Kidnie. New York: Oxford University Press, 2000.
Jonson, Ben. *Every Man in His Humour*, ed. Robert Miola. Manchester: Manchester University Press, 2000.
Jonson, Ben. *Every Man out of His Humour*, ed. Helen Ostovich. Manchester: Manchester University Press, 2002.
Jonson, Ben. *Bartholomew Fair*, ed. G. R. Hibbard. London: New Mermaids Series, A&C Black, 2007.
Jonson, Ben. *Discoveries*, ed. Lorna Hutson. *The Cambridge Edition of the Works of Ben Jonson Online*. Cambridge: Cambridge University Press, 2014. Available at http://universitypublishingonline.org/cambridge/benjonson/ (accessed 28 January 2016).
Joseph, Bertram Leon. *Elizabethan Acting*. London: Oxford University Press, 1952.
Kahn, Coppélia. *Roman Shakespeare: Warriors, Wounds, and Women*. New York: Routledge, 1997.
Kendall, Gillian Murray. '"Lend me thy hand": Metaphor and Mayhem in *Titus Andronicus*', *Shakespeare Quarterly* 40 (1989): 299–316.
Kiefer, C. 'Music and Marston's *The Malcontent*', *Studies in Philology* 51 (1954): 163–71.
Knapp, Jeffrey. *Shakespeare Only*. Chicago: University of Chicago Press, 2009.
Knowles, James. *The Roaring Girl and Other Comedies*. New York: Oxford University Press, 2001.
Knutson, Roslyn Lander. *The Repertory of Shakespeare's Company, 1594–1613*. Fayetteville: University of Arkansas Press, 1991.
Knutson, Roslyn. *Playing Companies and Commerce in Shakespeare's Time*. Cambridge: Cambridge University Press, 2001.
Korda, Natasha. *Shakespeare's Domestic Economies: Gender and Property in Early Modern England*. Philadelphia: University of Pennsylvania Press, 2002.
Korda, Natasha. *Labors Lost: Women's Work and the Early Modern English Stage*. Philadelphia: University of Pennsylvania Press, 2011.
Kyd, Thomas. *The Spanish Tragedy*, ed. Clara Calvo and Jesus Tronch. Arden Early Modern Drama. London: Arden Shakespeare, 2013.
Lindley, David. *Shakespeare and Music*. London: Thomson Learning, 2006.

Lodge, Thomas. *A Looking-Glass for London and England*. London: Malone Society at the Oxford University Press, 1932.
Lodge, Thomas. *The Wounds of Civil War*, ed. Joseph H. Houppert. Lincoln, NE: University of Nebraska Press, 1969.
Loewenstein, Joseph. 'Marston's Gorge and the Question of Formalism', in *Renaissance Literature and Its Formal Engagements*, ed. Mark David Rasmussen. New York: Palgrave, 2002, pp. 89–112.
Long, A. A. and D. N. Sedley, *The Hellenistic Philosophers*, vol. 1: *Translations of the Principal Sources with Philosophical Commentary*. Cambridge: Cambridge University Press, 1999.
Lopez, Jeremy. *Theatrical Convention and Audience Response in Early Modern Drama*. Cambridge: Cambridge University Press, 2003.
Low, Jennifer A. and Nova Myhill, eds. *Imagining the Audience in Early Modern Drama, 1558–1642*. New York: Palgrave Macmillan, 2011.
Luis-Martinez, Zenón. *In Words and Deeds: The Spectacle of Incest in English Renaissance Tragedy*. Amsterdam–New York: Rodopi, 2002.
MacKay, Ellen. *Persecution, Plague, and Fire: Fugitive Histories of the Stage in Early Modern England*. Chicago: University of Chicago Press, 2010.
Mackenzie, Agnes Mure. *The Playgoer's Handbook to the English Renaissance Drama*. London: Jonathan Cape, 1927.
McMillin, Scott. 'Acting and Violence: *The Revenger's Tragedy* and its Departures from *Hamlet*', *Studies in English Literature, 1500–1900* 24 (1984): 275–91.
McMillin, Scott and Sally-Beth MacLean, *The Queen's Men and their Plays*. Cambridge: Cambridge University Press, 1998.
McMullan, Gordon and Jonathan Hope, eds. *The Politics of Tragicomedy: Shakespeare and After*. New York: Routledge, 1992.
McNeill, David. *Gesture and Thought*. Chicago: University of Chicago Press, 2005.
McPherson, David. 'Ben Jonson's Library and Marginalia: An Annotated Catalogue', *Studies in Philology* 71 (1974): 1–106.
Manley, Lawrence. 'From Strange's Men to Pembroke's Men: *2 Henry VI* and *The First Part of the Contention*', *Shakespeare Quarterly* 54 (2003): 253–87.
Marlowe, Christopher. *Tamburlaine, Parts One and Two*, ed. Anthony B. Dawson. London: New Mermaids–A&C Black, 1997.
Marmion, Shackerley. *The Antiquary*. London, 1641.
Marmion, Shackerley. *The Dramatic Works of Shackerley Marmion*. New York: B. Blom, 1967.
Marshall, Cynthia. *The Shattering of the Self: Violence, Subjectivity, and Early Modern Texts*. Baltimore: Johns Hopkins University Press, 2002.
Marston, John. *The Works of John Marston*, 3 vols, ed. A. H. Bullen. London: John C. Nimmo, 1887.
Marston, John. *The Plays of John Marston*, 3 vols, ed. H. Harvey Wood. Edinburgh: Oliver and Boyd, 1934–9.
Massumi, Brian. *Parables for the Virtual: Movement, Affect, Sensation*. Durham, NC: Duke University Press, 2002.
Maus, Katharine Eisaman, ed. *Four Revenge Tragedies*. New York: Oxford University Press, 1998.

Mazzio, Carla. *The Inarticulate Renaissance: Language Trouble in an Age of Eloquence*. Philadelphia: University of Pennsylvania Press, 2009.
Mazzio, Carla and David Hillman, eds. *The Body in Parts: Fantasies of Corporeality in Early Modern Europe*. New York: Routledge, 1997.
Menzer, Paul, ed. *Inside Shakespeare: Essays on the Blackfriars Stage*. Selinsgrove: Susquehanna University Press, 2006.
Michie, Donald, ed. *A Critical Edition of The True Chronicle History of King Leir and his Three Daughters*. New York: Garland Publishing, 1991.
Middleton, Thomas. *Thomas Middleton: The Collected Works*, ed. Gary Taylor and John Lavagnino. Oxford: Clarendon Press, 2007.
Milsom, John. 'Sacred Songs in the Chamber', in *English Choral Practice, 1400–1650*, ed. John Morehen. Cambridge: Cambridge University Press, 1995, pp. 161–79.
Miola, Robert. *Shakespeare and Classical Tragedy: The Influence of Seneca*. Oxford: Clarendon Press, 1992.
Mohrmann, Gerald P. 'Oratorical Delivery and Other Problems in Current Scholarship on English Renaissance Rhetoric', in *Renaissance Eloquence: Studies in the Theory and Practice of Renaissance Rhetoric*, ed. James J. Murphy. Berkeley: University of California Press, 1983, pp. 56–83.
Montrose, Louis. 'Renaissance Literary Studies and the Subject of History', *English Literary Renaissance* 16 (1986): 5–12.
Montrose, Louis. 'New Historicisms', in *Redrawing the Boundaries: The Transformation of English and American Literary Studies*, ed. Stephen Greenblatt and Giles Gunn. New York: Modern Language Association of America, 1992, pp. 392–418.
Morley, Thomas. *A Plain & Easy Introduction to Practical Music*, ed. Alec Harman. New York: W. W. Norton, 1963.
Mullaney, Steven. *The Place of the Stage: License, Play, and Power in Renaissance England*. Chicago: University of Chicago Press, 1988.
Mullaney, Steven. 'Affective Technologies: Toward an Emotional Logic of the Elizabethan Stage', in *Environment and Embodiment in Early Modern England*, ed. Mary Floyd-Wilson and Garrett A. Sullivan. Basingstoke: Palgrave Macmillan, 2007, pp. 71–89.
Munday, Anthony. *A Critical Edition of Anthony Munday's Fedele and Fortunio*, ed. Richard Hosley. New York and London: Garland Publishing, 1981.
Munro, Lucy. *Children of the Queen's Revels: A Jacobean Theatre Repertory*. Cambridge: Cambridge University Press, 2005.
Murphy, James. 'One Thousand Neglected Authors: The Scope and Importance of Renaissance Rhetoric', in *Renaissance Eloquence: Studies in the Theory and Practice of Renaissance Rhetoric*, ed. James J. Murphy. Berkeley: University of California Press, 1983, pp. 20–36.
Nabbes, Thomas. *The Works of Thomas Nabbes*, 2 vols, ed. A. H. Bullen. New York: B. Bloom, 1968.
Neill, Michael. '"What strange riddle's this?": Deciphering *'Tis Pity She's a Whore*', in *John Ford: Critical Re-Visions*, ed. Michael Neill. Cambridge: Cambridge University Press, 1988, pp. 153–79.
Neill, Michael. 'Amphitheaters in the Body: Playing with Hands on the Shakespearian Stage', *Shakespeare Survey* 48 (1995): 23–50.

Neill, Michael. *Issues of Death: Mortality and Identity in English Renaissance Tragedy*. Oxford: Clarendon Press, 1997.
Newman, Karen. 'City Talk: Women and Commodification in Jonson's *Epicoene*', *ELH* 56 (1989): 503–18.
Novak, Maximilian and George Guffey, eds. *The Works of John Dryden*, vol. 10. Berkeley: University of California Press, 1970.
Nunn, Hillary M. *Staging Anatomies: Dissection and Spectacle in Early Stuart Tragedy*. Aldershot and Burlington, VT: Ashgate, 2005.
Oliver, H. J. *The Problem of John Ford*. New York: Cambridge University Press, 1955.
O'Neill, David G. 'The Influence of Music in the Works of John Marston, II', *Music & Letters* 53 (1972): 293–308.
Orlin, Lena Cowen. *Locating Privacy in Tudor London*. Oxford: Oxford University Press, 2007.
Orme, Nicholas. 'The Early Musicians of Exeter Cathedral', *Music and Letters* 59 (1978): 395–410.
Orme, Nicholas. *Education and Society in Medieval and Renaissance England*. London: Hambledon Press, 1989.
Ostovich, Helen. '"To Behold the Scene Full": Seeing and Judging in *Every Man out of His Humour*', in *Re-Presenting Ben Jonson: Text, History and Performance*, ed. Martin Butler. New York: St Martin's Press, 1999, pp. 76–92.
Owens, Margaret E. *Stages of Dismemberment: The Fragmented Body in Late Medieval and Early Modern Drama*. Newark: University of Delaware Press, 2005.
Palfrey, Simon and Tiffany Stern. *Shakespeare in Parts*. Oxford: Oxford University Press, 2007.
Palisca, Claude V., ed. *The Florentine Camerata: Documentary Studies and Translations*. New Haven, CT: Yale University Press, 1989.
Paré, Ambroise. *The Workes of that famous Chirurgion Ambrose Parey Translated out of Latine and compared with the French by Th: Johnson*. London, 1634.
Park, Katharine. 'The Criminal and the Saintly Body: Autopsy and Dissection in Renaissance Italy', *Renaissance Quarterly* 47 (1994): 1–33.
Parker, Patricia. *Shakespeare from the Margins: Language, Culture, Context*. Chicago: University of Chicago Press, 1996.
Parker, Patricia. 'The Novelty of Different Tongues: Polyglot Punning in Shakespeare (and Others)', in *Esthétiques de la nouveauté à la Renaissance*, ed. Francois Laroque and Franck Lessay. Paris: Presses de la Sorbonne Nouvelle, 2001, pp. 41–58.
Parker, Patricia. 'Shakespeare's Sound Government: Sound Defects, Polyglot Sounds, and Sounding Out', *Oral Tradition* 24 (2009): 359–72.
Paster, Gail Kern. *The Body Embarrassed: Drama and the Disciplines of Shame in Early Modern England*. Ithaca, NY: Cornell University Press, 1993.
Paster, Geil Kern. *Humoring the Body: Emotions and the Shakespearean Stage*. Chicago: University of Chicago Press, 2004.
Paster, Gail Kern, Katherine Rowe and Mary Floyd-Wilson, eds. *Reading the Early Modern Passions: Essays in the Cultural History of Emotion*. Philadelphia: University of Pennsylvania Press, 2004.

Peacham, Henry. *The Garden of Eloquence*. London, 1593.
Peele, George. *The Dramatic Works of George Peele*, ed. R. Mark Benbow, vol. 3 of *The Life and Works of George Peele*. New Haven, CT: Yale University Press, 1952–70.
Peele, George. *The Battle of Alcazar*, in *The Stukeley Plays*, ed. Charles Edelman. Manchester: Manchester University Press, 2005.
Pepys, Samuel. *The Diary of Samuel Pepys: A New and Complete Transcription*, 11 vols, ed. Richard Latham and William Matthews. Berkeley: University of California Press, 1976.
Picker, John M. *Victorian Soundscapes*. New York: Oxford University Press, 2003.
Pollard, Tanya. 'A Kind of Wild Medicine: Revenge as Remedy in Early Modern England', *Revista Canaria de Estudios Ingleses* 50 (2005), pp. 57–69.
Pollard, Tanya. *Drugs and Theater in Early Modern England*. New York: Oxford University Press, 2005.
Pollard, Tanya. 'Tragedy and Revenge', in *The Cambridge Companion to English Renaissance Tragedy*, ed. Emma Smith and Garrett A. Sullivan, Jr. Cambridge: Cambridge University Press, 2010, pp. 58–72.
Pollard, Tanya. 'Greek Playbooks and Dramatic Forms in Early Modern England', in *Formal Matters: Reading the Materials of English Renaissance Literature*, ed. Allison K. Deutermann and András Kiséry. Manchester: Manchester University Press, 2013, pp. 99–123.
Puttenham, George. *The Art of English Poesy*, ed. Frank Whigham and Wayne A. Rebhorn. Ithaca, NY: Cornell University Press, 2007.
Quintilian. *The Institutio Oratoria of Quinitilian*, trans. H. E. Butte, vol. 3. The Loeb Classical Library. Cambridge, MA: Harvard University Press, 1966.
Raman, Shankar. 'Hamlet in Motion', in *Knowing Shakespeare: Senses, Embodiment and Cognition*, ed. Lowell Gallagher and Shankar Raman. New York: Palgrave Macmillan, 2010, pp. 116–36.
Rastell, John. *Les Termes de la Ley*. London, 1624.
Rath, Richard Cullen. *How Early America Sounded*. Ithaca, NY: Cornell University Press, 2003.
Rather, Susan. 'Stuart and Reynolds: A Portrait of Challenge', *Eighteenth-Century Studies* 27 (1993): 61–84.
Read, Alexander. *The Manuall of the Anatomy or dissection of the body of Man*. London, 1638.
Rebhorn, Wayne. *The Emperor of Men's Minds: Literature and the Renaissance Discourse of Rhetoric*. Ithaca, NY: Cornell University Press, 1995.
Riggs, David. *Ben Jonson: A Life*. Cambridge, MA: Harvard University Press, 1989.
Roberts, Jeanne Addison. *The Shakespearean Wild: Geography, Genus, and Gender*. Lincoln, NE: University of Nebraska Press, 1991.
Rutter, Thomas. 'Marlowe, *Hoffman*, and the Admiral's Men', *Marlowe Studies: An Annual* 3 (2013): 49–62.
Rymer, Thomas. *A Short View of Tragedy*. London, 1693.
Sacks, David Harris and Michael Lynch. 'Ports 1540–1700', in *The Cambridge Urban History of Britain*, vol. 2, ed. Peter Clark. Cambridge: Cambridge University Press, 2000, pp. 377–424.

[Sanderson, William]. *Aulicus Coquinariae: Or a Vindication in Answer to a Pamphlet Entitled The Court and Character of King James*. London, 1650.
Sawday, Jonathan. *The Body Emblazoned: Dissection and the Human Body in Renaissance Culture*. London: Routledge, 1995.
Schalkwyk, David. *Speech and Performance in Shakespeare's Sonnets and Plays*. Cambridge: Cambridge University Press, 2002.
Schoenfeldt, Michael C. *Bodies and Selves in Early Modern England: Physiology and Inwardness in Spenser, Shakespeare, Herbert, and Milton*. Cambridge: Cambridge University Press, 1999.
Seigworth, Gregory J. and Melissa Gregg. 'An Inventory of Shimmers', in *The Affect Theory Reader*, ed. Gregory J. Seigworth and Melissa Gregg. Durham, NC: Duke University Press, 2010, pp. 1–25.
Shakespeare, William. *The Tragicall Historie of Hamlet Prince of Denmarke*. London, 1603.
Shakespeare, William. *The First Part of King Henry VI*, ed. Andrew S. Cairncross. Arden Shakespeare. London: Methuen, 1965.
Shakespeare, William. *A Midsummer Night's Dream,* ed. Harold F. Brooks. Arden Shakespeare. London: Methuen, 1979.
Shakespeare, William. *Hamlet*, ed. Harold Jenkins. Arden Shakespeare. London: Methuen, 1982.
Shakespeare, William. *Titus Andronicus*, ed. Eugene M. Waith. Oxford Shakespeare. New York: Oxford University Press, 1984.
Shakespeare, William. *Titus Andronicus*, ed. Jonathan Bate. Arden Shakespeare. London: Routledge, 1995.
Shakespeare, William. *Henry VI, Part Three*, ed. Randall Martin. Oxford Shakespeare. Oxford: Oxford University Press, 2001.
Shakespeare, William. *King Henry VI Part 1*, ed. Edward Burns. Arden Shakespeare. London: Thomson Learning, 2001.
Shakespeare, William. *King Henry VI, Part 3*, ed. John D. Cox and Eric Rasmussen. Arden Shakespeare. London: Arden Shakespeare, 2001.
Shakespeare. William. *King Henry VI, Part 2*, ed. Ronald Knowles. Arden Shakespeare. London: Arden Shakespeare, 2002.
Shakespeare, William. *Hamlet*, ed. Ann Thompson and Neil Taylor. Arden Shakespeare. London: Thomson Learning, 2006.
Shakespeare, William. *King Richard III*, ed. James R. Siemon. Arden Shakespeare. London: Methuen, 2009.
Shapiro, Michael. *Children of the Revels: The Boy Companies of Shakespeare's Time and Their Plays*. New York: Columbia University Press, 1977.
Shirley, James. *The Gratefull Servant*. London, 1630.
Shirley, James. *Dramatic Works and Poems*, 6 vols, ed. William Gifford and Alexander Dyce. New York: Russell & Russell, 1966.
Sidney, Phillip. 'The Defence of Poesy', in *Sidney's 'The Defence of Poesy' and Selected Renaissance Literary Criticism*, ed. Gavin Alexander. New York: Penguin, 2004.
Silverstone, Catherine. 'Fatal Attraction: Desire, Anatomy and Death in *'Tis Pity She's a Whore*', in *'Tis Pity She's a Whore: A Critical Guide*, ed. Lisa Hopkins. London: Continuum, 2010, pp. 77–93.
Slights, William. *The Heart in the Age of Shakespeare*. Cambridge: Cambridge University Press, 2008.

Smith, Bruce R. *The Acoustic World of Early Modern England: Attending to the O-Factor*. Chicago: University of Chicago Press, 1999.

Smith, Bruce R. *Phenomenal Shakespeare*. Malden, MA: Wiley-Blackwell, 2010.

Smith, Jeremy L. *Thomas East and Music Publishing in Renaissance England*. New York: Oxford University Press, 2003.

Smuts, R. Malcolm. 'The Court and its Neighborhood: Royal Policy and Urban Growth in the Early Stuart West End', *Journal of British Studies* 30 (1991): 117–49.

Stallybrass, Peter. 'Patriarchal Territories: The Body Enclosed', in *Rewriting the Renaissance: The Discourses of Sexual Difference in Early Modern Europe*, ed. Margaret W. Ferguson, Maureen Quilligan and Nancy Vickers. Chicago: University of Chicago Press, 1986, pp. 123–44.

Stallybrass, Peter, Roger Chartier, J. Franklin Mowery and Heather Wolfe. 'Hamlet's Tables and the Technologies of Writing in Renaissance England', *Shakespeare Quarterly* 55 (2004): 379–419.

Stern, Tiffany. *Documents of Performance in Early Modern England*. Cambridge: Cambridge University Press, 2009.

Strunk, Oliver. *Source Readings in Music History from Classical Antiquity through the Romantic Era*. New York: Norton, 1950.

Sugg, Richard. *Murder After Death: Literature and Anatomy in Early Modern England*. Ithaca, NY and London: Cornell University Press, 2007.

Syme, Holger Schott. 'Unediting the Margin: Jonson, Marston, and the Theatrical Page', *ELR* 38 (2008): 142–71.

Taylor, Gary and John Lavagnino, eds. *Thomas Middleton and Early Modern Textual Culture: A Companion to the Collected Works*. New York: Oxford University Press, 2007.

Teague, Frances. 'The Phoenix and the Cockpit-in-Court Playhouses', in *The Oxford Handbook of Early Modern Theatre*, ed. Richard Dutton. New York: Oxford University Press, 2011, pp. 240–59.

Thompson, Ann and John O. Thompson, *Shakespeare: Meaning and Metaphor*. Brighton: Harvester Press, 1987.

Thompson, Emily. *The Soundscape of Modernity, 1900–1933: Architectural Acoustics and the Culture of Listening in America*. Cambridge, MA: Massachusetts Institute of Technology Press, 2002.

Tiffany, Grace. '*Hamlet* and Protestant Aural Theater', *Christianity and Literature* 52 (2003): 307–24.

Tomlinson, T. B. *A Study of Elizabethan and Jacobean Tragedy*. Cambridge: Cambridge University Press, 1964.

Traub, Valerie. 'Mapping the Global Body', in *Early Modern Visual Culture: Representation, Race, and Empire in Renaissance England*, ed. Peter Erickson and Clark Hulse. Philadelphia: University of Pennsylvania Press, 2000, pp. 44–97.

Traub, Valerie. 'The Nature of Norms in Early Modern England: Anatomy, Cartography, *King Lear*', *South Central Review* 26 (2009): 42–81.

Tricomi, Albert H. 'The Aesthetics of Mutilation in *Titus Andronicus*', *Shakespeare Survey* 27 (1974): 11–19.

Vicary, Thomas. *The Englishemans treasure, or treasor for Englishmen with the true anatomye of mans bodye*. London, 1586.

Watson, Robert N. *Ben Jonson's Parodic Strategy: Literary Imperialism in the Comedies*. Cambridge, MA: Harvard University Press, 1987.
Webster, John. *The Duchess of Malfi*, ed. Leah Marcus. Arden Early Modern Drama. London: Methuen–Arden Shakespeare, 2009.
Weimann, Robert. 'Society and the Individual in Shakespeare's Conception of Character', *Shakespeare Survey* 34 (1982): 23–32.
Weimann, Robert. 'Mimesis in *Hamlet*', in *Shakespeare and the Question of Theory*, ed. Patricia Parker and Geoffrey Hartman. New York: Methuen, 1985, pp. 275–91.
Weimann, Robert. *Author's Pen and Actor's Voice: Playing and Writing in Shakespeare's Theatre*, ed. Helen Higbee and William West. Cambridge: Cambridge University Press, 2000.
West, William N. '"But this will be a mere confusion": Real and Represented Confusions on the Elizabethan Stage', *Theatre Journal* 60 (2008): 217–33.
Wilde, Oscar. *The Importance of Being Earnest: A Trivial Comedy for Serious People*, ed. Russell Jackson. New York: W. W. Norton, 1980.
Willis, Deborah. 'The Gnawing Vulture: Revenge, Trauma Theory, and *Titus Andronicus*', *Shakespeare Quarterly* 53 (2002): 21–52.
Wilson, Eric. 'Plagues, Fairs, and Street Cries: Sounding out Society and Space in Early Modern London', *Modern Language Studies* 25 (1995): 1–42.
Wilson, Thomas. *The arte of rhetorique*. London, 1560.
Wittgenstein, Ludwig. *Philosophical Investigations: the English Text of the Third Edition*, trans. G. E. M. Anscombe. New York: Prentice Hall, 1958.
Woodbridge, Linda. *English Revenge Drama: Money, Resistance, Equality*. Cambridge: Cambridge University Press, 2010.
Wynne-Davies, Marion. '"The Swallowing Womb": Consumed and Consuming Women in *Titus Andronicus*', in *The Matter of Difference: Materialist Feminist Criticism of Shakespeare*, ed. Valerie Wayne. Ithaca, NY: Cornell University Press, 1991, pp. 129–51.
Zucker, Adam. *The Places of Wit in Early Modern English Comedy*. Cambridge: Cambridge University Press, 2011.
Zucker, Adam and Alan B. Farmer, eds. *Localizing Caroline Drama: Politics and Economics of the Early Modern English State, 1625–1642*. New York: Palgrave Macmillan, 2006.

Index

References to images are in *italics*; references to notes are indicated by n.

acting, 51–2, 106–7
alarums, 3, 4, 13, 25
Alchemist, The (Jonson), 82, 129, 131
Alphonsus, King of Aragon (Greene), 3, 25, 26, 27
amphitheatres, 2, 55–6, 77
anatomy
   as discipline, 6
   texts, 8–9, 28, 69–70, 108, 159–60
   see also ear, the
Antiquary, The (Marmion), 162–3
Antonio and Mellida (Marston), 73, 79, 99–100n43
Argalus and Parthenia (Glapthorne), 144–5, 167n6
Art of Rhetoric (Wilson), 35–6, 37
audiences, 12, 45, 56–7, 74, 79, 94, 147, 149, 164
   and Cockpit playhouse, 141, 142–3, 152
audition, 2, 9–10, 15–18, 109–10, 176–7; *see also* hearing
Aulicus Coquinariae (Sanderson), 165–7

Bacon, Francis, 77
balconies, 147, 153–5
Ball, The (Shirley), 14, 143, 148–52, 160, 161
Banister, John, 28, 160, 171n47
banquets
   and revenge, 3, 44, 158
   and *'Tis Pity She's a Whore*, 152, 158–9
   and *Titus Andronicus*, 51–2, 120
Barish, Jonas, 66

Bartholomew Fair (Jonson), 45–6, 87, 96, 164
Battle of Alcazar, The (Peele), 4, 25, 27, 30–1
battle plays, 3–4, 25–7, 30–1, 40, 41, 46
battle scenes, 25, 40
Beaumont, Francis, 129–30
Berger, Harry, 18n4
Bird, Theophilus, 1–2
Blackfriars playhouse, 14, 77, 112, 140–1, 161
blank verse, 23–4, 30–1
Blind Beggar of Alexandria, The (Chapman), 78
Bloom, Gina, 6, 12, 170n
Boring of the Eare, The (Egerton), 9–10, 111
Bowers, Fredson, 31
boy actors, 73, 74, 141
Bradley, A.C., 124–5
Bride, The (Nabbes), 144
Broken Heart, The (Ford), 159

cannon fire, 10, 13
Case is Altered, The (Jonson), 112
Chapman, George, 67, 72, 78, 79
Chaste Maid in Cheapside, A (Middleton), 129, 131
Cicero, 35
city comedy, 2–3, 7, 13–15, 18
   and Ben Jonson, 63–5, 75, 77–9, 85, 87–9, 107–8, 111–12, 134
   and Cockpit playhouse, 141–2, 153
   and John Marston, 72–5, 85, 86–7, 107–8

and noise, 4–5, 10, 65–6, 94–6
and polyphony, 82–7, 91–4
and sound, 72–5, 76–7, 79, 105, 106–7
post-*Hamlet*, 129–31
Cockpit (Phoenix) playhouse, 14–15, 131, 140–6, 161
and structure, 154, 156, 170n35
and theatre culture, 146–8, 152, 156–8, 163–4
comedy (genre), 54–5; *see also* city comedy
conceits, 37, 71–2
conclusions, 35–8
costume, 43, 51
Covent Garden (Nabbes), 175
Cowper, William, 110–11, 113
Crooke, Helkiah, 8, 9, 28–30, 33, 58n22, 69, 97n20, 108
Curtain playhouse, 55–6
Cynthia's Revels (Jonson), 112

Davenant, William, 140, 141, 143
Davenport, Robert, 145
David and Bethsabe (Peele), 4, 23, 25, 44
de Grazia, Margreta, 126
Dessen, Alan C., 23
Dido, 52–3
and Aeneas, 47–8
dirae, 38–9, 52
Donne, George, 143, 164
Douglas, Mary and Baron Isherwood, 17, 166
Dowland, John, 89, 91
drums, 3, 4, 13, 25, 31, 54
Duchess of Malfi, The (Webster), 129, 130
dumbshows
and *Hamlet*, 120, 122, 132
and *The Spanish Tragedy*, 38

ear, the, 6, 10, 15–16, 28, 69–70
anatomy of, 28, 29, 58n22, 69–70, 97n20, 97–8n21
and *Hamlet*, 104–5, 108–9, 111, 123, 128
in painting, 15–18
and religion, 10, 111, 114
see also hearing
eavesdropping, 142, 143, 145–8, 165–7
and *The Ball*, 148–9, 151–2
and *Every Man out of His Humour*, 87–8

and *The Revenger's Tragedy*, 132
and *'Tis Pity She's a Whore*, 153–6
Edward I (Peele), 25
Edward II (Marlowe), 25
Egerton, Stephen, 9–10, 111, 113
English Grammar (Jonson), 83
Epicoene, or the Silent Woman (Jonson), 4–5, 82, 95–6, 108, 112, 129, 131, 148, 176
Every Man in His Humour (Jonson), 63–4, 65–72, 73, 74, 75–6, 77, 80–1, 82, 108, 117, 147
and music, 83–4
and sound, 107
Every Man out of His Humour (Jonson), 72, 74, 82, 83–4, 85, 87
and Paul's Walk, 87–9, 90, 91, 94
Example, The (Shirley), 141, 163–4
explosions, 22

Fedele and Fortunio (Munday), 26, 27, 30, 55
First Booke of Songes or Ayres (Dowland) 89, 92, 93
'fit similes', 71–2, 81
Floyd-Wilson, Mary, 35
Ford, John, 1, 2, 14, 142, 143, 152, 157, 158, 160–1, 163

Garden of Eloquence, The (Peacham), 7–8, 75–6
ghosts, 22, 141, 162
Glapthorne, Henry, 144, 145
Globe playhouse, 74
Gosson, Stephen, 1–2, 11
Gouge, William, 111, 113
Grateful Servant, The (Shirley), 140
Greene, Robert, 3–4, 23–5, 30, 37, 40
Greene's Groatsworth of Wit (Greene), 39–40, 43, 44
grief, 32–4

Hamlet (Shakespeare), 14, 104–8, 124–7, 131, 134
and audition, 109–10, 111, 112–13
and hearing, 104–6, 108–15, 116–18, 123–4, 125, 127
and soliloquies, 128–9
and theatre, 118–23
Harris, Henry, 173, 174
hearing
and city comedy, 65, 66–7, 68–72, 73–4, 77, 80–1, 82, 83–4
and ethical action, 76–7

hearing (cont.)
  and gender, 12, 44, 116
  and Pepys, 175–7
  and revenge tragedy, 28–31, 35–8, 41–2, 43–5, 47, 48–9, 50, 52–3
  and taste, 5, 13, 73, 96, 108–11
  see also audition; eavesdropping
Henry VI, Part 1 (Shakespeare), 26, 27
Henry VI, Part 2 (First Part of the Contention betwixt the two Famous Houses of York and Lancaster) (Shakespeare), 26, 43
Henry VI, Part 3 (True Tragedy of Richard Duke of York) (Shakespeare), 13, 26, 27, 39–45, 46, 51, 55, 56, 64
Hercules and Omphale (van Thulden), 15, 16, 17
Heywood, Thomas, 119, 141
Historie of Man (Banister), 28, 159–60, 171n47
history (genre), 25–6, 27–8, 54–5
Histriomastix (Marston), 74, 82, 86
humours, 10–11, 67
humoral comedy, 67, 72, 77, 94
Humorous Day's Mirth, An (Chapman), 67, 72
hunting, 47
Hutson, Lorna, 66, 81

I Selimus (Greene), 25
Importance of Being Earnest, The (Wilde), 175–6
Islip, Adam, 89, 91

Jack Drum's Entertainment (Marston), 73–4, 82, 84–5, 86–7, 94, 107
Jacques of Liege, 82–3
James I and VI, King, 165–6
James IV (The Scottish History of James the Fourth) (Greene), 3–4, 25, 28
James, Heather, 47
Jew of Malta, The (Marlowe), 141
Jonson, Ben, 7, 13, 45–6, 73
  and language, 72, 111–12
  and music, 83–4, 85, 94
  and poetry, 76–7
  and revenge tragedy, 75, 79
  and sound, 4–5, 63–5, 95–6, 107, 108
Just Italian, The (Davenant), 140

King John (Shakespeare), 26
King John and Matilda (Davenport), 145
King Leir (anon), 26–7
Knight of the Burning Pestle, The (Beaumont), 129, 130–1, 134
Kyd, Thomas, 13, 31–2, 37, 39, 57n4

Lady of Pleasure, The (Shirley), 143–4
Lady's Trial, The (Ford), 1, 144
Lake, Anne, 165, 166
language, 66–9, 71–2, 81
literacy, 6
Locrine (anon), 26, 27, 31
Lodge, Thomas, 25, 26, 59n49
London
  in comedy, 4–5, 88–9, 91, 95–6
  and soundscape, 10, 11, 65–6, 94–5
  see also urban growth
Looking-Glass for London and England, A (Greene/Lodge), 25, 27, 28
Love's Labour's Lost (Shakespeare), 145
Love's Mistress (Heywood), 141

Marlowe, Christopher, 23–4, 24–5, 30, 37, 40, 66
Marmion, Shackerley, 162
Marshall, Cynthia, 56
Marston, John, 73–4, 78, 79, 81, 82, 83, 84, 85, 91, 94
masques
  and genre, 141
  and revenge, 44, 120, 133
Manuall of the Anatomy (Read), 69–70
Massacre at Paris (Marlowe), 27, 55
Master of the Revels, 6
Mei, Girolamo, 85–6, 89
Menaphon (Greene), 23
Mennonite Preacher Cornelis Anslo and His Wife, The (Rembrandt), 15–16
metaphor, 7–8, 112, 153
Microcosmographia (Crooke), 8, 9, 28, 29, 69, 97n20, 108
Middleton, Thomas, 129, 147, 158, 163
mishearings, 5, 113–14, 116
Morley, Thomas, 82, 84, 89
Munday, Anthony, 26
music, 7, 72–3, 74, 82–6, 117
  and print, 89, 91, 92–3, 94
  and Restoration theatre, 174–5
  see also polyphony

Nabbes, Thomas, 144, 147, 175
Nashe, Thomas, 23, 24, 54
Neill, Michael, 152
Newman, Karen, 4
noise, 22, 25–6, 56–7, 65–6, 89, 94–5, 129, 130, 140, 143, 144
  and Ben Jonson, 63–4
  and *Henry VI, Part 3*, 40, 41–2, 45
  and revenge, 4, 27–8, 30–1, 51, 54–5, 109, 130
  and *Titus Andronicus*, 46–8, 51
  and violence, 3–4, 13, 28–30, 108

Opportunity, The (Shirley), 146
oratory, 7–8, 24, 32, 35–6, 51, 53, 56, 133, 144
outrage, 32–4, 37–8, 49
Ovid, 49, 50, 52

Paré, Ambroise, 160
Parker, Patricia, 7
Paster, Gail Kern, 35, 128
Peacham, Henry, 7–8, 52, 76
Peele, George, 4, 40, 46
Pepys, Samuel, 173–5
Perkin Warbeck (Ford), 143
Plato, 5
plays-within-the-play, 32, 34–8, 43–5, 51–3, 118–23, 149; *see also* banquets
Poetaster (Jonson), 77–9, 107, 134, 162
poetic style, 24, 37–8, 83–4
  and Jonson, 64–5, 72
  and sound, 76–7, 78–9
Poets' War(s), 73, 77, 98n25, 140
polyphony, 82–3, 84–7, 91–4
props, 51
  bloody napkin, 43–4
  heart, 158–9, 160–1
  skull, 131
prose, 66, 86–7
Protestantism, 6, 9–10, 111–12, 114
Puritanism, 9–10, 110, 116

Quintilian, 35

railing, 142, 143–5, 147–8, 150–1, 152, 158, 159, 161
rape, 47, 48–9, 50
Rare Triumph of Love and Fortune (Munday), 26
Read, Alexander, 69
Rebhorn, Wayne, 7
Red Bull playhouse, 141

religion *see* Protestantism; Puritanism
Rembrandt, 15–17
repetition, 37, 50
Restoration theatre, 173–5
revenge, 26–8, 30–1, 54–5
  and *The Ball*, 149–51
  and *Hamlet*, 114, 118–20, 122
  and *Henry VI, Part 3*, 40–5
  and *The Spanish Tragedy*, 31–3, 34–6, 38–9
  and *'Tis Pity She's a Whore*, 156, 157–9, 160
  and *Titus Andronicus*, 49–52
  see also revenge comedy; revenge tragedy
revenge-comedy, 14, 131, 148
revenge tragedy, 2–3, 4, 7, 12–13, 55
  and Cockpit playhouse, 141–3
  and definition, 22–3
  and *Hamlet*, 105–6, 107, 109, 119–23, 126–8
  and parody, 75, 77–9, 162–3
  and post-*Hamlet*, 130, 131, 133, 134
  see also battle plays
Revenger's Tragedy, The (anon), 3, 4, 5, 44, 129, 131–4
rhetorical training, 6, 7–8, 83
Richard III (Shakespeare), 25
roaring *see* railing
romance (genre), 74, 144
Rose playhouse, 55–6
Rowe, Katherine, 35
Rymer, Thomas, 104

Sanderson, William, 165, 166
School of Abuse, The (Gosson), 1
Schoenfeldt, Michael, 128
Scottish History of James IV, The (Greene), 3–4, 25, 28
secrets, 34, 36, 156
senses, the, 5–6, 8; *see also* hearing
sermons, 9–10, 110–11
  Gertrude's closet, 124–6
Shakespeare, William, 12, 13–14, 39–40, 56
  and Jonson, 107–8, 111–12, 117, 126, 130
  and sound, 107
Shirley, James, 14, 140, 141, 143, 145–6, 147
Short, Peter, 89, 91, 92, 93
Short View of Tragedy, A (Rymer), 104
Smith, Bruce R., 6, 11–12, 56, 65

social status, 12, 109–10, 111, 116–18
  and city comedy, 13–14, 67, 69, 70–2, 73–4, 77, 80–1, 84, 112
  and the 'University Wits', 23
soliloquies, 128–9
sound, 3, 4–6, 7, 55–7, 65–6, 176
  and definition, 8–9, 10–11
  and genres, 54–5
  and *Hamlet*, 108
  and pain, 28, 30
  and *Titus Andronicus*, 46–8
  and verse, 76–7, 78–9
  and war, 25
  and weapons, 13
  and wounds, 41
  see also noise
Spanish Tragedy, The (Kyd), 13, 27, 31–9, 43, 45–6, 49, 51, 55, 56, 127–8
  and date of first performance, 31, 59n40
  and parody, 75–6, 77–9, 107, 162
  and *'Tis Pity She's a Whore*, 157
speech, 3, 4
  and bombast, 13, 24, 46
  and hearing, 68–9
  and Stoics, 115–16
  and violence, 22, 48–9
  as weapon, 13, 23, 35, 125, 153
staging, 43–4, 46, 51, 87–9; *see also* balconies
Staple of News, The (Jonson), 112
Stoics, 115–16

Tamburlaine (Marlowe), 24–5, 40, 46, 144
Tamburlaine II (Marlowe), 25, 27
taste, 10, 110–11
Tempest, or the Enchanted Island, The (Shakespeare, Dryden and Davenant), 173, 174–5
theatre, 11, 12, 18, 51
  and aurality, 2, 9
  and genres, 74

and *Hamlet*, 106–8, 118–23
and venues, 55–7, 140–1
thunder, 13, 22, 27–8, 30, 31
Timber or Discoveries (Jonson), 64, 76–7
Tinctoris, Johannes, 82
'Tis Pity She's a Whore (Ford), 14, 44, 142, 143, 152–61
Titus Andronicus (Shakespeare), 13, 27, 45–53, 55, 120
tragedy (genre), 54–5
tragicomedy (genre), 141, 142, 160
Traitor, The (Shirley), 145–6, 147, 149, 152
Troilus and Cressida (Shakespeare), 145
trumpets, 3–4, 22, 25, 46

urban growth, 6, 10, 65

van Thulden, Theodore, 15, 16, 17
vengeance *see* revenge
verbal quirks, 66–7
Vicary, Thomas, 97n20
violence, 3–4, 13, 22, 149–51
  and *Titus Andronicus*, 46, 47, 48–9
  see also revenge

war, 25, 40; *see also* battle plays
Warning for Fair Women, A (anon), 53–4
Webster, John, 129, 163
Wilde, Oscar, 176
Wilson, Thomas, 35
Wistreich, Richard, 89
Wit in a Constable (Glapthorne), 145
Women Beware Women (Middleton), 129
Woodbridge, Linda, 27
wormwood, 123
wounding words, 22
Wounds of Civil War, The (Lodge), 25, 26, 27

Zucker, Adam, 147

EU representative:
Easy Access System Europe
Mustamäe tee 50, 10621 Tallinn, Estonia
Gpsr.requests@easproject.com

www.ingramcontent.com/pod-product-compliance
Lightning Source LLC
Chambersburg PA
CBHW051059230426
43667CB00013B/2371